C000246583

BLACK EVERYDAY LIVES, CULTURE AND NARRATIVE

This book is a ground-breaking exploration of everyday life as experienced through the lens of Black British cultural history and creative practice, through a multiplicity of voices and writing styles.

The structure of *Black Everyday Lives, Material Culture and Narrative* examines life through a personal study of the family home – room by room, object by object – as a portal through which to examine the intricacies and nuances of daily considerations of African heritage people living in Britain in the modern era (post-1950). Using Small Anthropology methodology, this book foregrounds the experiences of Black British lives by bringing the threads of history and culture into the relevancy of the present day and demonstrating how the personal sphere directly links to wider public and political concerns.

This book will be of interest to a wide range of disciplines, including Black studies, anthropology, cultural studies, history, visual culture, photography, media communication, sociology, community development, art and design, and by any course that studies ethnographic methodologies, material culture, migration, everyday life, and British society.

Shawn-Naphtali Sobers is Professor of Cultural Interdisciplinary Practice at University of the West of England, Director of the Critical Race and Culture Research Group, and teaches photography. As a visual anthropologist he has carried out many research projects, ranging from legacies of slavery, African presence in Georgian and Victorian Britain, disability and walking, Rastafari language and culture, creative citizenship, and Rastafari and Ethiopian connections with the city of Bath. As a filmmaker and photographer his work has been exhibited and screened nationally and internationally, and he has directed and produced documentaries with Firstborn Creatives for BBC1, ITV, and Channel 4.

DIRECTIONS IN CULTURAL HISTORY

Series Editors: Gillian Swanson and Ben Highmore

The *Directions in Cultural History* series directs history towards the study of feelings, experiences and everyday habits. By attending to the world of sensation, imagination, and desire at moments of change, and by coupling this to the materials and technologies of culture, it promotes cultural history as a lively and vivid arena for research. The series will present innovative cultural history in an accessible form to both scholars and upper level students.

The Making of English Popular Culture
edited by John Storey

Light Touches
Cultural Practices of Illumination, 1800–1900
Alice Barnaby

Photography
The Unfettered Image
Michelle Henning

Cultural Ideals of Home
The Social Dynamics of Domestic Space
Deborah Chambers

Black Everyday Lives, Material Culture and Narrative
Tings in de House
Shawn-Naphtali Sobers

For more information about this series, please visit: www.routledge.com/Directions-in-Cultural-History/book-series/DICH

BLACK EVERYDAY LIVES, MATERIAL CULTURE AND NARRATIVE

Tings in de House

Shawn-Naphtali Sobers

Routledge
Taylor & Francis Group

LONDON AND NEW YORK

Designed cover image: Mahalia Sobers

First published 2023
by Routledge
4 Park Square, Milton Park, Abingdon, Oxon OX14 4RN

and by Routledge
605 Third Avenue, New York, NY 10158

Routledge is an imprint of the Taylor & Francis Group, an informa business

© 2023 Shawn-Naphtali Sobers

The right of Shawn-Naphtali Sobers to be identified as author of this work
has been asserted in accordance with sections 77 and 78 of the Copyright,
Designs and Patents Act 1988.

All rights reserved. No part of this book may be reprinted or reproduced or utilised
in any form or by any electronic, mechanical, or other means, now known or
hereafter invented, including photocopying and recording, or in any information
storage or retrieval system, without permission in writing from the publishers.

Trademark notice: Product or corporate names may be trademarks or registered trademarks,
and are used only for identification and explanation without intent to infringe.

British Library Cataloguing-in-Publication Data
A catalogue record for this book is available from the British Library

ISBN: 978-0-367-40869-5 (hbk)
ISBN: 978-0-367-40867-1 (pbk)
ISBN: 978-0-367-80962-1 (ebk)

DOI: 10.4324/9780367809621

Typeset in Bembo
by Newgen Publishing UK

In dedication to…

JAH Rastafari

BEMSCA Elders

Mahalia, Aisha, Jacob,
and the next generation…

CONTENTS

FIGURES

ACKNOWLEDGMENTS

Huge thanks to…

Adam Murray
Aisha Sobers
Alice Liddell
Andrew Dolman
Amanda Harman
Bath Ethnic Minority Senior
    Citizens Association
    (BEMSCA)
Ben Highmore
Benjamin Zephaniah
Bonita Bennett
Brera – London
Carlton Joseph
Damian Thornhill
David Cummins
Deighton Smith
Digital Cultures Research
    Centre
Dionne Draper
ECHOES Research Project
Ed Robinson
Enid Swaby
Fairfield House CIC
Family Ties Network
Gillian Swanson

Glenis Simms
Helen Bates
Lubaina Himid
Luann Sewell Waters
Mahalia Sobers
Marcus Brown
Mearl Spalding
Michael McMillan
Mr Stuart
Meenu Manro
Nadia Williams
Naomi Williams
Natalie Foster
Nick Triggs
Nicole Justice
Norma Sobers
Opio Chung
Pauline Swaby-Wallace
Ping Wu Grant
Ras Benji
Richard Dixon
Rob Mitchell
Holly Bush Gardens
    Gallery
Jennifer Vennall

Jennifer Sharratt
Jessica Jardine Crymble
John Amos
Julie Smith
Juliette Sobers-Cummins
"Kate"
Kelly O'Brien
Lisa Robinson
Lois Francis
Lorna May Wadsworth
Louise Lynas
Samenua Sesher
Sandra Swaby
Sandra Trotman Meadows
Sireita Mullings
Sonia Swaby
Sue Johnston
Tekla Selassie
Theophilus Sobers
University of the West of
    England
Valda Jackson
"Veronica"
Wendy Leocque
Yuko Edwards

INTRODUCTION

Why Study Material Culture through a Black-Heritage Lens?

This book is an exploration of everyday life as experienced through the lens of Black British cultural history and creative practice. The structure of the book examines everyday life through the exploration of a family home, room by room, object by object, as a portal through which to examine the intricacies and nuances of daily considerations of African heritage people living in Britain in the modern era (post-1950). Crucially the book will also explore how different artists and creative practitioners have approached related topics in their work, mapping a continuum of how the family home has been used as a vehicle to discuss the "Black experience" for decades.

The family home has been used in television and film as a backdrop to explore various narratives of the "Black experience," such as British sit-coms such as *The Fosters* and *No Problem!*, filled with large characters and colourful storylines. This book takes away those characters and looks at the house itself, and the stories that are told from the objects that remain – the souvenirs, food, hair products, music, religious iconography, cooking utensils, and much more. The study draws upon personal experience, as well as the experiences of others and existing research, to explore the loaded cultural histories of objects found in rooms of the home, to tell unheard stories and connections through time. This work is unique in foregrounding the experience of Black British life in the context of the domestic space and demonstrates how the personal sphere directly links to wider public and political concerns.

This book is timely, being produced in a timespan where the first generation of post-war arrivals in the 1950s are now in their 80s and older, a generation which are sadly decreasing. As a process of bereavement of their parents and grandparents, the younger generations find themselves as custodians of lots of stuff, material objects

DOI: 10.4324/9780367809621-1

which are holders of memory, having witnessed family events, secrets, fears, and hopes (Tulloch, 2018: 257), stuff as symbols of the family psychology (McMillan, 2009). This book captures such generational shifts and how certain objects around the home have taken on new meanings over time.

The author is from the second generation of this demographic, and is well placed to have witnessed the dynamics of the domestic space, from a pinnacle vantage point of seeing how the older and younger generations have embodied aspects of a plurality of cultural heritages in the personal sphere.

The premise of this book is based upon the notion that, in context of the African diaspora, knowledge has transferred through generations in often turbulent and demanding circumstances. On the African continent pre-1600s, knowledge was communicated predominantly through an oral tradition. This continued under severe duress through the circa 400+ years of slavery, years of transatlantic slavery (transatlantic slavery began with Portugal in 1444, and ended in America in 1865). Traditions from the continent travelled and survived across the globe in what we now know as the African diaspora. The timely factor of this book now is, as expressed above, we are at the apex of the transition of histories in the African diaspora, with the older generations making way for the younger.

In the 2000s there have been increased debate regarding the need to decolonise physical and notional spaces – such as the curriculum, museums, and other entities. While we (Black activists) become co-opted and preoccupied in cleansing such external spaces, this book argues that our own intimate spaces are often taken for granted, that the liberatory lessons and narratives of our cultural identities and values remain hidden in plain sight, that are often searched for in those same external spaces that are already acknowledged as problematic. At a neighbourhood level, our community centres become derelict buildings while the decolonised museum in the adjacent postcode gets a multi-million-pound renovation. At a human level, we can celebrate the archives and collections of mainstream institutions, while the things we inherit from our parents and grandparents remain unexamined and become increasingly discarded through less-interested family generations.

Some narratives in this book may be highly subjective and expose the fragility of the author's mind. Other examples will be more widely known, common tropes referenced in popular culture. They all add up to tell the story of how cultural identity is a language which leaves traces in unexpected places. Objects do not speak on their own and need narrators and interpreters. Therefore, this book acts both as a time capsule and a communicator, passing on embodied knowledges from the past and protecting them for the future.

What follows is an exploration of the ideas which certain objects evoke, rather than a study of how they were practically used. The selected objects are launch pads to dive into broader narrative investigations, rather than as destinations. The book uses the basic structure of a generic UK terraced house as the framework for the chapters. As we move through the house, we pause in each room and focus on one object at a time. We take a deep dive into the socio-cultural history of that thing through an African heritage lens of analysis and find out what makes it meaningful in a contemporary context of Black studies and in our lives in the real world.

The study of things and objects, the material culture in our lives, has an important role to play in understanding how we as humans navigate the world, our place in it, and our relationship to others. Too often studies of material culture gets misinterpreted as a fetishisation of the object or a frivolous celebration of materialism over more holistic, spiritual, and emotional concerns. What I have attempted to do with this book is break that assumption, and to show, even when an object is not fetishised and/or given primacy over human relations, there is still something in the analysis of that object that can teach us more about ourselves, not only about our history, but also in relation to our presence and agency as African heritage people. A key concern of this book relates to intergenerational communication and understanding – for example, what can a sewing machine teach me about what life was like for my parents' generation living in the Caribbean in the 1950s, and how has that translated into the attitudes and practices of later generations born in the UK, and our relationship to craft and self-sufficiency? Also, what is the meaning of the things in our spaces when the longevity of your own body is called into question?

Material culture has an important part to play in all aspects of our lives: it is needed for the very survival of human existence in the forms of food, clothes, and shelter; it is present in all areas of education, leisure, and entertainment; and it is relied upon in the more personal and sensitive areas of our lives – such as in physical and mental health care, in our personal relationships, and also in our religious lives and forms of cultural, spiritual, and identity expression. The humble agenda of this work is to try and understand how certain selected items of material culture fit within the wider context of African-centred discourse and life experience through time, and in essence, what is it that makes them meaningful and recurrent in the narratives of many in the African diaspora. This is not striving for a position of "all Black people think this, that or other," but rather to tentatively suggest my offerings as examples of how connections can be made between things that may surround us day to day, and our sense of selves and knowledge of African heritage history and discourse. Therein leads to the path to dialogue and overstanding (as we say in Rastafari culture – above mere understanding).

Small Anthropology Methodology

What follows is not a "traditional" academic book. The research and the subsequent writing-up has been conducted using a multidisciplinary approach, with each chapter written in a different style, informed by, and sympathetic to, the topic of each section, including interview transcripts, autoethnography, photo essay, fiction, collaborations, production of creative works, as well as traditional academic essays. Each chapter stands alone as separate entities, rather than a continual narrative weaving developmentally throughout the book.

Given the subject matter of the book, I have been ultra-sensitive to the criticisms that have been levelled at academic researchers embarking on such studies. For example, Johan Gultung, the founder of "peace and conflict studies," tells the story of aspects of traditional academia's complicit role in the European project of colonial expansion.

> A painting used to hang in the ante-room of former President Kwame Nkrumah. The painting was enormous, and the main feature was of Nkrumah himself, fighting, wrestling, with the last chains of colonialism. The chains are yielding, there is thunder and lightning in the air, the earth is shaking. Out of all this, three small figures are fleeing, white men, pallid. One of them is the capitalist, he carries a briefcase. Another is a priest or missionary, he carries the Bible. The third, a lesser figure, carries a book entitled 'African Political Systems': he is the anthropologist.
>
> *Quoted in Kuper, 1996: 96*

Linda Tuhiwai Smith, a Māori professor of Indigenous Education, speaks of the consequences of the complicity of early academic disciplines with the colonial infrastructures, and the subsequent impact on contemporary indigenous communities.

> The term "research" is inextricably linked to European imperialism and colonialism. The word itself, "research," is probably one of the dirtiest words in the indigenous world's vocabulary.
>
> *Tuhiwai Smith, 2006: 1*

The common perception of such disciplines is one of white men travelling to far off lands full of dark-skinned people, conducting ethnography by gathering images, artefacts, and observations of "native" people's behaviours, customs, and rituals. Some areas of academic research continue such colonial practices and have the tainted reputation, of parachuting into communities, extracting knowledge for their agendas, and rapidly leaving when their temporal interest had been satisfied. This form of cultural exploitation is further problematised when those researchers/commentators analyse their collected material, and attempt to make grand narratives about the communities they have "studied," when the people themselves look at the final outcomes curiously, not recognising what has been said about them or the way they have been represented. Having previously worked full time in television, and now as a professor in academia, I am fully aware of these valid criticisms and share the arguments of the ethical pitfalls and challenges of research that engages "human participants" (regardless of the ethnicity of the scholars, as researchers with a heritage from the global south can be as guilty of exploitative practices as the colonial Victorians). This book advocates for academic inquiry to embrace a more transparent and humbler approach in both its data gathering and presentation. Therefore, the approach of both the research process and the writing-up has been developed as a "Small Anthropology" methodology as an antidote to these colonial sins of the past. This book is an experiment in this approach of a Small Anthropology – narrative fragments where we can learn lessons from instances and insights of storytelling, without making claims that our findings are universal truths or grand narratives about whole sets of people and their behaviours.

No longer inclined to only travel to "exotic" lands, anthropologists and other researchers are now also staying closer to home, exploring the habits of life and culture of their own people, in their own backyards (Powdermaker, 1966; Oakley, 1996; Cieraad, 2006), and no longer viewing culture in terms of binary oppos- itions, through the patronising evolutionary spectacles of the eroding primitive and progressive civilised. Jomo Kenyatta, the revolutionary founding father and first President of independent Kenya, was an accomplished anthropologist who trained under Bronisław Malinowski (Kenyatta, 1938). Many modern anthropologists are the former studied, have come to reclaim the discourse and speak for oneself using it as a tool for empowerment, and rather than having assumptions and values imposed upon them by others are "returning the gaze" (Jacobs-Huey, 2002). As articulated by Tuhiwai Smith (2006: 4),

> To acquiesce is to lose ourselves entirely and implicitly agree with all that has been said about us. To resist is to retrench in the margins, retrieve what we were and remake ourselves. The past, our stories local and global, the present, our communities, cultures, languages and social practices – all may be spaces of marginalization, but they have also become spaces of resistance and hope.

As such, Small Anthropology is an emerging space of resistance and hope, as enacted, examined, and tested throughout this book. As expressed by Nigerian writer and activist Ken Saro-Wiwa in a lecture in 1993 (Wiwa, 2001: 63),

> The writer cannot be a mere storyteller; he cannot be a mere teacher; he cannot merely X-ray society's weaknesses, its ills, its perils. He or she must be actively involved shaping its present and its future.

As an African heritage Rastafarian, I freely let the Gultung's researcher flee, whilst also being curious about what they (think they) observed. Whatever researchers observed about Africans in those times was taken back and used in British (and other European) institutions to strengthen their knowledge about us, to better inform their political and cultural expansions in African territories (Somé, 1995), even when their observations and findings were based on misunderstandings and ignor- ance. Small Anthropology methodology pulls back from making universal "truth" claims about whole sets of people, recognising the tendency to do so is also part of the colonial mentality of coveting ownership of land, culture, and knowledge. Small Anthropology is a more intimate enterprise, of gaining knowledge about ourselves for our own self-empowerment – the power of knowledge remaining with the people and strengthening from within, rather than is being extracted from us and used for our subjugation from without.

The qualities which Small Anthropology promotes have been categorised into five themes, as follows:

Challenging Knowledge Hierarchies

- No inherent hierarchy between academic and "community" sources of knowledge
- No inherent hierarchy between text, visual, and audio material
- Engaging with narratives from family, friends, and people with close proximity to the subject at a non-academic level

Knowledge Values

- Not making grand narratives or universal claims
- Learning from the everyday and the mundane
- Reflexivity of the researcher and inclusion of autoethnographic positionality and vulnerability

Creative Inquiry

- Privileging intergenerational dialogues and learnings
- Interdisciplinary and multidisciplinary theoretical positioning
- Mixed methods in research approaches and output style

Showing behind the Scenes

- Celebrating and accepting nuance, serendipity, and embracing the unplanned
- Making the method transparent, conflating process, and output

Output Values

- Storytelling
- Narrative fragments
- Plain language and accessibility

The theory behind each of these themes and sub-categories will not be exhaustively discussed in this book, but the ideas of them will be worked through and put into practice in the following chapters. To find out more about Small Anthropology and the theoretical thinking behind it, please visit www.smallanthropology.wordpress.com, where I provide a video of a lecture where I discuss each of the above 14 qualities of Small Anthropology in more detail.

Small Anthropology is not a methodology that is limited to the analysis of domestic space or everyday objects and can be applied in any context. It is an unapologetic qualitative discourse, rooted in the arts and humanities (more social than science), and the pedagogic belief that every interaction between humans within a context of related phenomena can enlighten both parties to some aspect of human experience. As Paulo Freire (1977: 61) says:

> If it is in speaking their word that people, by naming the world, transform it, dialogue imposes itself as the way by which they achieve significance as human beings. Dialogue is thus an existential necessity. And since dialogue is the encounter in which the united reflection and action of the dialoguers are addressed to the world which is to be transformed and humanized, this dialogue cannot be reduced to the act of one persons "depositing" ideas in another, nor can it become a simple exchange of ideas to be "consumed" by the discussants ... Dialogue cannot exist, however, in the absence of a profound love for the world and for people. The naming of the world, which is an act of creation and re-creation, is not possible if it is not infused with love.

The writing of Small Anthropology is both a dialogue with others and with oneself. Whether it is a chance encounter or an arranged meeting, every interaction has a planned or post-rationalised methodology. Drawing on Deleuze and Guattari's (2001) notion of the Rhizome, which advocates a non-hierarchical application of interconnected knowledge, Small Anthropology recognises and embraces the messiness of human relations, interactions, knowledge transfer, and impacts to transformation. Even with this book written, the methodology of Small Anthropology is still being developed, the thinking is peppered throughout the following chapters, and is a journey of discovery which I invite you to join.

This book is a first long-form exploration of putting Small Anthropology into practice, investigating the meaning of material culture in the domestic space from a personal African-centric perspective. The work has a simple structure, wherein complexity dwells. My own narrative is present in many areas of the book's narrative, and it celebrates reflexivity of the presence of the researcher in the inquiry, in some sections I start with the self and work outwards, other times, starting with the wider context and referencing inwards.

What Is Meant by Black Everyday Lives?

During the process of proposing and writing, this book has had many different names, the most recent version before the final iteration was *Black Everyday Life, Material Culture and Narrative*. The difference is subtle but also arguably seismic. Everyday Life is the popular field of study in cultural studies, sociology, photography, and many other disciplines, and they use the singular of *Life* under no illusion that what lies underneath is a multiplicity of life experience being explored and represented, rather than a singular universal narrative. However, for me to adapt it to the plural of *Lives* was a gesture to shift the notion and perception away from a singular essentialist cultural narrative, which often still gets projected onto Black people when we are the subjects of research study. Therefore, it was particularly important to make this semantic adaptation to the title of this book, as in Black studies discourse any hint of an essentialist singular Black life experience would be rightly criticised as a form of colonialist anthropological othering and generalising.

This book is not attempting to define Blackness or put limits on what constitutes the so-called "Black experience" and has attempted to avoid such pitfalls of making such simplistic claims. Lives (rather than Life) acknowledges the problematics of studying and writing about the "Black experience" and suggests tentative knowledges rather than definitive. In practical terms, the Lives plurality is reflected in the interdisciplinary and mixed media methodology of the study, and narrative voices have been drawn from a wide range of both formal and informal sources, including personal experience, interviews, YouTube videos, newspapers, social media, blogs, roundtable discussion, books, music, informal conversation, journals, short films, fictionalised characters, and any other place where stories are shared.

In 1903, W.E.B Du Bois coined the term *Double Consciousness* to describe the effect a particular form of Black experience can have on an individual's sense of self, when you become aware of how your presence as a Black person is being watched and perceived by a dominant and predominant white gaze. *Double Consciousness* attempts to describe the experience held by many but which can be hard to articulate, of what it is like to navigate a world in which hostile tensions become embodied, and how it can create a burdensome hyper-aware self-consciousness as a survival mechanism.

> It is a peculiar sensation, this double-consciousness, this sense of always looking at oneself through the eyes of others, of measuring one's soul by the tape of a world that looks on in amused contempt and pity. One ever feels his twoness, —an American, a Negro; two souls, two thoughts, two unreconciled strivings; two warring ideals in one dark body, whose dogged strength alone keeps it from being torn asunder.
>
> *Du Bois, 1903: 168*

Possessing the sensibility of *Double Consciousness* can be both a blessing and a curse, depending on how well we consume and navigate stressful situations. There are times when I spot a small action in another person (an action which is too mundane to even attempt to give an example of) and know in that instant that the reason of that action or behaviour was in response to my presence as a Black person in that space. But to try and explain that to someone else often feels futile, and to try and unpick it could be a descent into paranoia. Often, you shrug things off and carry on with your day. (Psychologist Guilaine Kinouani presents an excellent study of these kinds of experiences and how to emotionally deal with them, in her 2021 book *Living While Black: The Essential Guide to Overcoming Racial Trauma*.) This book you are holding, however, has a different emphasis; it attempts to shift the directional focus of Double Consciousness away from being perceived as a burden, and privileges the Black gaze towards the phenomenon of material culture to extract their hidden narratives to recharge your sensibility to become a superpower, to be able to navigate the physical world with a refreshed perspective.

Arguably every individual on the planet has their own version of Double Consciousness as every person has had experiences that inform and affect how they relate to the world and people around them, and how they feel about themselves. That however does not lessen the importance of Du Bois naming this experience for Black people. The activist elements of Black cultural history, which have been manifest in various iterations over the years in movements such as the Civil Rights Movement, Rastafari, Afrocentrism, and more recently Black Lives Matter (and in academic with fields such as Black Studies and Critical Race Theory) have been trying to argue that everyday life experiences are different to what has been catered for in mainstream politics, education, healthcare services, etc., and the neglect to recognise specific needs has resulted in unequal and unjust policies with Black people being disadvantaged in the majority of social structures. This resistance has been met with seeming indifference by the dominant non-Black social hierarchies, either not understanding what the Black people are complaining about, or not considering it important enough to act.

It could be said then that the constant battle for Black activists from an academic perspective is to argue that a Black cultural history is significant and does have an effect and impact, which infiltrates as racism across all nine areas of human relations, namely: economics, education, entertainment, labour, law, politics, religion, sex, and war/counter-war (Fuller Jr, 1984). In her study "Post Traumatic Slave Syndrome," Dr Joy DeGruy argues that the impact lasts generations and has a detrimental effect on not only the individual, but also on wider society. She states,

> Post Traumatic Slave Syndrome is a condition that exists when a population has experienced multigenerational trauma resulting from centuries of slavery and continues to experience oppression and institutionalised racism. Added to this condition is a belief (real or imagined) that the benefits of the society in which they live are not accessible to them.
>
> *DeGruy, 2005: 121*

This book then is concerned with the intricacies of a Black cultural history that has for decades been invoked, debated, legislated, and campaigned on, but seldom analysed, and looks to explore and meditate on the material items found in the Black cultural history of everyday life, as experienced as everyday occurrences.

Throughout the book, particular interest is placed on how creativity has been embraced as a form of cultural expression of reclamation, through the use of domestic furniture, design, music, arts, cinema, photography, and other forms of creative practice. The study includes examples of how the topics in question has been explored in various area of the creative practice and popular culture, and a discussion of how representations of those themes add to our wider understanding of the histories and its role in the contemporary world.

1
(FRONT DOOR/HALLWAY) – SIGNS

On entering my own parents' house, you are immediately greeted with two signs, which contain three overlapping elements – a universal welcome, a witty poem, and a statement of national representation (see Figure 1.1).

> When you come here
> What you see here
> What you hear here
> What we do here
> What we say here
> When you leave here
> Let it stay here.
> *Barbados*

The enthusiastic singular message of the "Welcome" sign is immediately cautioned with the more reluctant sentiments contained in the poem, which is hung directly beneath, tied with the same string. In smaller letters the name "Barbados" lies underneath the poem, yet we know that the repeated "here" of the poem is not speaking about Barbados. We understand the country name speaks the accepted language of a souvenir, communicating the place of purchase (LaSusa, 2007: 274). The repeated "here" of the poem is (of course) referring to the place where your feet are planted when you are standing there reading the sign in real life – this house. If we are still under any illusion where the "here" is referring to, the wooden plaque that the poem is printed onto is in the shape of a house. The collective messaging of these signs is

You are welcome here....but....

DOI: 10.4324/9780367809621-2

FIGURE 1.1 Welcome signs, 2020 (© author)

Houses, and the stories they tell, are full of contradictions. When we see such signs in any place we visit, we do not usually stand and analyse them line for line looking for the hidden meaning, especially when they are hung in a hallway, where the physical movement is usually a fluid in or out (rather than when you're invited in to sit on the sofa, where your eyes have more time to linger).

This chapter will examine the idea of cautionary messaging when thinking about the history of Black households in the UK, and some cautionary tales from history about the entertaining of strangers.

Both dad and mum were from lower-working class families in Barbados and arrived in England in 1960 and 1962, respectively, both aged 21 in those years. Dad settled in the city of Bath, and when Mum arrived two years later, she went to Leicester to stay with her elder sister who had arrived a few years before, who herself was staying in a house with two other families. The three-bedroom house was owned by one of the families, and they had one bedroom, the other family in the second bedroom, my mum and her sister lived in the third room, and all the older children slept in a converted room downstairs. All the occupants ate together and shared the communal spaces. Moving to Bath to be closer to her future husband, mum took work at the hospital, and found a room in the same shared house as my future dad, owned by an Italian landlady. After they were married in 1964, my parents continued to live there, moved into a single room and saved for their own house.

We were lucky with our landlady, but we were aware some of our friends had a more difficult time. Landlords would exploit them, for example taking money to put in the electric metre, but never actually putting it in the machine, they were left in the dark and without hot water. We decided to save for our own place. We knew about saving because of our families back in Barbados, they always say, if you got 10 cents then save one. We put it in the Post Office, because if you left it in your purse of course you would spend it. We would also save money and send back home.

One of my first lessons in life, handed down to me by my parents, involved the idea of the front door as a border, and testing my self-awareness of individual responsibility and my potential impact on the family. When I was old enough to go out by myself and with friends, my mum told me sternly, waving her finger in my face.

Do not bring the police to my front door. You hear me? Do. Not. Bring. The. Police. To. My. Front. Door!

That was all she said, and all she had to say. Her instructions were clear, and a preemptive strike at whatever behaviour she imagined I could get up to. The demand is clear, and on the surface, it is not culturally specific (though what this book attempts to show is the specific cultural positioning beneath first appearance). For a mother to warn her son to not get in trouble with the police is easily understood, and is not the basis of this further analysis. What I am more interested in is the phrasing of "… to my front door." That is the part that rang in my ears. It is in fact a two-part instruction: (1) do not get in trouble and (2) do not bring the trouble back here.

The subtext of my mother's message is, "After all what our people went through, do not bring shame on them and me by bringing police and trouble to our door." At a holistic level, my mother's instruction dug deep into a historical collective consciousness and reached back to the time when Ghana's Elmina's Castle slaving port was in operation in the 1400s, the message was carried across the Atlantic and taken to the Caribbean, remembered in the plantation fields, and carried back across the Atlantic from Barbados with my parents in the early 1960s, and delivered to me circa 1982 aged 10 as I was heading out the front door, unaware of the antecedents of the instruction. The use of the front door specifically in this instruction, speaks to a Du Boisian Double Consciousness awareness (Du Bois, 1903: 168), of the judgement of the external others, and is not neutral simile to simply mean "this house." The gaze of the ancestors and family upon me would be internal, though the gaze upon the front door would be an external gaze from a hostile external world.

It was this awareness of the external observation and judgement of others that in part motivated my mother's stern lesson, which she embodied and translated as her own first strike as parental advice. Her instruction was to not direct the attention of the hostile world towards our own house, by invitation of my own (possible) foolish acts. These overt and covert messages were absorbed into my 10-year-old body and have been honoured to this day, though, the pressure of the pre-emptive inhouse warnings and external judgements has not evaporated, and works to make Du Bois' Double Consciousness more pronounced and visceral. Her words betrayed a fear communicated as worried anger. For many of the Caribbean settlers who arrived in the UK between the 1940s and 1970s, everyday living was to find oneself in a state of perpetual protest. Rather than placards and marches, negotiating daily domestic tasks, negotiating employment and visiting consumer spaces became moments of heightened awareness and tension as everyday forms of activism of survival (James, 1993: 245). The essence at the root of these tensions was the exhaustiveness of attempting to decipher the hostile gazes from the friendly ones, evaluating the strangers from the friends (BEMSCA, 2022).

My sister has a memory of me as a child in the 1970s in Bath, whenever the doorbell rang, I would run to the window to see who it was. If it was an unfamiliar white person, I would mock look scared and whisper to my sister with exaggerated tones, "There's a white person at the door!," and leave my mouth hanging open wide in comedy dramatics. I might have only been around 7 years old, but in my own cheeky, irreverent and playful way, I was enacting the echoes from my West African ancestors (DeGruy, 2005: 117), and in my childlike mind positioned our own family home as our safe castle, with any imagined enemies blocked at the front door. Of course, the notion of a family house as a safe space is not unique to African heritage people, though this book takes into account the argument advocated by Windrush Foundation co-founder Arthur Torrington, that in the British Empire, the existence of a stable African diaspora family unit is a phenomenon less than 200 years old (Torrington, 2014), arguing that before slavery was finally abolished on 1st August 1834, the idea of an African family on a plantation was a challenged existence, with the "overseers" systematically fragmenting any meaningful loyalties and bonds amongst the enslaved population. Considering the precarity of the existence of the African body throughout modernity – from the capture on African soil, transport across the ocean, surviving the plantations, descendants relocating to live in the land that enforced the initial enslavement – the existence of a Black child in an English city, playing mock-scared in this way cannot be taken for granted. Rather than a mere piece of wood or metal, the front door itself becomes both a symbol of survival and a re-enactment device as the first line of defence.

For the first post-war settlers from the Caribbean, the experiences of living in a modest Victorian terrace versus a high-rise block of flats were very different, though on first arrival any illusions of class difference was often neutralised. Whole groups of barely acquainted individuals forced to sleep on floors squashed with a whole room of others, as they worked to try and get their own shelter and stability (BEMSCA, 2022). Whether looking to rent or buy, the experience of the arrivals to actually get through a front door was not easy. According to a study on 1950s Caribbean migration and housing by Carter, Harris, and Joshi:

> Many local authorities, on a variety of pretexts…refused to house black people yet were not penalised by the minister of housing. Rather [Harold]

Macmillan, as housing minister in 1954, announced a reduction in council-house building for the following year from 250,000 to 160,000. For black people the alternative to council housing was the private sector, and here discrimination, made easier by the relaxation of controls in 1954, ensured that only areas designated for slum clearance and/or areas with short-lease properties were generally available. The difficulties of finding accommodation were underscored by the reluctance of local authorities to implement redevelopment programmes which might rehousing black tenants for fear of antagonising white tenants on long waiting lists.

Carter, Harris, and Joshi, 1993: 63

The experiences of achieving house ownership by the Caribbean newcomers are less documented in previous research, concentrating instead on the challenges of renting and social housing, but according to Wendy Webster in a study on gender and race from 1945 to 1964:

Getting a house – especially a new house – was seen as miraculous, and the house itself often named a "palace" in comparison with what had gone before.

Webster, 1998: 165

It was common to have two or three jobs in the effort to save, working night shifts and overtime, and making small amounts of money stretch a long way (BEMSCA, 2022). As my mum said, "We knew we didn't come here to just sit about. It's just what we had to do." The employment landscape was fierce, with employment exchange offices under pressure from trade unions and employers to not place Black workers in jobs where they would be superior to their white workers, and to limit the rates of pay. According to Harris (1993: 29):

As more and more black workers became trapped in labouring jobs so too did these jobs become identified as "black jobs". In a brief prepared by Ministry of Labour for a 1958 House of Commons debate, the MP Miss Hornsby-Smith was informed that white unemployed people are "not suitable for the kind of jobs held by the coloured people".

ibid.

Harris goes on to say that if the argument that post-war labour shortage was valid for recruiting Black workers, then why was there an emphasis on only filling "unskilled" jobs from the "bottom" up, rather than also focussing on the Black professional workers who had gained their education and training in their homelands, as the higher-paid jobs would also have had a labour shortage. Harris (ibid.: 30) concludes, "extensive evidence on the downgrading experienced by black workers casts serious doubt" on the argument that the Black workers were predominantly unskilled and not capable of the higher-paid positions.

Discrimination in white-collar work was underlined when Prime Minister Winston Churchill, at a cabinet meeting in December 1952, instructed the Chancellor of the Exchequer to arrange for the examination of the possibility of restricting the number of coloured people obtaining admission to the Civil Service.

ibid.: 31

Such was the welcome of the new arrivals, in their Caribbean homelands being enticed and seduced to board the boats and planes by the colonial recruiters, selling narratives of streets paved with gold, while upon arrival the story was rather different. In her study of the London borough of Newham's housing and planning decisions and the effect they have on young people, Joy White describes the council's 1967 housing policy of imposing a five-year clause of residency in Greater London and a one-year residency requirement in the Newham area, before a person was even eligible for a council house, meaning that Black and Asian people had little access to social housing (White, 2020: 15). White quotes the councillor at the time justifying the policy, he casually states it was put into forces to make it as difficult as possible for the new arrivals to access council housing. Such policies were similarly enacted in different areas of the country, meaning many had no choice but to turn to private accommodation (ibid.).

Those Everyday Signs

The "No Blacks, No Irish, No dogs" signs placed in property windows in the 1950s and 1960s have been well-documented across a wide range of sources, from academic research (Parker, 2019), media interviews (Harris, 2016), song titles and lyrics (Pelembe, 2019), in poetry (Chambers, 2007), and even designs on clothing merchandise (O'Reilly, 2016). In a letter to the *Guardian* on 21 October 2015, reader John Draper tried to cast doubt on the veracity of the signs, arguing:

> A much-reproduced photograph is held by the Irish Studies Centre of London Metropolitan University. It depicts a front window with handwritten signs saying "Bed & breakfast" and "No Irish, no blacks, no dogs". The photograph emerged only in the late 1980s, and the university has conceded to me that it is of "somewhat uncertain" provenance. They have been unable to discover who took the picture, where or when.
>
> *Guardian, 2015a*

A week later, on 28 October, Dr Tony Murray from London Metropolitan University responded:

> When Mr Draper contacted me about it two years ago, I explained that its provenance was, as he quotes, "somewhat uncertain" because there was no acquisition record in our files. However, I also explained that we had no reason

to doubt the authenticity of the image and that the archive had received it in good faith. Mr Draper appears to be confusing authenticity with provenance. Numerous artefacts with minimal provenance are held in archives but this does not necessarily mean they are not genuine. Like most of your readers, I'm puzzled by what exactly Mr Draper is trying to prove. Ample evidence exists in numerous oral history interviews with both Caribbean and Irish migrants that such signs existed well into the 60s.

Guardian, 2015b

In his original published letter John Draper does concede that, "Notices aimed at Commonwealth immigrants ('no coloureds,' 'no West Indians') certainly did exist, evidence for which exists in the BBC film archive."

Draper is confident himself of the existence of the other signs, so quibbling over the wording seems like a moot point, and evading the bigger issue at hand, which is how actual people were treated upon their arrival and the desire to secure accommodation, rather than the semantics of how the hostility was worded. Engaging in a piece of close-to-home primary research, I ask my mother about the signs. She said although she did not see the signs personally, she did hear about them, "especially in London," but by her own recollection she says she did not experience much racism that she noticed. Of course, everyone has different experiences, and many white British people did welcome the newcomers warmly and sincerely, and formed lifelong friendships.

However, the trauma of negative experiences and how people made you feel can equally last a lifetime, and transcend generations. Johannesburg-born musician Skinny Pelembe, who moved to Britain with his parents aged three (circa 1993), released a song titled "No Blacks, No dogs, No Irish" in 2019, a cultural mixture of UK drum and bass, funk rock, trip hop, with South African style melodies in the opening bars leading up to the lyrics.

• MUSIC SEARCH – *No Blacks, No dogs, No Irish* Skinny Pelembe – *PRESS PLAY*

Pelembe repeats the words of the title, from the infamous signs, continually in the song outro like a mantra chant. To evoke these words in such a sustained way, Pelembe acknowledges both the visibility and invisibility that Black people can feel in space where you are still viewed as "other" and alien even when you are home (as Ralph Ellison explored in his 1952 novel "Invisible Man"). The ability, however, to not allow such sentiments to crush you, is, I believe, reflected in the composition of Pelembe's song – the harsh lyrical content balanced with a dreamlike soundtrack – heavy drums holding up a somewhat ethereal musical arrangement. Somehow the listener is reminded of some of the harsh realities of life and the impacts of racism, while at the same time managing to find peace in the moment, taken to another place in the long instrumental parts of the music – from violent visibility to the safeness of internal invisibility. However, the words on the window signs, whether there was only one, or one hundred thousand, is something that once seen, cannot be unseen, cannot be unheard. The sentiments pierce your understanding of the very meaning of a civil society and repeats in the consciousness like Pelembe's mantra. According to Kinouani (2021: 62)

> How can your home be truly your home if entry into it and your right of abode is conditional? When this right can so easily be denied under the racist fantasy that some other home will always be yours for you to claim and return to. Even when that connection barely exists. Even if that presumed home is in fact much more unfamiliar than your usual place of dwelling.

Even when having secured a property, the front door continued to be the battleground for resident tensions, with one side facing outwards the front door is the vulnerable skin of the house, and on occasion racist graffiti, faeces, and other obscenities were daubed onto front doors by hostile locals, which became particularly prevalent in the 1970s with the increase of the racist factions of the skinhead movement and the National Front targeting Black and Asian homes and businesses (Sinclair, 2018; Grey, 2018; Mir, 2020). Throughout 2019 and up to early 2020, reports of front doors being targeted with racist graffiti and posters telling the residents to leave the country were reported, with the UK's decision to leave the European Union being cited as the reason for these outpouring of racist attacks, sometimes admitted by the perpetrators themselves (Sharman, 2019; Weaver, 2020). In this context, the front door represents the symbolic battleground of nationhood. Contemporary discourses relating to immigration are dominated by media stories of brown skin people trying to enter westernised national spaces, such as Europe, the United States, and Australia, with the front and back door being used as metaphors for legal and illegal entry, respectively (Wright & Clibborn, 2018).

Entertaining Strangers

The use of the metaphor of a house as a site of battle with invading forces, was the focus for British reggae artist Macka B in 1986, with his song *Invasion*. He evokes the idea of the house as a site of battle when meeting colonial visitors, being made an illegal presence in your own home, and forced to live in the back garden. He sings, "If a man in your house, told you to come out, and told you to live in the garden, if it happened to you tell me what would you do, wouldn't you fight and fight and fight them?" (MacFarlane, 1986).

•   MUSIC SEARCH – *Invasion Macka B* – *PRESS PLAY*

Macka B performed this song on BBC 2's Black-themed comedy series, The Real McCoy in 1993. At 6 minutes 40 seconds, it is a whole history lesson describing the behaviours of the colonialists as they invaded different terrains, telling the story of the marginalisation of Native Americans and Black South Africans in their own lands. Macka B directly asks the question of the audience to contemplate their response, of whether they would be prepared to defend their land and fight for their autonomy. The use of the house as a metaphor for these colonial conquests is significant, as the European forces were largely initially invited in as guests and did not need to enter by force. Asking the audience to contemplate the same happening to them in their own homes is a potent creative device.

The narrative of the colonial visitor, entering a domestic space and turning hostile against the rightful owners of the land, was explored in detail in the acclaimed 1958 novel *Things Fall Apart*, by Nigerian writer Chinua Achebe. Set in a pre-colonial 19th-century Nigeria, Chapter 17 deals with the arrival of European missionaries to the village of Mbanta. The missionaries ask for permission to settle in the village and for a place to build their church, and are invited in, rather than arriving using physical force. The elders of Mbanta conspire to give the missionaries part of the evil forest to build their church, in the hope that harm will come to the visitors, and they would abandon their plans and leave. Weeks pass and no harm befalls the missionaries, and subsequently their influence and presence spread amongst the village and the surrounding areas.

> [S]tories were already gaining ground that the white man had not only brought a religion but also a government. It was said that they had built a place of judgment in Umuofia to protect the followers of their religion.
>
> *Achebe, 1971: 136*

The missionaries' initial toehold presence is leveraged for the eventual takeover of the whole region, with the installation of new laws which the native villagers were now subjected to. As readers we can only passively witness the village and the region being taken away from indigenous inhibiters by the missionaries and colonial representatives in plain sight, and it happens so smoothly, you can imagine as one of the African villagers, by the time you realise what has happened it is too late. The front door cannot be closed.

What the Macka B and Achebe examples have in common is showing the precarity of comfort, and how ownership is relative to the power and danger which exude from entitlement. All anyone wants is to feel safe at home, and when your existence is threatened from those outside, the house becomes your fortress. In Macka B's use of the house as the very site of the conflict, there is nowhere left to run but their own backyard. In Achebe's example, although the village creates more space than the confines of the house, the highly communal way the people lived in Mbanta village meant the presence of the missionaries in the nearby evil forest consumed their every waking hour with concern. Both scenarios ask, *what did pre-colonial African safe spaces feel like, and how were they lost so easily?* As succinctly stated by anthropologist and Kenya's first independence president Jomo Kenyatta (Ombati–Simon, 2012: 31).

FIGURE 1.2 Mrs Sobers – Lockdown portrait, 2020 (© author)

> When the Missionaries arrived, the Africans had the land and the Missionaries had the Bible. They taught how to pray with our eyes closed. When we opened them, they had the land and we had the Bible.

I think back to my mum's warning about not bringing police (aka trouble) to the front door. I wonder if the mothers in West Africa before colonialism told that to their children when they went out to play. Strangers came to the village doors bearing gifts, and as hospitable African people were, they were invited in. In the modern world, with scammers looking for any opportunity to gain access to your home, bank account, email account, social media passwords … the list is endless. There are lessons to be learned about who to let in the front door, and in 2020, in the era of Covid-19 pandemic when many were confined to their homes, that worry took on an added meaning, with people feeling more vulnerable (Figure 1.2). Maybe more cautionary lines need to be added to the witty poem in our hallway.

2

(LIVING ROOM) – PHOTO WALL

These words are being written in the living room of my childhood home. My mum has reached the stage in her health where she needs someone in the house with her most times in the day, and I'm now back at home more than any other time since I left aged 18 (32 years ago). In the context of writing this study, things have come back full circle, and I find myself embodied in the physical space with a very personal motivation of family care, whilst trying to balance the academic pursuit of analysing the fabric of the space I am in. The medium which best captures the essence of embodied personal connection with spatial presence is the photograph, and particularly the family photograph displayed in the home.

Opposite me as I type, over the gas fire mantelpiece, is the chimneybreast wall covered in photographs of all shapes and sizes, mostly displayed as montages fixed within frames (see Figure 2.1). The wall is a teaser for the stacks of family albums in the cupboard, packed together in a series of large over-stretched plastic bags. The wall is the visitor-facing family album, the trophy wall of posed moments, perhaps reminders of what to be thankful for, and the equilibrium to be sustained as the ideal family unit.

According to ethnographers Drazin and Frohlich in their study of framed photographs in English homes, "domestic photographs are double materialisations. In their content they materialise experiences, while in their framing they comprise a representation of a moral community involved in exchanges" (Drazin & Frohlich, 2007: 53). By 'framing' they mean the context of how any photograph is treated with care, 'including in frames, on boards, in books, and in envelopes' (ibid.) – not specifically a literal physical frame. The photographic display of frames within frames of intergenerational exchange is a subjective discourse happening between the image content and the relationship of the viewer. We each understand photographs differently according to our own proximity and understanding of the scenes represented.

DOI: 10.4324/9780367809621-3

FIGURE 2.1 Photo wall, 2021 (© author)

All the handiwork of my mum, it is in keeping with the domestic aesthetic. The display of photos themselves – not the content of the images – speaks volumes about the limitations in how we perceive identity in relation to our personal pursuits and achievements. For example, I asked my mum to list all the roles she played in society and the family sphere, the list included – nurse, wife, mother, grandmother, committee member, Christian … and at no time did she say photographer, curator, or archivist, yet growing up she operated in all those roles. She was the photographer of our house; I do not recall ever seeing dad hold a camera. Mum is the custodian of the family photo archive, compiler and keeper of the family albums, and responsible for their "public" display in the home.

According to Michael McMillan, a long-standing chronicler of West Indian domestic space and material culture, "the formal mise-en-scène of the front room is also a site of photographic production providing a safe, controlled space for family portraiture" (2009: 142). In my mum's display, the photographs predominantly consist of episodes relating to my parent's children (me, my sister, and brother), and grandchildren. Proximity in the frame of group shots means the photographs also include other family members and friends, our current and former partners, our current and former friends, and some key group family shots from visits to Barbados, and reciprocal visits from family to the UK. There is a smaller representation of photographs solely of my parents and their friends. The family albums however tell a much wider story, but the photo wall is more specific. I can see through mum's image choices that this is a celebratory display of my parent's legacy, rather than a survey documenting their presence. The wall speaks of connection, attachment, recognition, and evidence of existence, the memory of which will only remain in the lifetime of the knowledge of those in proximity. With each generation, purveyors of such familial knowledge diminish, to the extent when such images, which feel as familiar to me as my own face, will be rendered alien to future generations who carry none of the information or recognition that is needed to make sense of the family images and their embedded codes. If I need to know information about a family photo now, I tend to first ask my sister, then my mum. Following the question would be a look at the image, and a narrative would follow which enlarges the frame of the photo itself. The flat surface of a photograph belies the swell of stories that are contained within.

Within the context of a Black British home, displays of intergenerational family photographs speak to not only a narrative of kinship, but also of international and historical realignment. Franz Fanon posits the notion of "passionate research" – the activity which African heritage people do to reclaim their identities from the colonial project, which sought to destroy both the present reality and past imaginary of African people (Fanon, 1962: 169). Stuart Hall draws upon this reference, arguing that the seeming innocence contained in both the display and interrogation of Black representation lays a personal quest with subconscious political urgency.

> The question which Fanon's observation poses is this: what is the nature of this "profound research" which drives the new forms of visual and cinematic representation? Is it only a matter of unearthing that which the colonial experience buried and overlaid, bringing to light the hidden continuities it suppressed? Or is a quite different practice entailed – not the rediscovery but the production of identity? We cannot and should not underestimate or neglect the importance of the act of imaginative re-discovery.
>
> *Hall, 1992: 24–26*

When looking at family photographs that you have a personal connection with, the umbilical link between you and it is lined with the presence of memory and knowledge. The photograph is speaking to you in a language that you and only a select number of other privileged few can decipher. Collectively, you have the knowledge to decode the visual references in what Barthes (1977, 42) calls the "denoted" (literal) image. I can confidently state that in Figure 2.2 – that is my grandfather stood at my left shoulder, and my little cousin Damian stood in front of me, and my older cousin Mary (Damian's mum) stood on my right-hand side.

Without further instruction, it should now be quite easy for the reader to identify which one I am, even without you knowing anyone's names or relational connection. To a certain level, you are now complicit in the decoding, and take away a knowledge of the photograph that widens the number of select few that can decipher the language the photograph speaks. As a newcomer to the image, you

FIGURE 2.2 Barbados group shot, circa 1986 (© author)

could be forgiven for humbleness in arguing that your knowledge is only partial, yet even though I know every person in the image and can talk about my perspective of each of their lives at some length, my knowledge of the photograph is also only partial, and there is an infinite number of questions that can be asked. Some questions will forever remain unanswered, frustrated that memory can only account for so much, and not all the protagonists are within proximity or still alive to speak for themselves. However, the passionate research Fanon/Hall speak of need not be deterred by such perceived barriers such as poor memory and death, and remain resolute in reframing questions so they can be answered – *How do you remember him? Was this your first time to Barbados together?* – and encourage into the information flow the presence of feeling. The umbilical link between you and your family photograph will remain subjectively partial without the addition of a third element to add to memory and knowledge – dialogue.

Personal Archaeology

In 2012 I was contacted by my friend, actress Nadia Williams, to re-create two old photographs of her mother, for her mum's birthday. The photographs had been on display in their home for as long as Nadia could remember and they were her favourites, so she thought it would be a fun thing to do. During the photo shoot I asked Nadia about the images, and she admitted she did not actually know much about them (Figure 2.3).

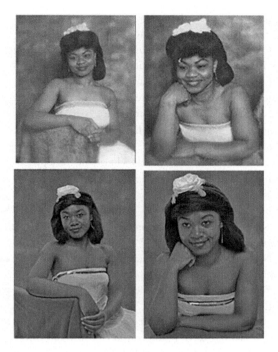

FIGURE 2.3 Mrs Williams and Nadia Williams revisited portraits, 2012 (© Sobers and Williams)

A few weeks after the shoot I asked Nadia if she could interview her mother about the photographs. I did not want to be there to steer the conversation; it should just be between the two of them, without me as a distraction. I was interested in knowing whether the conversation between Nadia and her mum would create a dialogue of unearthing long forgotten memories and the becoming of new stories. On request I offered Nadia a few opening questions, and gave some tips on how to record it using her mobile phone. About a week later I was emailed an unedited audio file, an extract as follows.

Nadia What do you remember about the day that you had these photos taken? Where were you?
Mrs Williams I was at home.
Nadia At home? (surprised) And where was that?
Mrs Williams [Redacted] Street, Bristol
Nadia And what was the occasion? Why were you having these photos taken?
Mrs Williams I just fancied getting dressed up and having a nice photograph of myself.
Nadia Was this the first time you had a photo session of yourself, and how old were you?

Mrs Williams Yes it was, and I think I was 22.

Nadia Okay, and did you pay for the occasion?

Mrs Williams I paid for the photographer, but I did the make-up myself.

Nadia Now when you look at these pictures, what do you see?

Mrs Williams I see a very nice young lady back in the day.

Nadia And what were you doing? Were you working at the time?

Mrs Williams No, I think I've stopped to have a baby.

Nadia Oh, what baby did you stop to have?

Mrs Williams I think it was you.

Nadia Okay, interesting. I thought it was when you were pregnant with my older brother [name redacted].

Mrs Williams No, I had him before.

Nadia And what is the story of this dress that you're wearing? Did you buy it?

Mrs Williams No, this dress I'm wearing was bought by your dad.

Nadia Did you go with him to buy it?

Mrs Williams No, he bought it for me about two weeks before, and it fit.

Nadia So would you say these pictures are important to you?

Mrs Williams Yeah. Because it reminded me of when I was young and how attractive I did look.

It was clear that new things were being found out in that conversation, most notably that the mother was pregnant with Nadia herself when the photograph was taken. The exercise became a form of photo-elicitation, with Nadia finding out more about her mother but also something about herself. Photographs are treated as small fragments of facts in and of themselves, and the need to question further is not always apparent, deemed relevant, or urgent. Family photographs provide familiar comfort, but they contain gates to unknown histories, many of which remain locked, un-elicited. Ben Okri suggests,

> Time weaves a spell round the image – preserves it, changes it. Portraiture keeps the subject in its time and yet projects it into ours. Portraiture is always time travel. It is time travel that keeps all the secrets of its time concealed behind the subject. It freights over to us only the image, mute with all the passions of life. Silent stories stare out from our eyes. They will no longer look upon the light or dark of our day. And yet they look at us as through a transparent medium, beyond even death. What is the true nature of that almost mystic medium?
>
> *Okri, 2011: 47–48*

We seldom ask questions of familiar photographs, until a time when we are forced by circumstance. Photography is a time-weaving shape-shifting medium, full of flux and movement even though it looks still. Barthes called the multiple readings, meanings, and narratives of photography its *rhetoric* (1977: 32–51), and Gillian Rose (2002: 17) specified that the meaning of an image is made across three critical overlapping dimensions (as Rose calls them, "sites") – (1) the circumstances of how the image was made, (2) what the image itself is depicting, and (3) how the image is experienced and received by an audience. As stated in the Drazin and Frohlich study quoted earlier in this chapter (2007: 53), one of the natures of photography is it "materialises experience" and represents "exchange." The narratives of photography exist beyond the image itself, in the case of family photos, subconsciously embodied in the memory of those who own them and hold them dear, and is present even when the photographic object is not.

At a friend's birthday garden party in Bristol 2021 (after the easing of the second coronavirus lockdown), my friend Sandra Trotman Meadows made a point of seeking me out to specifically ask me which part of Barbados I was from, as she was Bajan also, and had often wondered if there were any family connections. I have known Sandra for many years, albeit not immensely close, and we had never had this type of conversation with each other before. Explaining where my family was from on the island, we soon realised any connection was extremely remote. I suggested she speak with my partner Julie Smith, also Bajan (born in Reading), who had moved to Bristol from Leicester just the year before. They soon got into an excitable conversation, quickly establishing that their families were from the same small village in St John parish, and recognised some of the names of each other's relatives. The following weeks they stayed in touch regularly, doing more detective work to find out more connections, and came upon the realisation that they were in fact cousins. Sandra sent Julie two photographs – one of a Christening, the second of a wedding – asking if she knew anyone in them, as they were largely a mystery to her, not knowing many people in the pictures other than her own parents. In the Christening photograph Sandra's mum is seated holding a baby. The second, Sandra explained, was from an unknown wedding, her own parents were the guests at the front. I watched Julie with tears in her eyes as she spoke to Sandra on the phone. To paraphrase…

> Sandra, you're not going to believe this. In the first photo, that is my mum and dad stood next to your parents. And the second picture, that is a photo of my mum and dad's wedding! Your parents are stood next to them. Mum always told us that there were two photos of her wedding, but we have only ever seen one of them and she never knew where the other one was. This is that second photo!

The one wedding photograph that any of Julie's large family had ever seen was hung on the wall in our house, and now she was looking at the "lost" photo on her phone, "found" after 53 years, as she spoke to Sandra. Photography lends itself readily to such serendipity, faces and places waiting patiently to be identified. Images of famous faces and places have an easier job and do not need to wait for long, however, the faces and places of our everyday lives often need a more thorough investigation, and a willingness of exchange from both invested parties. It is rather apt that this exchange between Julie and Sandra happened one to one (albeit over video chat), and the photo sharing was an intimate exchange between two people, rather than a scattergun post query on social media. Evidence of the photographs vindicated their initial exchange and communications over the previous weeks, and solidified the connection between Julie and Sandra's families, satisfying the investigations in a way that mere memory and anecdotal words ever could. Sadly, Julie's parents are also no longer here to be able to share this moment or get to meet their newly discovered family member from many miles away.

When Sandra reached out and asked me her initial question, she was enacting an embodied sense of national cultural narrative, and seeking the reconstruction of a national identity that related to the self. Narrative identities provide a framework from within which we are able to navigate an understanding of proximity with the familiar. This framework is particularly so in spaces where we do not originate from, or have made homes away from home. According to Stuart Hall (1996: 623),

> National cultures are composed not only of cultural institutions, but of symbols and representations. A national culture is a discourse – a way of constructing meanings which influences and organizes both our actions and our conception of ourselves. National cultures construct identities by producing meanings about "the nation" with which we can identify; these are contained in the stories which are told about it, memories which connect its present with its past, and images which are constructed of it.

National cultural narratives face both ways – from the state outwards in the form of nation building, and from the citizens inwards in the form of identity formation. Family photographs contain codes of both – the structures of kinship and the clues of connection.

Finding and buying lost photographs of Black people is the preoccupation of UK-based Black American artist Yuko Edwards. When in the US, she would spend her time trawling through antique shops and flea markets looking for discarded images of Black people that could be reclaimed. Now being based in the UK, the search has moved online. Yuko's father grew up in the segregated American South in the 1940s and 1950s, and moved to the West Coast in the 1960s believing passionately in the idea of integration. Her father was predominantly around Black people all his life in the South, moving to the West as an adult and raising his family. By the time his daughter Yuko was born in the 1970s, the values of integration and belief in the idea of non-race-specific human family were the reality he expected to see reflected back for his children to be able to enjoy. We know, however, the reality of America from the 1960s onwards was very different from this dream of utopian idealism. Yuko grew up in a predominantly white environment yearning for the presence of Black people that her father had previously taken for granted.

> I didn't have Black people like he had Black people. He **only** had Black people. So, I lived in this somewhat false world where I was one of the few Black people. So, all this family that I would hear being talked about,

I didn't actually know. It was like knowing my Black family was supposed to happen through osmosis, I regretted their absence. So, at the beginning of my searching, all the people in these photographs were like my family. When I grew up and watched TV in the 70s and 80s, Blackness was not reflected back at me. I learned how to see myself in people who did not look like me, but then I also started searching out people who did. I was searching for kinship in magazines and in newspapers. I went looking for them, going into antique shops and asking, "Do you have any pictures of Black people?" My collection of images continue to bring me joy.

Yuko has now amassed hundreds of these photographs, some sent to her from friends and family. The images have begun to enter Yuko's creative work, but the repurposing of the images is not her prime motivation. It is simply to own them, and reclaim them from otherwise being discarded alone in the world. The physicality of the photographs is a key in Yuko's search, and she has no interest in downloading digital files from the internet. The condition of the physical prints – creases, rips, dates, and names written on the back – that is the way the images speak, adding to the narrative providing clues of who the people are and what they were doing. Digital images remain largely pristine, where physical prints show signs of age, as do real people. The photographs and the people within them form for Yuko a community of fictive kinship, bonds which extend beyond the ties of blood relations (Chatters, Taylor, & Jayakody, 1994). Yuko is fully aware how, like all families, family photographs can also be problematic, and can perpetuate lies and hide the more complex dynamics of family life.

What I'm learning from this collecting is that a photograph can stimulate a memory that has nothing to do with the photograph. What we wish we had photographs of are the things that we remember, but instead, we have photographs of a time. If we look through the lines of those photographs, we start to remember what was happening at that time. I mean, imagine if we actually had pictures of how we felt, what hurt us, the faces of the people that we'd like to forget. Instead, we see these happy families or moments, you know, which may not have been like that in reality. For some people family albums are torture. They are often a façade, in that people were made to stand in this way with their hands in this position. It is more that narrative which is behind the image that I'm interested in, that is how you can make stories.

The lived experience of living within a state-sanctioned segregated society, as Yuko's father did, or from living in a failed or flawed integrated society, as Yuko herself did, are both visible and absent in photographs of those times. Searching these photographs out and becoming their custodian today offers the Black people represented in the images a new opportunity for a renewed story, and offers us the imagination of how we would like to live and what we would like that reality to be.

Complex Emotional Attachment

Thinking back to mum's photo wall display, there is one photograph that is no longer visible. I stole it from the domestic gallery when I was a teenager, much to mum's annoyance. In 1977, aged 5 years, despite my protests I was put forward to participate in a Royal Scene in celebration of the Queen's Silver Jubilee. My strong memory of this event is not being happy to take part, as I had to wear Union Jack shorts. (This is a memory that my mother readily concurs with, while laughing heartedly.) The lasting legacy of the event revolves around a transient memory and a permanent product: the memory of not being happy to take part, and the permanent product reminder of the resulting photograph (see Figure 2.4). Immediately I became embarrassed by the photograph, feeling straight away what Barthes refers to when seeing himself in an image as the "terrible spectacle" of the "spectrum of the photograph" (Barthes, 1980: 9, 12). Any embarrassment about

1977

2009

FIGURE 2.4 Silver Jubilee revisited, 1977–2009 (© author)

being a participant in such a nationalist and royalist propaganda flag waving scene would not come until my later teenage years, an affront to my by-then evolved Pan-African sensibilities.

The original reluctance to take part in the event, and the disempowering feeling of shame of not being in control of one's representation, would not have been sustained in me, if it had not been for the product of the event – the photograph – particularly when on display in the home for all my friends to see. Without the photograph the event would be consigned to the past with few witnesses, but the photograph rendered the event perpetually present. Mum would put it up, and I would take it down, and thus the cycle continued until age 18 when I left home, and hid it in various places, only to be unearthed again each time I moved house, then re-packed away in a box to be conveniently forgotten, even taking it with me to a different town aged 21 (1993) when I left for university.

Even though the experience of the school's photo-opportunity had the opposite effect on me than the school intended – one of shame rather than pride – I realise now while writing this chapter that between myself and the photograph a complex emotional attachment was formed. Even though I commonly said I hated the photograph, I never destroyed it, or attempted to. The fact is, although I loathed it, I now realise that I still protected it. I grew up in a household that cherished the value of photographs, and possibly that same level of affection had been subconsciously passed to me. Even though I hated the embarrassment that the photograph evoked in me, paradoxically I seem to have still respected the artefact that carried the contested memory. According to Drazin and Frohlich (2007: 51),

> Family photographs demand of us that they be treated right. They seem ubiquitous in modern life, spread throughout the home … Yet these everyday casual objects are nonetheless demanding. For some reason, photographs should not be thrown away. They are given and received, transmitted hand to hand and home to home, but rarely disposed of.

As the typical brash teenage boy that I once was, I am surprised that I did not rip it up and throw it away. I now thank my younger-self for this restraint, yet still slightly disappointed by my apparent lack of rebelliousness that I thought I possessed. My embarrassment of the image was based on damaged ego shrouded by a perceived evolved sense of identity. At first it was about not being comfortable with wearing embarrassing clothes at the actual event, then later shame at the photographic evidence. Latter, in my late teenage years and early twenties, my renewed sense of African identity was at odds with the celebratory sense of unadulterated British patriotism expressed in the scene. There is nothing new about an older-self being shamed by the activities of the younger-self. The image represents a power that was taken away from me, a reminder of being imposed upon by adult ideas. Dressed as a childhood trophy for a contest I did not believe in.

The first time I voluntarily showed the photograph to anyone was in 2008, 31 years after its capture, when as part of my PhD I had the idea to reclaim the moment and remake it. I began to see the image through the framework of visual anthropology rather than from the perspective of a tortured actor. It became a fascinating historical document of a moment in, not only my history, but also in the histories of the other children I shared the 1977 event with, collectively captured. After a year of searching and organising, in 2009 the six of us met back together again in our old infant school for the first time since 1977, and with the help of photographer Amanda Harman and filmmaker Rob Mitchell, we re-made the infamous image. We all agreed to simply stand in place as we wanted to be seen, or as Barthes would have it, to "imitate" ourselves (1980: 13). The relative neutrality of the image, of each individual in "normal" attire and casual poses, visually speak to the participatory aim of giving a platform for a group to represent themselves as they are and want to be seen, and not dressed as caricatures according to someone else's agenda.

Since reclaiming the moment and remaking the image, I now show both versions in lectures to students, have exhibited them in galleries, and now reprinting them in this book. If you told my teenage-self I would be doing this, I would have bet any money that would **not** be happening. Such is the power of reclaiming and owning the narrative for oneself.

The nationalist cultural narrative captured in the original 1977 Silver Jubilee photograph is self-evident in the royal attire and the Union Jack flags and clothing designs. However, the act of using children to make the scene is the most potent nationalistic narrative symbol of all, added with the layer of ethnic and gender diversity. What the school did as an apparent cute thing to do can paradoxically also viewed suspiciously as propaganda and coercion, an afront to my latter Pan-African Rastafari identity. When speaking with the other members of the photograph, it was evident, and possibly not surprising, that I was the only one who attached it with such strong negative feelings. Some of them had not given it much thought since the day it happened 32 years previously. Such is the burden of resentment, that any Buddhist will tell you, hurts only yourself, as you carry the heat of the torment by energising it with feelings. "Attachment is the root of suffering" (Ñāṇamoli & Bodhi, 2009: 868), and I accept I am scarred. DeGruy (2005: 142) states,

> (W)e all bear the burdens of our ancestry to some degree. And make no mistake: though some of us bear them more than others, all of us have been affected. Three hundred plus years of slavery and oppression certainly have had their impact. A portion of the impact has given rise to weaknesses that we have to understand, confront and deal with if we are to thrive. Another portion has provided us with great strengths upon which to build. In both regards we all are slavery's children.

Though hard to read and possibly accept, DeGruy's argument is persuasive. Of course, being embarrassed by a childhood photograph is an extremely mild version of what DeGruy is talking about, when faced with the far more serious symptoms of – Black people living in poverty, experiencing mental health difficulties, the high percentage of us caught up in the criminal justice system, and the challenges of young Black people face in mainstream education. Part of the point of this book, however, is to show the symptoms of some of these more serious conditions in aspects of everyday life, and how we relate to the world around us. It reminds me of a seminar I ran with my class of all white photography students about representation. The conversation went something like this.

Me: I'm going to ask you a crass question, but please indulge me with your honest answers. What types of students might be most likely to make work exploring ideas relates to gender identity?

After a Slight Awkward Pause ...

Student 1: Most likely female students. (Student 1 was female herself.)

Me: And what type of students do you think would most likely be making work exploring ideas relating to race and ethnicity?

After a Short Pause than before.

Student 2: Hmmm ... probably students of colour.

What then followed was a discussion about intersectionality (Crenshaw, 1991). About how it is funny that, even though white students also have an ethnicity and race, yet unanimously they are less likely to feel the need to explore it as a topic in their work. Likewise, male students also have a gender identity, but again in the class it was agreed males are less likely to be the ones to feel the urge to explore it. We discussed why that might be the case, and what people of colour and women have in common, similar with the LGBTQ+ community, and people with disabilities. When you are forced to confront aspects of your identity every day of life as an act of mere existence, you are then prone to reflect on it more in your creative work, and for it to also inform and shape your principles and worldview.

Even in silent rooms, photographs speak volumes. They carry within them a complex entanglement of social codes which are both visible and invisible. The photographs people choose to have on display in their homes are some of the most cherished objects in the world, bursting with noise, yet appear to be the most silent.

3

(LIVING ROOM) – TELEVISION

Sitting down to watch Roots was like a window to a world and history we knew was out there, but it was the first time we saw it siding with the Black man.

Mr Stuart

There is a Ghanaian symbol called Sankofa, which depicts a bird looking back collecting a seed in its mouth. It is an ancient Adinkra symbol, which education scholar Kwadwo Asafo-Agyei Okrah defines as meaning "taking from the past what is good and bringing it into the present in order to make positive progress through the benevolent use of knowledge" (Okrah, 2008: 26). The allegory speaks of the importance of reclaiming your history in order to be able to move into the future as a whole person. On Friday, 8 April 1977 at 8.45 pm, Black Britain experienced a moment of collective Sankofa, with the transmission of the first episode of the *Roots* mini-series on BBC1. Based on the novel *Roots: The Saga of an American Family* by Alex Haley, through eight initial episodes broadcast on consecutive days, the series tells the multigenerational story of how, in 1750, a young Gambian man Kunta Kinte was captured into slavery, and survives the brutality of plantation life to become the ancestor of a modern African American family. Having previously aired in the USA in January 1977, *Roots* broke audience records becoming the largest viewed television programme in America of all time with over 98 million viewers (Wolper & Troupe, 1978: 154). When the series came to British television sets, my 5-year-old eyes were amongst the reported 19 million UK viewers who tuned in (Kwei-Armah, 2007), which was completely unexpected. Distributed by ABC television network, there was lack of confidence of how well *Roots* would perform in an international market, and the original transmission schedule was designed for it to be broadcast on consecutive days, to minimise the risk and cut losses rapidly if it

DOI: 10.4324/9780367809621-4

was a dismal failure (Havens, 2013: 30). A year after its first transmission, producer David Wolper reflected on its success.

> Roots was designed to reach a large television audience, not a small sophisticated group of intellectuals who wanted to increase their knowledge of the "slavery situation in America". I wanted to educate a mass audience. Television can and should be used as a mass cultural medium, not just to educate a chosen few – and the gigantic audience out there wants to be educated, but they want it their way.
>
> *Wolper & Troupe, 1978: ix*

As Mr Stuart (a 78-year-old Caribbean-born, London-based elder) alludes to in the opening quote, watching *Roots* was an eye opener to a history he was previously unable to visualise, it was like watching a reflection on screen and making sense of his sense of self. Even at 5 years old, I experienced those same complex emotions, sat on my dad's lap, crying and fascinated in equal measure. The safety of a living room is relative to the complexity of the surrounding society. Television creates a window out into wider society (Highmore, 2014: 65), and also emboldens wider society to have an opinion on other people's lives. The following Monday back at school, at which there were only a tiny handful of other Black children (I was the only person of colour in my class), the racist taunts and mocking *Kunta Kinte* name calling swiftly came. The television in the corner of our living rooms had shifted the reality of our precarious mutual existence. The shift in consciousness in my own Black body was to realise, no matter the racism I faced in the wake of *Roots*, that there was no shame in my Black skin or ancestry (as the Sankofa bird lesson anticipated).

Polish theorist Elzbieta Rokosz-Piejko alludes to the shift in white viewers consciousness, in the realisation there were other sides to a story, and they themselves had also been lied to in white-supremacy's suppression of the Black narrative. She goes onto say:

> For the first time, in a major television show addressed to the wide audience, whiteness was decentered and African American characters appeared as fully human. And for the first time in a production like this, the fact of white slave masters raping their female slaves and having children by them is conspicuously referred to, stressing that in American history whiteness and blackness are inextricably linked.
>
> *Rokosz-Piejko, 2018: 147*

For conscientious Black and white British audiences watching this cultural phenomenon in 1977, came a cognitive dissonance with the question of – *how does the UK and the Black British experience specifically, fit into the slavery narrative, with the material connections between the land we found ourselves in, and the history we are presented with?*

Watching *Roots*, England seemed like a long way away, an almost mythical place, seemingly unconnected to this period of history by its absence, yet with the knowledge that it is umbilically linked as the source of the brutal decision-making we saw on screen. During Britain's involvement in transatlantic slavery, between 1562 and 1834, the British landscape remained largely distanced from the brutal horrors that happened on its behalf on the plantations in the Caribbean, North and South America, and on the continent of Africa itself. *Roots* brought the heat of Africa, the sweat of the slaving ships, the tensions of crossing the Atlantic, and the blood and tears from the plantations, into the contemporary living rooms of the UK. The show provided validation for politicised and "conscious" Black people who were aware and vocal about the racist treatment they found in the UK. Alternatively, *Roots* also created a challenge for any of the Caribbean migrants whose survival strategy since arrival in the UK was to try and integrate, assimilate, and distance themselves from any overt "Blackness," wanting to find favour in the white gaze.

In the 2000s we can take the "Black and proud" mantras for granted, and the general acceptance of the African antecedence of Black/Caribbean/West Indian identities, but in the 1970s such sentiments were not so prevalent in many Black working class households, in some cases taboo. This was not a reflection that pride in their own Black skins was not present, just that the articulation of that pride was not necessarily overtly stated. In the wake of Enoch Powell's *Rivers of Blood* speech in 1968, the 1970s provided the apt conditions for the rise of the far-right National Front party and the racist factions of the skinhead movement amongst the white working classes (Brake, 1974). Amongst the first generations of children born in Britain to Caribbean parents, saw an increase in a politicised younger Black generation, exposing the African-centric ideas of Marcus Garvey and the Rastafari movement, inspired by the American Civil Rights movement discourse of Malcolm X and Martin Luther King Jr., and the arguments of US Black Power movement leaders such as Stokely Carmichael, H Rap Brown, Bobby Seale, and Huey P. Newton. The Caribbean-born generation who came to live in Britain in the post-war period laid steadily built foundations – got jobs, secured accommodation, and started families – and their UK-born offspring were hungry for change, trying to make sense of this pan-African vision in a Black British context (BEMSCA, 2022). In amongst this developing Black British identity came *Roots* which provided an accessible and widely consumed historical underpinning. Broadcast in 50 countries spanning five continents, the resonance within the African diaspora was visceral. This was Alex Haley's own comet with global impact. Descendants from the Caribbean looked at their own surnames, and felt the heat of the branding iron in the realisation they carried the names of their ancestors' former owners. According to writer and actor Kwame Kwei-Armah (2007),

> It was a moment that changed my life. By the end of the series I had told my mother that I would one day trace my heritage back to Africa and reclaim an ancestral name. Before I watched the programme I was called Ian Roberts but now my name is Kwame Kwei-Armah.

From the comfort of our living rooms, we watched as Kunta Kinte received the whip for not renouncing his birth name, refusing to adopt his "slave name" Toby. This moment, possibly more than any other, articulated the determination to try and erase African consciousness from the new world. There was no place in the British Empire for African tastes, values, sensibilities, or sympathies. The overseer would rather have us die than remember. The memory of Africa was a threat to the new world the Europeans were creating with the labour of the African body, the memory of the old world had to be erased. The African body and mind could only exist to service the needs of the oppressor.

In Plato's *Allegory of the Cave*, written in approximately 380 BCE (Plato, 2010), captured prisoners are held for so long, tightly bound in a dark cavern, they forget their former world, seeing only the shadows on the wall in front of them as their new reality. One prisoner manages to escape, and sees the world outside, and tells the others of their misunderstanding. The still captured prisoners reject him, telling him he's mad, that there is nothing more to reality than the flickering shadows. In 1977, television was the flickering shadow on the wall, and *Roots* became the fleeting glimpse at a wider challenging world of possibilities. According to Mr Stuart,

> What was lost was more than names, we lost everything. Roots restored some of my sense of pride. Water came to my eye, I'd never seen anything like it, I don't think any of us had. The power of that television (show) man ... we looked at each other different than before. Haley did us all a service. Black and white people I mean. It did good for everyone to see that.

Stories to Tell

The predominant regular representations on UK television of British Black families around the time *Roots* was broadcast, were two sides of the same coin, which can be seen in the examples to two comedies from that era – *Love Thy Neighbour* (1972–1976), and *The Fosters* (1976–1977), both broadcast on ITV. The former depicted the tense toxic relationship between neighbouring working class Black and white families, with verbal abuse, misunderstandings, stereotypes, and accusations coming from both families along problematic racial lines. In the landmark book *Black and White in Colour: Black People in British Television Since 1936*, edited by UK-based African American writer Jim Pines in 1992, Stephen Bourne interviews some of the key individuals involved with both shows. According to Rudolph Walker, *Love Thy Neighbour's* lead actor, the robust representation of racism being challenged by Black people was one of the unsung pioneering elements of the show.

> [It] was agreed that that is the bigoted white neighbour called me something I would call him the equivalent back. If he hit me I would hit him back. In other words, we were on a par ... [N]ow we had someone who was standing up for himself, and that had to be good for the youngsters.
>
> *Pines, 1992: 78*

Walker talks about how he became a role model for young people, them seeing for the first time on television a Black person defending themself in such a bold way. Alternatively, the other TV comedy, *The Fosters*, offered a more nuanced representation of an intergenerational Black family. Modelled on the USA sit-com *Good Times*, it showed Black people whose every waking moment was not dominated by thoughts related to race and racism. *The Fosters* portrayed a family that happened to be Black, rather than about the race dynamics of being Black, such as was the storylines in *Love Thy Neighbour*. Also interviewed by Bourne (Pines, 1992: 116), lead actor of *The Fosters* Norman Beaton said about the show,

> The Fosters was purely about a Black family – and to have a Black family portrayed on British television, without referring to the fact they were Black, but just dealing with the fact they ate food, went to church, and did quite normal things – that was really quite extraordinary.

Thus, according to Beaton, it was the everyday life-ness of *The Fosters* which made it revolutionary, rather than the depiction of racist struggle. Although these narrative positions are not static nor mutually exclusive dichotomies, this binary approach of critiquing representations of the Black family dynamic is a tendency that continues and has become exacerbated, especially within Black audiences ourselves. For example, growing up as a teenager watching the highly successful American export *The Cosby Show*, despite its huge popularity I was also fully aware of the critique that the show was "whitewashed," that it wasn't "Black enough". In a 1995 edition of the influential journal *The Black Scholar*, Carlos Nelson and Hermon George Jr argue that

> The Cosby Show's failure to comment on class and race, the raison d'être of US society, perpetuates a monstrous lie. It simultaneously performs a disservice to the millions of African-Americans who, unlike the Huxtables, must contend with class and racial discrimination as a part of their daily existence. The inescapable question, therefore, is whether this concession made in order to gain access to a European-American audience was too great. We assert that it was.
>
> *1995: 59*

The accusation is that to represent a non-racialised Black everyday life experience is not only a luxury, but an insult at a time when the racism faced by so many is so urgent and stark. As a naive teenager in the 1980s and later as a student in the 1990s, hearing such comments and reading like-minded editorials and letters in Black media outlets, my response was quite simplistic – *surely this shouldn't be an either/or situation, there should be enough space for both types of representation as I want to see both, and can relate to both.* It should be noted, that is still my view today, regardless of how naive and simplistic it may seem. I relate to Chimamanda Ngozi Adichie when she states

> All of these stories make me who I am. But to insist on only these negative stories is to flatten my experience, and to overlook the many other stories that formed me. The single story creates stereotypes. And the problem with stereotypes is not that they are untrue, but that they are incomplete. They make one story become the only story.
>
> *Adichie, 2009*

Being Programmed

In 2016 I had a conversation with a Rastafari female friend on Facebook, discussing the merits of live versus on-demand television. It was in response to a post from a mutual friend which asked whether anyone still watched scheduled television anymore, and questioning the need. The argument I put forward was that there was still a need for "event" television, where big parts of the population have a shared experience watching the same thing at the same time, such as sports events, live events, and other such cultural moments of popular significance. She said I had a point, but the way she sees it, "television has programmes, because it is programmed, so when we watch programmed television, we get programmed!" I *Liked* that. Jamaican theorist Stuart Hall, who is well-known for his version of "encoding and decoding" audience reception theory (Hall, 1980), may have sympathy with my friend's clever thinking and word play, though ultimately refute the subsequent resolution of writing-off all programmed television from fear of media manipulation. Hall acknowledges that an "event must become a 'story' before it can become a communicative event" (Hall, 1973: 2), mediated stories which are encoded with "dominant or preferred meanings" by producers, broadcast within a wider ideological framework which he calls a "*structure of dominance*" (ibid.: 13). Despite this dominant structural messaging framework that programmes are produced and broadcast within, Hall still argued that audiences are not as passive as often stated in previous theories, and that they can play an active role in decoding messages from programmes and make personal meanings, which are equally ideological, though informed by their own world views, class, race, and other discourses. Audiences have the ability to deconstruct given messages through our own negotiated and oppositional readings of what we are being fed via the media, with the agency to agree or refuse whatever message intentions were envisaged by the programme's producers. As Hall describes,

> The consumption or reception of the television message is thus itself a "moment" of the production process, though the latter is "predominant" because it is the "point of departure for the realisation" of the message.
>
> *ibid.: 3*

Media theorist Marshall McLuhan, however, might robustly support my Rastafari friend, saying the message and the meaning of this televised event, was the fact we were all watching television at the same time in the first place, regardless of what the details of the material was that we were seen to be individually consuming. The physical event **is** the message, meaning and the content, not the story on the screen. For McLuhan, the real power of the media is in how it makes you act, not in what you watch. For Hall, who was well aware of McLuhan's argument at the time he formulated his theory, each of us has our own individual agency and the power to make our own choices, in light of wider context and knowledge of structures of power.

Both perspectives are compelling, and arguably both are true at the same time, it is not a dichotomy. Both also have a strong echo in the discourse of Blackness, which was the context of the original Facebook post. A music playlist of Gil Scott-Heron's *Revolution Will Not Be Televised*, The Disposable Heroes of Hiphoprisy's *Television, the Drug of the Nation*, and Public Enemy's *She Watch Channel Zero* all reflect this. Understandably there are rather less songs celebrating the liberatory forces of television. (By the second verse of Dinah Washington's *TV Is the Thing This Year*, it is quite clear the message has been extended far beyond being a song about the box in the corner of the room, and used a sexual metaphor.) For signs of Hall's more optimistic intellectual empowerment position, hear the message in Bob Marley's line "Emancipate yourself from mental slavery, none but ourselves can free our minds" in *Redemption Song*. The encoding/decoding argument permeates the discourse of Hip Hop representation, with NWA, KRS One, Dead Prez, The Roots, Eminem, The 2 Live Crew, and many more, defending their music genre, saying their listeners are not as passive and impressionable as mainstream media accuses them of.

Racialising McLuhan's position lets us see how the politicisation of television and the media has long been present in Blackness discourse, and it is of no surprise why my Rastafari friend has suspicions about the media's intent. British media and television have had long-standing accusations of racist portrayals of Black people on its screens (Twitchin, 1990; Hall, 2003), and Black actors continue to leave the Britain for America, for the wider range of acting roles on offer (Seymour, 2013).

In the 1970s and 1980s, a collective announcement network existed, with the friends of my parents ringing each other up to tell us to watch a certain channel, to catch a glimpse of whatever Black actor or personality happened to be on screen at that moment. The bar of expectation in those times was low, and many of the televised representations being announced would likely have been quite problematic racist depictions. The details, however, were often overridden by the mere presence of a Black person on screen at all, and the actual dialogue of the programme drowned out by the voice of my parents making their own phone calls, extending the announcement network. As children, my sister and I could all but stare at the Black presence on the screen, not hearing what they were saying, but just thankful they were there.

Covid Television and the Black Atlantic

During the Covid-19 lockdowns of 2020, television became the source of solace for many, being cut off from being able to socialise with others. On 25 May 2020, our televisions and digital devices became alight with news that 46-year-old African American George Floyd was killed by a white policeman, who knelt on his neck for a period of 8 minutes and 46 seconds. The whole ordeal was filmed by numerous witnesses and were quickly shared online and reached global mainstream television news.

Black Lives Matter protests similarly spread across the world, and in my hometown of Bristol, the protest on June 7 culminated in the toppling of a statue of notorious Bristol-born slave trader Edward Colston. This action similarly was quickly shared online and reached global mainstream television news, and inspired the toppling of statues of slave traders in other parts of the world, including Europe and back in the United States. Add to this live televised connected dynamic, the Covid-19 virus itself, whose spread could be traced through people's local, national, and global interactions, and disproportionately affecting African and Asian heritage people at rates far higher than their white counterparts. The reasons for this disparity are still being researched, though strong indications pointing towards inequalities in society and unequal living standards (Elwell-Sutton, Deeny, & Stafford, 2020). This back and forth set of inspired empathetic activist actions and biological impacts ricocheted across the globe, not least between the USA and the UK. The summer of 2020 became a visual representation of the entangled and interconnected nature of African diasporic discourse and gave added meaning to Gilroy's persuasive notion of the Black Atlantic.

> Getting beyond national and nationalistic perspectives has become essential for two additional reasons. The first arises from the urgent obligation to re-evaluate the significance of the modern nation state as a political, economic, and cultural unit. Neither political nor economic structures of domination are still simply co-extensive with national borders ... [It] is a world-wide phenomenon with significant consequences for the relationship between the politics of information and the practices of capital accumulation. Its effects underpin more recognisably political changes like the growing centrality of transnational ecological movements which, through their insistence on the association of sustainability and justice, do so much to shift the moral and scientific precepts on which the modern separation of politics and ethics was built. The second reason relates to the tragic popularity of ideas about the integrity and purity of cultures. In particular, it concerns the relation-ship between nationality and ethnicity ... [It] reflected directly in the post-colonial histories and complex, transcultural, political trajectories of Britain's black settlers.
>
> *Gilroy, 1999: 7*

Television and disaggregated social media platforms are the carriers of this plural and porous discourse, and the humble television set does still have a role to play in the intergenerational flow of the Black Atlantic and other spatially entangled territories. In the 1970s, the mere representation of Black people on screen was deemed to be a key marker of achievement, and spoke to the integration strategy of many of the early Caribbean settlers in the late 1950s and throughout the 1960s, which was a strategy born out of necessity and sheer survival. In 2020s the conversation has changed, from the importance of on-screen representation, to the diversity of representation off screen, with challenges to assess how ethnically diverse the boardrooms are, the producers, commissioning editors, camera operators, and other behind-the-scenes roles, both technical and strategic. On-screen Black presence in programmed broadcast UK television has significantly changed, with mainstream drama and factual series having Black characters and presenters, where the key interest in their presence is not in the fact that they have black skin. On-demand television has also altered the perception of on-screen presence significantly, with films and boxsets available instantly to satisfy any cultural appetite or specific tastes, to watch a certain actor or the work of a particular director, at any time we specify.

However, a regional BBC1 news broadcast on 29 July 2020 highlighted the chasm between the quality of on-screen Black presence and the editorial decisions made by those off screen. Reporting on a suspected violent racist attack on a 21-year-old Black male NHS worker from Bristol, in an incident where a car mounted a pavement as he was leaving his workplace of Southmead hospital and ran him over, leaving him with significant physical injuries including a broken leg, cheek-bone, and nose. Happening at a time when NHS workers were roundly hailed as heroes for their work during the coronavirus pandemic, the television interview with the victim was rightly sympathetic towards him. Though, this tone was significantly marred by the editorial decision for the news reporter to speak in full the racist word *N****r*, which was heard to be shouted at the victim as the car drove directly towards him, in the 10.30 am broadcast. After the BBC first defended the use of the word in the news item, following 18,000 complaints including public statements from BBC's own Black staff, 11 days later the Director General Lord Tony Hall offered an apology, stating

> It should be clear that the BBC's intention was to highlight an alleged racist attack. This is important journalism which the BBC should be reporting on and we will continue to do so. Yet despite these good intentions, I recognise that we have ended up creating distress amongst many people. The BBC now accepts that we should have taken a different approach at the time of broadcast and we are very sorry for that. We will now be strengthening our guidance on offensive language across our output.
>
> *Points West & BBC News Channel, 2020*

The collective announcement network re-emerged in November 2020, with the broadcast of Steve McQueen's *Small Axe* series – five films about the historic Black British experience. On the night of the screening of *Mangrove*, the first film in the series, which told the story of police racial harassment against a London Black community in the 1970s, my social media platforms and text messages were alight with Black friends announcing the broadcast with a palatable excitement and expectation.

> @ACCOUNT NAME REDACTED
>
> The glorious buzz in the lead up to #SmallAxe is reminding me of the days it presents, when we used to call each other and say "Turn on … black people are on the telly!" ☺🖥 That's how rare it was. #Memories #History

This collective announcement of McQueen's films by people of all generations was different in quality from the announcements in the 1970 and 1980s, not just in the platforms of its delivery being social media rather than the house phone. In the 1970s it was mostly about the mere sight of Black actors on screen, yet with *Small Axe* it was the Director, McQueen's name, which was used as the selling point, not that of the actors. This shift reflected the anticipated authenticity of on-screen representation that comes with having a Black director, and inevitably raises the bar of expectation of what was delivered in that content. The fact that these organic collective announcements of Black presence on screen happened at all in the 1970s, 1980s, and 1990s, and to a lesser extent but still happening at the time of writing in 2022, demonstrates the enticement of representation, and the urgency and hunger for fair on-screen depictions of Black people in our media. These were not orchestrated activist events of mailing lists and scripted campaigning, this was simultaneously Black people in their 80s, 40s, 20s, and teenage years, recognising the importance of seeing someone who looked like them (like us) on their screens, and wanting to share that news with another from a shared cultural background. It speaks of a collective alienation of how a whole demographic of people felt (and feels), and any instance where the alienation is challenged with a glimmer of how things could look in a more equal British society is cause for sharing the good news.

Invariably however, my Rastafari friend on Facebook would have the last laugh, as when I was receiving the abundance of messages and notifications urging me to watch BBC2 to watch McQueen's *Mangrove*, I had my cable TV box set on pre-record to watch it at another time, ironically missing out on the collective broadcast event I previously championed for.

Black Gaze on the Life, Death, and Legacy of an Electric Media Princess

The island of Barbados has been known as "Little England" since 1940, when Bajan politician Grantley Adams (later the first Prime Minister) sent a telegram to King George VI saying "Go on England; Little England is behind you," in support of "big" England going to war against Hitler's Germany, with Bajan troops sent to fight alongside the allied forces. The mixed reactions of this label, which has continued to stick to the island, was described by Austin Clarke as being a feeling of "pride or embarrassment" by Bajans, depending on your politics and nationalistic affiliation (Clarke, 1998: 41).

This enactment of *Little England*, and the entangled relationship to the British monarchy, was alive and well in 1981, when collective live television came into its own on 29 July, with the wedding of Princess Diana and Prince Charles. Watched by 750 million people in 74 countries (BBC Anniversaries, 2019), including in the living room of my grandparents' house in Barbados.

Aged 9 years, with my sister aged 13, my grandfather woke us up at around 5 am Bajan time, and gathered us into the living room to watch the Royal wedding. I don't remember whether we asked to watch it, but it was definitely an event we knew about, and as children, had taken an interest in. On holiday with our mum, dad stayed behind in England. With flights to Barbados being so expensive, me and sister would only usually go there with either parent (only on one occasion with both, for my sister's wedding). This time was with mum, and she sat with us as we watched Diana and Charles walk down the aisle 6,775 km away. This scene, however, is not unique to Barbados, and was echoed across the Caribbean, even in households which would pride themselves as being anti-monarchist and highly politicised. The role of television in galvanising and shifting moods of nationalistic identity, whether that being in celebration of, or resistance to, the content being broadcast, was foreseen by Marshall McLuhan as early as 1964 when he wrote:

> As electrically contracted, the globe is no more than a village. Electric speed in bringing all social and political functions together in a sudden implosion has heightened human awareness of responsibility to an intense degree. It is the implosive factor that alters the position of the Negro, the teen-agers and some other groups. They can no longer be *contained* in the political sense of limited association. They are now *involved* in our lives, and we in theirs, thanks to the electric media.
>
> *McLuhan, 2008: 5*

The cultural positionality of McLuhan's voice is clear, and who he assumes his readership to be. He speaks to an assumed white middle class normative reader, speaking of the connectivity of people that electronic media affords, and anticipates the decoding agency of audiences that Stuart Hall describes. Once people are connected, they cannot be unconnected, as that original moment of connection cannot be undone. The "Negro, the teenager," to use McLuhan's terminology, have seen glimpses of the near and further world through the lens of electric media (namely television), and more importantly, its politics, and that means, with Hall's decoding, they have not only seen, but they also form opinions on what they have seen. As McLuhan states, this access to the world means our worlds are now entwined and involved.

What does this theoretical thinking mean to me as a Black 9-year-old, watching a white Princess and Prince getting married in England, the country of my birth, on a television set in Barbados, the country of birth for both my parents? In hindsight, from which is the only position I can confidently speak, it possibly relates to the realisation that there was a connection between this Royal family of the British Empire and my birth family in the commonwealth, which at 9 years old I would not have understood. At that age, it would have been manifest in the simple question, "Why are we watching this?." Though I did not ask that question, I went along with the spectacle. As I grew, the awareness of that connection grew, more understanding the links between my mother's country, the Mother Country, and the Motherland of Africa, building on my witnessing while watching *Roots* four years earlier. I took notice of the enthusiasm and the ambivalence of different people around me towards the wedding and towards the Royal family in general. By the time Princess Diana returned to television in 1995 in her (now contested) interview with Martin Bashir, to unravel the dominant fairy-tale narrative of her wedding 14 years previously, I was Rastafari, with a politicised African-centric worldview that had little time for the domestic spats between the aristocracy that had been made rich from the enslavement of my ancestors. However, then as a media studies student, I was interested to see how she was using the medium of television to have her own voice heard, an affordance denied to the average television viewer, who were now full of their own opinions but then had few platforms through which to express them.

Two years later I attended the wedding of my cousin Sharon and surrounded by my Bajan family in England, and woke up the next morning to the news that Princess Diana had died in a car crash in France, and was glued to the television news all day, and leading up to and during her funeral one week later. This fixation on the televised broadcasts of Diana's death was not due to any particular affinity or affection per se, though it was not difficult to sympathise with her against the power of the Monarchist machine she was up against. The death of Diana became a cultural event that millions across the globe tuned into witness, regardless of their personal politics. The crudeness of describing the event of a human being's death as a cultural event is acknowledged, but though the dynamics of the circumstance are very different to events such as the Olympics or football World Cup, the effects on the national and international imagination were arguably similar. Occasions when people who are not normally fans take notice and actively spectate and participate in the temporary cultural activities, and get emotionally involved. Any resistance to the event is also an active emotional choice of having to express non-interest, in the face of pervasive media exposure that is hard to avoid.

Twenty-six years after Princess Diana's tell-all television interview with Martin Bashir, came her son Prince Harry and his wife Meghan Markle's similarly revealing interview with Oprah Winfrey, on 8 March 2021, broadcast a few hours after the Queen's own globally televised speech for Commonwealth Day. The young Royal couple created a new explosive television Royal moment, with claims of racism from members of the Royal family, and people across the world took notice.

Amongst Black Britons that I spoke to, from my parents' age, people of my own age, and also my teenage children and other young people, there was little surprise of Meghan and Harry's accusations of racism levelled towards the members of the Royal family and UK media. None were in the least bit surprised, and were only shocked it took this long for the news to emerge. The explosive nature of Meghan and Harry's interview with Oprah Winfrey was magnified by the additional layers of amplification via countless online and social media platforms received through numerous digital devices. Four days before the Oprah interview, a Sky News interview with comedian Gina Yashere, actress Kelechi Okafor, and lawyer and activist Dr Shola Mos Shogbamimu became widely shared. Three Black British women interviewed at the same time on mainstream television speaking their unadulterated views about the Royal family, such a combination was previously unheard of. Dr Shogbamimu stated in her 8-minute-and-16-second interview:

> Can I just say, Prince Harry is the husband to Meghan, that Prince Charles never was to Diana, and that's saying something. This is a man who has understood that history can repeat itself, and is saying, "You know what", as Nigerians would say, "prevention is better than cure."
>
> *Sky News, 2021a*

Mainstream television news sought the views of citizens of Commonwealth countries, about their reactions to the Oprah interview, which was broadcast in 68 different countries (Carr, 2021). When Winnie Nyandiga, Vice Chair of the Commonwealth Students Association of Kenya, was interviewed on BBC News 24 by Washington-based Katty Kay and London-based Christian Fraser (BBC News 24, 2021), she clearly described the feelings for many,

> Young people, the progressive digital natives, saw this interview as helping us to expose, on a global stage, the institutionalised racism in the UK. We are looking at how the Royal family has reacted and responded to this. And even the notion from what Meghan said that there was nothing, no protection, there was no support on the alleged racism and its perpetuation within the palace itself. So, the issue of racism, coming up at a point when the wounds of Black Lives Matter are still very fresh, it elicited conversations among young people.

Gina Yashere was invited back to Sky News on the evening of the UK broadcast of the interview, presenting views that very much echoed the sentiments of many Black Brits that I had spoken with.

> We knew that there was racism. The heritage, the Royal family, all Britain's wealth is built on the backs of colonialism and slavery and people theft. So why would people be surprised that it's still trickling down and still running through the veins of the Royal family? It wasn't a surprise to me,

but I'm glad I watched it. I'm glad they completely let everything out into the open.

Sky News, 2021b

Polemic presenter Piers Morgan storms off his own ITV GMTV programme when challenged by his colleague Alex Beresford, the show's weatherman (who happens to be dual heritage), about Morgan's denial of Meghan's claims of racism against the Royal family and her saying it drove her to contemplate suicide. Morgan resigned later that same evening, and there was a domino effect of other fallouts and resignations in other parts of the UK press. (Most notably at the time of writing, the resignation of Ian Murray, the Executive Director of the Society of Editors, after their statement which roundly denied any racism in the UK press was widely criticised by its own members [BBC Online, 2021].)

The television set in the corner of the living room continues to play a significant role in the discussion of race relations in the UK. Its broadcast content symbolises the complexity of feeling, and the challenges faced in articulation of experience and reflecting contemporary Britain, not only in how society outwardly looks, but also reflecting the sensibility in how modern UK thinks. In the 1970s in the Black domestic home, the television set represented caricatures of how we were seen by the dominant white gaze, and in the 2020s it was a battleground of how we not only want to be seen, but also fully heard. I believe this is the true meaning of Gil Scott Heron's seminal song *The Revolution Will Not Be Televised*. No matter what changes appear on the surface, real change and revolution needs to happen within, behind the scenes, in the values and belief structures of actual people, which cannot be captured with a camera.

Postscript

Royal death as Event became even more apparent with the passing of Queen Elizabeth II in September 2022, televised solidly in the UK for the 10 days between death and burial, and the funeral itself broadcast live around the world. Government flags in the new republic of Barbados did not fly half-mast until the day of the funeral itself, but as noted in iNews,

there was little else in the way of public mourning for the island's former head of state… Barbadians have been reflecting on the magnitude of her historic impact but there are no signs of regrets over the decision to become a republic.

Francis, 2022

Sat under the photo wall, I was at my mum's house with her and my partner Julie watching television when the news was announced. My sister, who lives in England, was on a flight to Barbados at the time of the Queen's death, learning of the news when landing in Grantley Adams Airport.

Waiting to collect my luggage from the bag carousel, many around me had already logged on to their phones to catch up on the news and social media posts they had missed whilst in the air for 8 hours. I overhead someone casually say "The Queen has passed away. That news will be all over Facebook soon". I thought she was joking as she did not appear shocked. I collected my luggage and made for the exit. Once logged into the airport WiFi I spoke to my husband and he confirmed the news. At my aunt's house I started to catch up on the breaking news articles and watched BBC World News on tv. I'm no royalist, but let's face it, they have always been there, as it were. It's hard to ignore this scale of Royal event, regardless of your politics as it's on every TV channel!

Time will tell how the fortunes of these two formally entwined countries will manifest in the future – the UK with a new monarch in Charles III, who personally presided over the abolition of the monarchy in the new-formed republic of Barbados less than a year earlier – all televised with a global witness, with rich parallel social media commentary.

The Coronation of the new king Charles III will of course dominate the television schedules in the lead up and on the day itself, scheduled for 6 May 2023 (after this book has been published). The Crown we will see on his head was originally made in 1661 for the Coronation of King Charles II (Murphy, 2022), the first monarch after the royal family was restored in 1660. Charles II, along with his brother James II, the Duke of York, founded the Royal African Company in 1660, one of his first acts after restoration. This established England's dominance in the 'trade' with Africa, and renewal of the charter in 1663, confirmed the trading of African bodies as a commodity for enslavement (Davies, 1999: 42).

Similar to his marriage 42 years ago, I will be watching with interest at the television spectacle of the Coronation, now more as an academic than a curious child (though the difference between the two, I would argue, should be closer than we appreciate). It will be a curious watch, no doubt full of double-consciousness-type analysis swirling around in my mind and heart. Through the television screen and commentary, looking for signs of whether his namesake's crown weighs heavy on the new King's head.

4

(LIVING ROOM) – SEWING MACHINE

I don't know if any of you have heard this saying, "You eat the flour and wear the bag!"

Everyone on the Zoom call laughs, nodding in agreement.

In those days shopping used to come from the store in large 50lbs flour bags. You'd wash them and bleach them, they would come out so white. It would always get turned into something.

This is my mum talking about how children in Barbados used to joke about having to wear clothes that were obviously homemade, even though it was something that everyone wore. I have brought together elders from the Bath Ethnic Minority Senior Citizens Association (BEMSCA) to talk about some of the objects discussed in this book, sewing machines being one of them. BEMSCA have been providing social care services for Bath's African-Caribbean and Asian elder populations for over 30 years, including a day care service, lunch club, social and leisure activities, and well-being support. They are based at Fairfield House in Bath, the former residence of Emperor Haile Selassie I when he lived in the city. I am at mum's house for the Zoom call – she is downstairs on her iPad (that BEMSCA had provided its active members years before, now become more used during lockdown), and I am upstairs in her bedroom on my laptop. Behind mum's head in the Zoom window, I can see her 80th birthday cards on display.

In many of my parent's friends we visited when I was a child, particularly the friends from the Caribbean, I remember usually seeing a sewing machine somewhere in the room. It was often a Singer, either uncovered ready for action, or covered with the sturdy surrounding box. Sometimes they were on its own designed legs, or placed on top of a table or waist height cabinet. The sewing machines were

DOI: 10.4324/9780367809621-5

usually proudly displayed like a piece of furniture or ornament. It was not merely a utilitarian functional object, such as an ironing board, but a statement piece in full view. Jamaican poet Verna George captures the feeling in her poem "Dumb Things," in which she calls the Singer sewing machine "a member of our house" (George, 2008: 61).

I cannot help but wonder how the sewing machine got connected with the sense of identity of Caribbean elders of my parent's generation, and how that translates today. I ask the members of BEMSCA about their memories of this intriguing object in the Zoom call (of approximately ten people), and I was also sent the transcript of a similar conversation between other BEMSCA members, Mrs Enid Swaby, and her daughters. Extracts from both the Zoom call and the written notes are used seamlessly in the commentary below.

Mrs Enid Swaby

I did have a Singer machine that folded into the table with a pedal foot made of cast iron. I could do a little [sewing] and when I first came to this country made my underwear and dresses and slips for the two girls. Mrs Thomas helped me as she was an expert at sewing. I could knock up a curtain or two and let the breeze blow on them like other professionally made curtains.

Pauline

I love to hear a machine humming when it is in use. There were many variations of sewing machines, some that were stand alone, the one that mum had that came with its own table, some that you carried with a cover.

Sandra

Growing up we only knew of Singer sewing machines, but then later came the Husqvarna machines from Europe, which could do the overlocking and other fancy stitches and had the technology to make clothes look more professional. Another make was the Brother machine from America.

Mrs Enid Swaby

My mother didn't love sewing but she used to help others, and so that was her bargaining point, to get others more experienced to do her sewing, and she would help them out in other ways. I didn't teach my children as the [Singer] machine wasn't cheap, and I paid for it outright not on hire purchase. However, I gave the machine to the mother of my grand-daughter, as she was a very good seamstress and I know she would use it.

The above exchange shows a clear inherited interest and development of skills in using sewing machines, which has spanned across three generations in relation to the use of Mrs Swaby's original Singer machine. The protection of, and considered passing-on, the Singer machine by Mrs Swaby shows it was a valued object which was not just to be used, but treated with care. Pauline's immediate recollection of the way the machine sounded shows how the home itself was transformed by its presence when in action, for her in a pleasant way. Far from being a mere unattached inanimate object, it is something which evokes fond visceral feelings and memory, a nostalgia that can be practically used. The intergenerational flow of memories goes upwards as well as towards the present, and mum starts to talk about the relationship between the sewing machine and her life growing up in Barbados before she came to England.

> You'd have your school clothes, church clothes, and play clothes, most of it would have been made, by either your parent or local seamstress. We had a Singer sewing machine at home, that was the most popular make. It wasn't electric, it had a handle you had to turn, and [local seamstress] Mrs Maynard had a treadle foot-pedal machine, that's the one the tailors used to use.

Mr Joseph

> I used to have my clothes made by a tailor back in Antigua, get nice shirts made, and I always had black coats. It was cheaper going to a tailor than being from the shops. See a style that you wanted, even for a wedding, and find the material and take that to the tailor, and they would do that for you. You could pay them piece of the money each week, you didn't have to pay it all at once. That was good.

Mr Joseph jokes about how you'd need to walk past the tailor fast with your head down, embarrassed if they saw you out wearing the clothes before you had paid for them in full. In anthropologist Rebecca Prentice's study of sewing cultures in Trinidad (Prentice, 2012), she discusses the economics and how circumstances started to shift to the position we see today, where buying clothes in shops is now considered to be the normal and cheaper option, and getting bespoke clothes made by a tailor or seamstress reversed to become a luxury. Changes in import tariff laws in the 1990s saw the rise of industrialised mass-produced goods, predominantly made in Asia, or in factories with casualised labour on minimum-wage, fuelling high street shops and supermarkets across the Caribbean (ibid.: 403–404). The price of everyday wear dropped to more affordable levels, less than bespoke made garments, and in contrast the clothes made by the previously lower-paid skilled artisan, such as seamstresses and tailors, are now more costly and time consuming to produce. Any price they charge is likely now to be more expense than what can be bought directly from a shop, seeing the levels of value reversed, and the skilled artisans finding it hard to compete. "Trinidadian women who are devoted to making a living through sewing have therefore faced a formal sector of shrinking job opportunities and declining working conditions" (ibid.: 401).

In the Caribbean sewing cultures sits within Mintz's notion of "Caribbean Transformations" (1989), where Black society, through the times of slavery and beyond

> depended – had to depend – on creativity and innovation far more than on the indelibility of particular culture contents. Such creative adaptation is, of course, a form of culture change, in which the individual, or a whole mass of individuals sharing certain traditions and values, develops new forms.
>
> *Mintz, 1989: 14*

The sewing machines I witnessed as a child, proudly in view in the homes of my parents' friends, dualistically represents a people of invention and a people in motion. To never catch oneself in need of what is necessary, to not have any excuse to present oneself as less than they are, with a flexibility to both be in service to the community and one's own economic security as much as is possible. In short, the sewing machine is a humble symbol of the readiness to attend to necessity. Even when not in use, even when little interest is shown, the machine was present and ready to be used if the need were there, like a ready packed suitcase at the bottom of the wardrobe. The pride in being able to make garments, and having garments made, is still present across the Caribbean today, and the economic necessities of having to supplement multiple streams of personal income due to some of the precarious natures in the labour market (Prentice, 2012: 402), means there is still a healthy bespoke garments trade "despite the increasing availability of ready-made garments from abroad, neighbourhood seamstresses and tailors still play a significant role" (ibid.: 404).

Sewing Machine, a Girl's Best Friend?

For the use of tailors and seamstresses to be semi-standard route to acquiring new clothes is in contrast to the experience of living in the UK today, at least for working class people, where the use for such services would be unthinkable. Even for the British middle classes, bespoke made garments would mostly only be for special occasions such as a wedding, if ever used at all, and would be considered a luxury rather than the default of everyday life. However, in the UK bespoke garments are still being made for a market prepared to pay those rates, and for decades workers from the Caribbean, mostly women, have worked in those positions, sometimes as second jobs. In her autobiography "*And Still I Rise: Seeking Justice for Stephe*n," Doreen Lawrence (mother of Stephen Lawrence, who was murdered aged 19 in a racist attack in London in 1993) remembers the hard work and long hours her mother used to do, working as a machinist for someone else from home, when she first moved to England in the 1960s.

I know now how hard it had been for my mother, one of the early arrivals, when she came to England. She was a machinist, and she took in sewing at home on a piece-rate basis. She had to meet a basic quota in order to get paid, and I remember her crouched over her sewing machine from early in the morning working up women's dresses and suits, her feet pressing the pedals of the machine and her hands moving the cloth forward under the needle. At first the machine was in the corner of the dining room and you could hear it whirring and humming all day; when we moved later, she had her own small sewing room. She worked all the time, never lifting her eyes from the job in hand.

Lawrence, 2006: 25

Doreen goes onto talk about how, due to her mum was always working at the sewing machine, that she was "expected to be a second mother to her children, and to carry a lot of weight around the house" (ibid.), and from aged 10 or 11 she was already having to do lots of the domestic chores. This expectation on Doreen to be the replacement mother of the family is an experience that I have heard many times, not just in relation to research for this book, but in examples I can think of from different people I have grown up with and seen throughout my life. The eldest girl child would be expected to assume the service role in the house, and the same burden was seldom placed on male siblings. Often the echoes of these burdens on the eldest daughters can be seen in later life, and can continue to affect their relationships with their parents and younger siblings.

The gendered dynamics underpinning lots of the conversation and representations around the sewing machine are clear to see, and it is (unfortunately) far from a revelation that the association with sewing, and also the burden of household chores, is often pointed towards the female members of the house. Even though in my interviews and discussions about this topic there was talk of male tailors (more of which below), the female voice and connection with the sewing machine, as seamstresses or machinists, is strong, and tailors, who were all men, felt like a slightly separate special entity. Within the family unit, the expectation of using sewing machines was more placed on girls, and it was often used for functional needs within the immediate household, such as Mrs Swaby's curtains, and the children's clothes that my mum referred to, rather than working for outside clients. Making garments for others was a natural expected development of the skill, and some women in the Zoom conversation did talk about occasionally making clothes for people even though it was not their main work, though the reality was that sewing, in the first instance, was something that girls did and expected to do, feeling like a natural part of their growing up process. A comment from my mum further confirms this with an insight to how it can happen implicitly without the need of much overt external pressure.

My sister used to take sewing classes at Mrs Maynard's, and I followed after her, as I wanted to do everything she did. Growing up we had a song – (starts

to sing) – "Ohhh the sewing machine, the sewing machine a girl's best friend,
If I didn't have my sewing machine I'd a come to no good end …"

The singing trails off with her admitting she doesn't remember the rest of the
words, but that we would get the idea from that short beginning. When researching
the song at a later stage when transcribing the conversation, I find it to be the
"The Sewing Machine," from the opening scene from a relatively obscure 1947
film called "*The Perils of Pauline*" (Loesser, 1947), starring Betty Hutton. The film is
about a factory sewing machine operator called Pauline, who gets frustrated with
her job and wants to become an actress. In the song Pauline's lyrics continue, saying
how, if she didn't have a sewing machine, "a wicked life I'd lead." Perhaps the most
telling line is when Pauline sings about how she dreams about romance, but feels so
"weary" after a day of sewing "that I never get out to dance."

• MUSIC SEARCH – The Sewing Machine *Betty Hutton* – PRESS PLAY

Written by Frank Loesser and sung by Hutton, the song is energetic and funny, and
a knowingly mischievous take on how working at the sewing machine keeps her
out of trouble. At the same time, the song reinforces the traditional values of the
time, that, indeed, for a young woman being engaged in strenuous activity such as
sewing, would hopefully keep her away from boys ("dance" being a euphemism for
sex). My mum was 6 years old at the time that film was released, and she does not
remember how, where, or when she first heard that song, and demonstrates how the
tacit dominant values of wider society can seep into your consciousness as "norms,"
in ways that the individual themselves cannot even explain, and place expectations
on you that, at the time, you cannot necessarily detect (Turner, 1994: 4).

A more direct version of the same sentiments sung by Betty Hutton can be
found in the 1978 short story "Girl," by Antiguan writer Jamaica Kincaid. In
Hutton's version, the limitations attempting to be placed on female freedoms is
hidden behind a comical self-deprecating narrative. However, in Kincaid's writing
(1978), a mother gives advice about sewing to her daughter, and the apparent
criticism of the daughter by the mother is thinly veiled. Written as a series of
instructions to the daughter on how to navigate tasks in everyday life, the mother
offers personal digs at the daughter's character while simultaneously giving mundane practical advice, which presents an uncomfortable narrative experience for
the reader.

> [T]his is how to sew on a button; this is how to make a buttonhole for the
> button you have just sewed on; this is how to hem a dress when you see the
> hem coming down and so to prevent yourself from looking like the slut
> I know you are so bent on becoming.

Esther Ohito offers a Black feminist perspective reading of Kincaid's "Girl," arguing
that the text challenges a simple reading using Western literary expectations, and is

steeped in a Caribbean conscious voice that would easily be misunderstood using a solely Western lens of analysis. Ohito states that the mother, although no doubt stern, is motivated by a "declaration of devoted care rather than one of bitterness" (Ohito, 2016: 447), and at the root of the mother's discourse is deep "concern her daughter's welfare with regard to both the minutiae and the generality of life in that setting" (ibid.). The sharpness in the mother's words is a desperation of fear in wanting to keep the daughter safe, so is a tough love strategy of preparing the child for the harsh realities of life. Ohito draws other extracts from Kincaid's story as examples, such as the mother's instruction to "wash every day, even if it with your own spit" (Kincaid, 1978), arguing that even though the strategy may be hard to digest through a Western sensibility, the mother's focus is one of care for the daughter, and to prepare her for the emotional, financial, physical, socio-cultural challenges that life with inevitably throw at her (Ohito, 2016: 447), and to toughen up the daughter even at the sacrifice of the quality of their own relationship.

Kincaid's fictional mother's approach to parenting is a trait I have personally witnessed in others, though perhaps not at that same level of sharpness. According to Ohito (2016: 442), this extreme and challenging demonstration of care is an inherited behavioural instinct from slavery, and through the subsequent colonial period to the contemporary era (DeGruy, 2005: 158), mothers continuing the practice of having to go to some extreme lengths to keep their children safe (Bush, 2010: 70). However, the "tough love" cultural traits, is still upsetting and confusing, and can understandably be in conflict with modern and Western contexts of parenting, and challenge our notions of what care and love are "supposed" to look like. In his book "*Growing up Stupid under the Union Jack*," Austin Clarke reflects on life growing in Barbados in the 1940s, witnessing such challenging parenting messages from the perspective of a boy child, and further compounds the gendered perspective of the expectations on girls and the taken for granted structures of patriarchal society.

> Girls were expected to be dressmakers, sugar and silent, spice and stupid, and wash the boys' clothes. So [my friend's] sister would have helped her mother with the needlework which sustained the family.
>
> *Clarke, 1998: 71*

The expectations on Caribbean females to sew was not confined to their home islands, and continued long after they emigrated to Britain. Andrea Levy explored this tension in "Small Island," in an exchange between husband and wife, Gilbert and Hortense. Upset when she finds out that her teaching qualification from Jamaica is not considered valid in England, Gilbert tries to console her by saying she is capable of doing other things, and asks if she can sew. Hortense confirms she has been sewing since she was a small girl, but protests that she is now a teacher, not a seamstress. Gilbert's clumsy attempt at comforting her further provokes and angers her even more, when he tells her "And a teacher you will be even when you are sewing" (Levy, 2004: 464). This philosophical sleight of hand in discussing Hortense's self-identity and sense of self-worth echoes cognitive dissonance experienced by many who moved to Britain from the Caribbean in the post-war period – qualified to do work at a higher level than what UK society permitted them to do.

It should be noted at this point that not all of the women interviewed for this chapter could sew, or showed any interest in sewing machines, and in the Zoom conversation said so when asked for any memories to contribute.

Up ye Mighty Race!

In celebrated artist Lubaina Himid's 2019 painting "Six Tailors," we see five Black men sat around a table covered with pieces of material and sewing implements, and one man walking behind with possibly trouser material over his shoulder. Three of the seated men appear to be looking at the man on the far left, who is monochrome and less defined than the others, possibly dishevelled, more of a shadow of man, possibly lost in his own thoughts. Maybe the other five are making him a new outfit, or alternatively maybe he is the elder teacher passing on his skills to the younger generation (see Figure 4.1).

I offer this tentative personal reading of the painting, fully aware that the intentions of the artist, and the meaning attached to artworks by audiences, do not always align. Though both readings are subjectively valid, as the view of the artist does not necessary privilege over the readings of the audience (Barthes,

FIGURE 4.1 Lubaina Himid, Six Tailors (2019) (© Lubaina Himid)

1977: 142–148). Himid herself does not give much detailed narrative information away about the work, but in two different interviews she offered the following:

> Six Tailors – The whole exhibition was about making your way out of trauma, about creating your way through mourning, and through disaster.
>
> *2021*

> They're all trying quite hard not to be the most dominant man in the room. They're making something together, working quite hard on the moment, perhaps creating their way out of trauma. I do like their cotton reels … The idea was to get that many men in a space and have them not planning, exactly, but being and thinking.
>
> *Himid & Higgins, 2021*

Ideas of using creativity as a means of fostering unification, and to encourage cooperation and communication in the face of trauma, speak to Mintz's notion of "creative adaptation" and focusing one's identity on a common cause (1989: 14). Himid's second quote carries the idea of creative practice as a leveller of stereotypical masculine traits of competitiveness, stymying their want to be in positions of dominance. There are plenty of metaphors in the practice of sewing that can be utilised to represent larger ideas of society and our interactions with each other – the need for planning, listening to what others want for themselves, piecing fragments together, making presentable, repair, making beauty, being patient, attention to detail, and the desire to make others feel and look good. Around the table of the Himid's *Six Tailors* there is not much space for ego, and the success of whatever they are making relies on the cooperation of each of them. Mintz reflects this in his highlighting of the importance of inter-personal working relations, in the sustaining of a transformative and flexible market economy, for Black people trying to earn a living as traders in former colonial spaces.

> [A] highly complex network of individuals is engaged in the operation of the market system, and myriad series of interpersonal relationships link traders with each other, and with the [suppliers] and consumers who stand at each end of the chains of intermediation.
>
> *ibid.: 218*

It is not usual in a literal sense to see tailors working so closely together in this way, but in the realm of extending the above metaphors in context of Mintz's analysis, the Tailors represent the architects of civic society and actors in civil society, and people rely on them to deliver. It is not a stretch to infer social commentary in Himid's work, she says of herself, "I think of myself as a painter, and at the same time as a cultural activist" (Himid, 2018). In the same interview, directly after this quote, Himid speaks of growing up with her mother who was a textile designer, being surrounded by clothes and colour, spending a long time in shops looking and being fascinated by that world. The use of fabric and bright colour in different iterations is a constant trend in Himid's own work. With this personal insight into the construction of garments from a young age, it is not a surprise therefore to see her explore this direct narrative in her own work. Nine years before her painting of the Six Tailors, Himid worked with Manchester Art Gallery's West African textile collection and produced a series of portraits, one of which was The Tailor. Himid says of the work:

> This is the person who knows how to make the best of the human figure or to reveal a good one, to give elegance of line and to permit movement without disturbance to the actual look, style and fit of the costume. For me, the Tailor is like an architect for the body; how our clothes feel on the inside is as important as how they look on the outside. How we feel on the inside is what makes us act in a particular way in the world.
>
> *2011*

To explore this further, I interview Ras Tekla Selassie, a performance poet and member of the Rastafari community in South West England, who makes all his own clothes. Born in England, with parents who moved here from Jamaica, Tekla is holding onto the tradition of the skilled artisan, though (at the time of writing) not for monetary gain or selling to others, but more for principles of self-reliance and living a spiritual life, where everything on his body carries a meaning, and outward symbols of his adherence to Emperor Haile Selassie I. He recalls his earliest memories of sewing from childhood (Figure 4.2).

> I remember my gran had a sewing machine, but we didn't have one, as gran, we called her mama, used to do it for her. My mum used to sew by hand, and that's how I learnt to sew, repairing holes in socks, buttons and things like that. Repair was good, and I started to sew by hand. When I was about 10 years old, I repaired some socks but they looked rubbish as I didn't turn them inside out first. I learnt from that and now turn everything inside out first before I sew them.

Tekla talks about how he progressed from socks to repairing his "judging clothes," a Jamaican term for children's play clothes, or what you wear to do household chores (Woolery, 2014). Tekla explains,

> Judging clothes weren't necessarily clothes that were old, but they maybe too small or something wrong with it. Your parents aren't going to buy you judging clothes, and if they needed repair, you couldn't just dash them weh, so I repaired them myself.

It was through Tekla's gran that he first saw Rastafari clothes being made when he was a child, as she used to crochet hats (known as *tams*) for his uncle, who everyone

FIGURE 4.2 Ras Tekla Selassie, 2021 (© author)

knew simply as "Rasta." At the time, Tekla heard tams referred to as tea-cosies, and taking it literally, he had to learn for himself what it meant, and found out it to be the style of hat (known as a crown) that Rastafari men would wear. As an adult Tekla became inspired by the Rastafari tradition commonly known as Bobo Shanti (known officially as the Ethiopian African Black International Congress – EABIC). They are distinct in wearing turbans and long robes which they make themselves, and in Jamaica particularly they are known to make brooms which they sell to provide income for their community (Kamimoto, 2015: 45). These practical life-style choices are a manifestation of their philosophy of self-determination for all African people, and to live a spiritual frugal life of prayer, not distracted by the ego and temptations of the world. They hold close the philosophies of Jamaican pan-African leader Marcus Mosiah Garvey, who worked towards unifying Black people across the world with the rally cry "Up you mighty race, accomplish what you will" (Clarke, 1974: 15). In 1998 Tekla spent time in the EABIC village in Jamaica known as Bobo Hill, and there had his dreadlocked hair wrapped in a turban, and wore the distinct robes for the first time.

> Self-reliance is about looking after ourselves, and Rastafari people should be looking after ourselves. When I spent time at the Bobo camp, I could see how they were self-reliant and everything they ate, drank, wore, smoked, even the

instruments they played, they made themselves. I could see they were serious, they really lived it.

Returning to England, Tekla taught himself to make his own clothes on a sewing machine given to him from a family member, who inherited it from her gran. Laying one of his tracksuit tops over a large piece of material, he cut around it, improvised, and made up patterns in his head. His first attempts failed, but he eventually worked out the format, and has now been wearing only his own clothes for the past 20 years.

> I still don't have a pattern for my clothes, I do them by eye. Even though they all look identical as I've been doing it for so long, only I know how each one to be unique, so I don't want a pattern to work to.

His clothes even have details hidden from public view which carry spiritual significance. For Tekla his clothes are a constant reminder to himself of the sacrifices he is making for his chosen spiritual path, and a symbol to others, inspired by Marcus Garvey, that the betterment of a nation (self-determination) begins with the betterment of the individual (self-reliance). Tekla is now considering making clothes for other people to buy for the first time, but is wrestling with the dilemma of whether the garments he sells should continue to carry the spiritual significance he attaches to them, or whether he would be happy for them to be sold to anyone to be used for any purpose. Even though he has been making his own clothes for two decades, Tekla does not consider himself to be a tailor, as he is not providing a service to others. This is the tension that Hortense in Small Island found so challenging in the face of Gilbert's clumsy attempt at comfort, as the act of service to others defines your identity in their eyes – she was a teacher not a seamstress, and did not want to be seen as a seamstress. In contrast, even though Tekla is only ever seen wearing his own clothes, it is seldom thought about by other people who know him (mutual friends that I discussed this interview with), they just know that is his style, not giving a thought to where the clothes come from, and were surprised to learn he made them himself.

During the interview Tekla gave me one of his poems to read, which he said should sum up his thinking on the subject, an extract of which is below, with no further analysis necessary.

> We are those whose clothes make a statement.
> We seek no argument.
> We move with an honourable intent.
> With our own personal garments in our vestments,
> As if it were the season for Lent,
> We visibly separate ourselves in any event,
> not often, not frequent, but constant.
> We are those, we are those that are clothed with order

Clothed with culture
Clothed with the Kushite flavour.
We are those that are clothed,
light in weight,
dark and bright and colour smooth in texture.
We dressed up not to impress,
but to remember
we are those that wear our own style.
We measure we cut
We sew
we compile,
then create with our own profile.

© Tekla Selassie, 2022

5

(LIVING ROOM) – THE ARMCHAIR (FICTION)

Mortley Grant sat in his chair. Every time he blinked, it took just that little bit longer for his eyes to re-open, and each time they opened just that little bit narrower.

The etches in his ebony-tone skin fell deep with time. Seventy years previous this was virgin skin, cradled by his mother's love and untouched by breath. He was then born into this world. Age began its relentless pace. This skin has encased his soul on all its travels. Now it was time for his soul to travel alone.

Mortley was a tall heavy man. His sturdy Armchair carried his weight well. Dusty green, frayed at every edge. Armchair knew Mortley well, maybe better than anyone. The wooden ends of each of its arms sported four worn spots in its varnish, from the constant drumming of Mortley's well-worked fingertips. Particularly in these latter years, Mortley would sit in front of a switched-off television set and stare at the blank screen. To an observer he would appear to be waiting. Waiting for the phone to ring, the door to knock. Armchair felt it knew what Mortley waited for, even though Mortley himself never knew. Whenever Mortley sat in Armchair and thought, Armchair knew he was praying. What Mortley really waited for was God.

Mrs Grant once bought a brand-new three-piece suite. Mortley insisted that Armchair stayed. From that day onwards Armchair felt indebted to its owner, and paid Mortley back in the only way it knew how. Always be there for him. There was one day in particular that this relationship intensified considerably. This was the day the spirit of the room changed. The movement slowed. The talking stopped. Mortley Grant was now, officially, alone.

The living room stayed as it did in the time of Mrs Grant. Her glasses still rested on the mantle-piece. Flowery slippers discreetly placed by the side of one of the new chairs, next to the wool box. Adjacent to this was Armchair.

If Armchair was ever moved for any reason, which was unlikely, the carpet would expose four dents so worn in its surface the floorboards could be felt through the underlay. Mortley never felt the need to re-arrange anything. He left that kind of

DOI: 10.4324/9780367809621-6

activity to Mrs Grant, and she also wasn't fond of drastic change. Maybe a new vase in spring, a change of curtains in the summer. Once every couple of years she would initiate a sabbatical indulgence, the last time being, of course, the new chairs. The flowered wallpaper was the next thing on the hit list, but that was before …

Mortley hated the wallpaper when it was first put up ten years in memory. He frowned every time he looked at the entwining pastel flower stems which repeated every third row. Mrs Grant was always the more vocal presence of the two, and simply said, "you'll get used to it." She was right.

Mortley found himself thinking of Tyrone, his only grandchild, whenever he concentrated on the now faded wall covering. When the child was only 3 or 4 years old, he was fascinated by the flow of the shapes and colour. He would sit and try and draw the patterns using his gnarled Crayola crayons and imagination. That was one of the reasons the wallpaper had stayed up so long. Mortley would sit forward in Armchair watching, fascinated by the child's patience and attention to detail. Mortley then began to find himself trying to search for the same interest in the wallpaper that this child so obviously found in its patterned arrangement. There was no denying the pattern was mildly interesting in a bland way, but Mortley could never recreate the aura in himself with which Tyrone seemed to approach the wallpaper each time, with new eyes. Mortley thanked the Lord for children's innocence and sense of wonder, a trait which adults rarely possess.

The alcove of the fire-side wall was covered almost completely in old photographs and postcards. Only a hint of wallpaper could be glimpsed through the gaps in the Blu-Tak'd pictures. This was the feature which caused the most excitement in the visitors to the house, even the regulars. The tiled 1950s fireplace and mantle were framed in a wonderful overlapping array of clashing colours and images. This was something which Mr and Mrs Grant were most proud of in their home, and by which their children were most embarrassed.

Constantly the three now-adult children would try to persuade their parents to redecorate, although none of them even lived at home anymore. Once Beverly, the mother of Tyrone, took it upon herself to buy ten rolls of wallpaper and went as far as hiring the decorators to do the job. Needless to say, her parents turned them away without hesitation. The wallpaper stayed in the cellar for years and the nagging continued until Mrs Grant conceded and said she would agree to have the living room redecorated, but only when she was ready. She half said it just to keep the children quiet, even though she also reluctantly admitted to herself it was probably time for a change. Mrs Grant's submission came just two weeks before she passed on. The subject has never been raised since.

The Album Wall, as it was affectionately called, could spark hours of colourful conversations and stories about Barbados and the "old times." This was one of the reasons the house was such a magnet for friends who were "just passing by." Hours later the elders would still be reminiscing and recounting the funny tales of Home.

What did ever 'appen to ole Swing Foot Jones?
He mus' dead now fa true.

No he ain' dead yet! Aunt Lou se she pass he by Bibby's Lane when she did home
de las' time.

Fi true? Well praise de Lord. Swing Foot mus' be in he nineties now innit? I did
t'ink he did dead ever since.

Praise de Lord.

Nineties? I hear he already pass t'rough he hundredth birt'day, ya know.

Fi true?

Praise de Lord!

The conversations would meander and journey into the small hours of the night.
When the friends had left and Mr and Mrs Grant laid down to sleep, nothing could
stop dreams from entertaining the night. It was on such a night which Mrs Grant
floated to her Father's Home.

Mortley relaxed in Armchair and drummed his fingers against the varnished
grain. He cast his eyes over the Album Wall and closed them to meditate under the
solitude and stillness of his eyelids. The thud of four fingers was the only sound.

Among the images on the wall were postcards from Barbados, Jamaica, America,
Cornwall, Leicester, The Isle-of-Wight, Bath, Bristol, London, France, Morocco,
and Amsterdam. These were from their children, friends, relatives, old work-friends,
and some bought by Mrs Grant herself because she simply liked the picture on
them. The photographs told the story of generations. Photographs taken on the
day of their wedding 48 years ago were pinned side-by-side with Tyrone's school
photographs and his mother's, aunt's, and uncle's baby pictures. There was no
obvious order to the wall, not as may be found in a photo album book. Images
from day trips were scattered on all corners, likewise with "event" photos such
as weddings and christenings. Mortley and Mrs Grant knew exactly where each
photograph was without really realising the skill involved. The wallpaper on either
side of the alcove carried the repetitive pattern of flowers. The Album Wall, however, carried the fragmented chaos of sweet memories.

The last memory Mortley saw before he closed his eyes was that of his
mother.

The sepia-toned photograph showed a woman heavy in stature and gentle in
eyes. She stood uncomfortably straight and stiff-backed clutching a handbag. Her
Sunday-hat tilted slightly as she shifted to find a natural pose.

Mama. Keep still nuh! I wan' fi tek one more so I can sen it back fi ya.

Wha I wan' pic'cha of mi self fa? You know se mi own a mirror already!

Mama relentlessly paced over to Mortley and adjusted the collar of his shirt and
blazer.

Fru time you reach Englan' you haf "fi save ya money, ya hear? If anyt' ing you
sen' back, mek it a likkle money fi ya bruddah an sista, ya hear?

Mortley rescued his clothes from his mother's clutches and put his arm around her.

Listen mama. I gon' miss ya, ya know dat. Tek care of ya self.

Mama discreetly escaped her son's embrace. She was never a person to outwardly show her emotions, particularly if she was sad. Mortley knew her ways well and wasn't offended. He kept a firm hold of her earth-hardened hands.

"Listen."

Mama spoke in a matter-of-fact manner.

> Don't even bod'da worrying 'bout me. It's you dat ya haf" fi look afta', ya hear? The Lord protec' me in all I do, an' I pray Him will look afta' you in Englan'. Have faith an' de Lord will be wid you. You know I always tell ya dat.

Mama snatched back her hand and rummaged around in her handbag.

> Mama, mi know dat but …

Mama wouldn't let him speak.

> Look 'ere! I wan! you fi tek dis. Ya know how I does treasure it, so when you done mek ya money an' come back in five years, I wan' ya fi give dis back in de same condition as mi give it to ya, ya hear?

Mama handed Mortley a book which was as much a part of the family as anyone.

> I c'yan tek ya Bible frum ya Mama. When I reach Englan' I'll buy one, mi promise.
> Chuh! Just tek what mi give ya an' hush ya mout'. I put ya in Jesus trust frum now. Ya bes' pray an' show your appreciation to de Father.
> Mortley was told.
> T'ank ya mama. Mi love ya.
> Love de Lord!
> Mortley kissed his mother on the cheek and slowly parted.
> Thaf" fi go now. De ship soon lef'.
> Well tek dis now before ya lef it. God be wid ya my son. I pray fi ya.

Mortley took the Bible, picked up his small suitcase, and left for the New World.

Mortley sat in Armchair. The trusty friend carried his weight well. The wooden varnished ends felt the texture of its master's worn, still left hand. The movement ceased. The thudding stopped. The spirit of the room changed. Armchair was now, officially, alone.

Armchair knew quietly it wasn't strictly alone. There was still one dedicated companion which Armchair had always known. A heavy book which always lived on its right arm. Mortley's hand was tightly clutched around the rough leather-bound cover. His nails were dug deep into the well-thumbed pages of text. He waited no longer. Mortley had finally floated to his Father's Home (Sobers, 1998b).

6

(FRONT ROOM) – RADIOGRAM

The significance of the radiogram (Figure 6.1) in the front room of many Black British homes in the 1970s and 1980s is offered by Michael McMillan, he states,

> Often excluded from pubs and clubs, [and for fears of their safety], many West Indian migrants would entertain themselves in the front room, and central to this was the prized 'Blue-Spot' radiogram … made by the German manufacturer Blaupunkt.
>
> *McMillan, 2009: 151*

McMillan has produced the largest number of published articles, books, chapters, and other projects on the topic than any other writer or artist, as well as reproducing Front Rooms as art/museum installations that have been exhibited across Europe (McMillan, 2007), the Caribbean itself (Coussonnet, 2012), and in the Tate Britain (Tate, 2022). In line with the Small Anthropology ethos of transparency, it is only right for me to admit that, as McMillan is such an authority on the subject, when planning this section on The Front Room, I felt as if I was encroaching on his research area. Having met Michael a few times I know he would not think that, but in this context, it feels only right that his words about the Front Room and the radiogram sets the tone.

> I grew up learning that cleanliness was next to godliness and regardless how poor we were, if the front room looked good, then we were respectable. Having been ritually hoovered, dusted and polished on Saturday, the front room was always immaculate awaiting the unexpected visitor; the insurance man, salesmen selling the Encyclopaedia Britannica, the "Avon Lady" selling cosmetics, teachers, the police, the pastor of course, and the guests who my parents wanted to entertain. This was usually Sundays when big people came

DOI: 10.4324/9780367809621-7

FIGURE 6.1 Radiogram – Blaupunkt "Bluespot" at Fairfield House

> around for the big Sunday dinner of rice and peas and stewed chicken. Belly full, the big people retire to the front room for big people chat. Jim Reeves playing on the radiogram. Me and my siblings are invited into people we didn't know but who knew us.
>
> *McMillan, 2019: 189*

McMillan's recollections take me back to my experiences, and the feelings I had about the front room in my house growing up. The radiogram was a poignant feature of his memory, as it is in many others who have written or spoken autobiographically about growing up in Black British households, for example Benjamin Zephaniah (2018: 37–38), Andrea Levy (1994: 30, 99–100, Mykaell Riley (2014: 104), David Johnson (2018), and Vanley Burke (Holmes, 2020). McMillan, Zephaniah, Riley, Johnson, and Burke all talk about how the Blaupunkt "Bluespot" model was "the preferred record player/radiogram amongst West Indians" (Riley 2014: 104).

The Bluespot radiogram plays a role in the pilot episode of *Love Thy Neighbour* in 1972, we see new homeowners Bill and Barbie, a Black couple, unpacking items in their new home, amongst which is the radiogram (see Figure 6.2). Bill soon ends up in an altercation with his racist neighbour Eddie, and later in the episode Eddie and his wife Joan pay a visit to apologise. Sat in the front room while Barbie goes to find Bill to tell him of the surprise guests, Joan and Eddie have the following exchange.

FIGURE 6.2 *Love Thy Neighbour* – Unbroadcast pilot episode, Thames Television, 1972

Joan Hey Eddie look, they've got some nice stuff.
Eddie Aye, it's alright. A bit flashy though!
Joan They got a lovely radiogram back there.
Eddie Well, it's always to be expected. They do a lot of dancing.

This thinly veiled racist comment, in this context born out of a mild jealousy, is mild in comparison with the more overt racist slurs Eddie delivers each episode. The liberal use of racist language was one of the reasons why the show became controversial and labelled as racist, while its defenders say Eddie was the ultimate butt of the jokes and that Bill gave as good as he got (Malik, 2002: 97–98).

My parents threw away our radiogram at some point in the 1980s. I remember it standing across the left-hand wall of our front room, but the make and model is long forgotten. It was smaller than the Bluespot model in Figure 6.1 but similar in style, and even though it was smaller, it still dominated that side of the room. On top of it were crocheted doilies with an array of souvenirs and ornaments, but for me the main area of interest was the drawers underneath, areas which, as a child, we were seldom permitted to open (even though we often did). In the top left-side section was a record turntable, accessed by either lifting the lid (after removing the ornaments), or it slid forward on its base. The turntable had a stem in the middle which held a stack of seven vinyl records, which automatically dropped and played each one sequentially. The top right was an amplifier with radio and the buttons to control the unit. The large bottom section with the double doors between the speakers was a large area, which in our house had a stack of vinyl albums propped up on the left side, and the right used as a drinks cabinet, and it was from there I had some of my first illicit tastes of alcohol when my parents were not at home. I ask my sister if she has any memories about the radiogram or what make it was, her immediate response – "What, the one stopped working when you broke the turntable?" That is an unfortunate memory I do not recall (demonstrating the unreliability of personal memory as a sole research method).

The radiogram was a commanding piece of furniture, with its plush gloss wood varnish, the style was a mixture of formality and classic lines with a strong bold presence. They sold for approximately £50–£70 at the time, with top of the range Decola model by Decca selling for £200 (Cook, 2010: 265), the radiogram was a relatively expensive arrival, especially in modest working class homes. Mum confirms ours was at the cheaper end of the spectrum. The formal exterior design and the adult pleasure of the interior (which could be locked with a key) spoke to the promise of what the radiogram represented in the house – a statement of both arrival and existence, a financial commitment to have fun and enjoy life, while maintaining the grown-up presence of having worked hard to be able to afford to be surrounded by "nice things" (McMillan, 2009: 147).

In the conversation with the BEMSCA elders, I ask them about money and how such an item would have been paid for. Some talk about using hire-purchase methods paying in monthly instalments, with mention of using catalogues to buy relatively expensive items such as this, as it could be delivered to the house as well, having an easy-to-arrange instalment payment system. The talk turns to saving, with some saying they knew people would save up for months to pay for large items such as this upfront, to avoid the burden of instalments and the interest that had to be paid on top of the item's price. Lois Francis then talks about a very specific approach to saving that existed within the British-based Caribbean community called *Pardna*.

> With pardna you had certain number of people who were saving together, that would be the idea. If you had, say, 10 people and they're contributing £20 each week into the pardna, you called it "throwing", you're "throwing a pardna". That's the language. Each person will then have the whole lot of money on one particular week, you called it a "hand". So, each of the 10 people would be throwing their £20 each, and when it's your hand you get the full £200. You'd keep throwing until it was turn for your hand, which might be, say, in week 10. You had to keep throwing right through the whole thing until everybody had their amount before you could drop out, you can't just take your hand and run. You had to keep going. But it was a good way

of saving, especially to buy quite expensive things. It was a good community thing, and a great way of managing money.

Mr Joseph jokes "you couldn't take your hand and run, someone would find and catch ya!"

I remember pardna from childhood, mum would meet "aunt" Urseline in either our or her front room, and give her some money, which would get diligently noted in aunt Urseline's well-worn notebook. As a child I should not have been noticing what was going on, and I certainly did not ask, but over time I put different fragments of information together, along with asking my older sister, and came to the understanding of what was going on. Anthropologist Clifford Geertz was one of the first people to conduct an extensive study of what he termed Rotating Credit Associations (RCA) (Geertz, 1962: 242), and conducted a survey showing the striking similarities of RCAs across different areas of the world, such as Java, China, Japan, Vietnam, Cameroon, Nigeria, and Ghana. In all cases, it was identified as being an activity mostly present in "developing countries" and their diasporas, amongst communities who were not wealthy, but who were likely to be in work and therefore had access to money to contribute their hand, though still needed a support structure to encourage saving and access to further funds (ibid.: 261).

> The rotating credit association is also found in various parts of Negro Africa, most especially in the more commercially developed regions of West Africa, from where it evidently spread via the slave trade to the Caribbean, and perhaps to parts of the southern United States … [A]mong the Bulu people of the French Cameroon … the economic aspects of the association are thus completely embedded in tribal social structures.
>
> *ibid.: 255*

Therefore the presence of the radiogram in the front room was, for some, the result of pardna meetings that took place in those same rooms, unknowingly part of a tradition that spread across the continents of Africa and Asia, as well as back through time to a point before slavery.

Vanley Burke, often called the "Godfather of Black British Photography," spoke to fellow photographer Claudette Holmes about the radiogram, on how it had a gendered representation in the house, and how it related to the idea of home (Holmes, 2020). He stated that while many areas of the Black British front room in the 1960s, 1970s, and 1980s had a strong female presence and sense of ownership, such as the glass cabinet, the radiogram alternatively was "definitely the man of the house." Burke says that as the radiogram was a significant purchase, the man and woman would likely have chosen it together, but likely that "he would have bought it … it's his prerogative" (ibid.). Ben Highmore, who chronicled the appearance of objects and their use in the home (Highmore, 2014: 124), corroborates the maleness of the radiogram also in white working class households of the same era, describing an interview in which a husband bought a radiogram with winnings from the betting shop, much to the delight of his wife but to the horror of his mother-in-law, and draws upon a study which argues that men were the main purchasers of radios and similar equipment in that period, due to listening habits and also the gendered trends of that era (ibid.: 125). In the Black British family home, the apparent male aura of the radiogram was certainly tempered by the crocheted doilies and ornaments that were inevitably perched on top.

Another aspect that Vanley Burke discusses with Holmes is how many couples bought them with the aim of sending them back to the Caribbean at some point, as a switch at the back of the radiogram allowed them to be used with the alternative electrical current, making them compatible. According to Burke, "a lot of these large items that were bought, were initially bought to be taken back to Jamaica" (Holmes, 2020). The motivation of buying significant items with the aim of returning to the Caribbean with them is concurred swiftly by my mum when I mention Vanley's comments:

> That's right! We thought that would be nice to keep and take back home. We only thought we'd be here for five years. The gram, cabinet, even the table and chairs, we thought we'd send back to Barbados. [chuckles] We still have some of them now, over fifty years later!

Why Jim Reeves?

In the group conversation with the BEMSCA elders, the memories of the radiogram started to take on a distinct pattern, where the thought of one member cascaded the memories of the others in a form of "reciprocal influence" (Goffman, 1956: 8).

> *Lois* My strongest memories that were the records played on a Sunday morning. Jim Reeves was always really popular.
> *Glynis* The radiogram would play in our house especially on Sunday morning and special occasions. We played Jim Reeves too.
> *Alice* We had a neighbour who was a policeman, and all of us from the village used to go and listen to the music. That was in Kenya where I grew up. We also listened to Jim Reeves music.

These memories concur with McMillan's description of the radiogram in his parents Front Room at the beginning of this chapter. I ask them about Jim Reeves, and why he seemed to be so popular with their generation of Caribbean elders. There is an embarrassing moment after my question preamble when I ask "Why Jim Reeves?," and some in the group thought I said, "White Jim Reeves." I try to correct their mishearing, but as it is on Zoom, I am not sure my correction was heard, however, the immediate responses are insightful.

Glynis Well he sang gospel, spiritual, hymns, that was the sort of thing we used to listen to, good Christian songs.

Mum He used to sing nice music. We never thought of it about what colour he was, we just liked it, gospel and spiritual music, really nice.

Glynis And not just gospel, he used to sing all kinds of music, country music, love songs, Christmas songs and things like that, different types. I used to like listening to him, also on my tape player.

The strong popularity of Jim Reeves amongst our Caribbean households has long been a running anecdote and amusement in our communities for decades on both sides of the Atlantic, though the phenomenon has largely escaped academic study, other than in the work of McMillan. He states (2009, 151), "Reeves was reappropriated by the 'older generation,' though he is still popular across diaspora. 'Gentleman Jim' sang about transcending the trials and tribulations of everyday life in recurring themes of loneliness, love, infidelity, and loss that echo the hymns, spirituals, and gospels of the black Christian church, which sang of the 'intense desire and yearning to transcend the misery of oppression' (Mercer, 1994: 140)."

A prolific artist, having recorded over 400 songs (ibid.), Reeves commanded a strong following also across the African continent, as alluded to by Alice in her comment above. According to music writer Randall Grass, in the early 1980s, "[Bob] Marley ... one of the best-selling musical artists on the continent ... [came] second only to the country singer Jim Reeves" (Savishinsky, 1994: 22).

Biographer Larry Jordon and South African academic Michael Titlestad both outline a more troubling narrative of the complex relationship between Reeves and Black audiences. Titlestad discusses Reeves' relationships with apartheid era South Africa and his tours there in 1962. Reeves had a "vast" following amongst the Afrikaans community, and initially had fears about visiting Africa, "he publicly expressed the fear that he would be abducted at spear-point by savages" (Titlestad, 2014: 498), and afraid that "half naked natives with spears" would capture him and cut out his vocal chords (Jordon, 2011: 403–404). According to Jordon, Reeves held this fear until he saw photographs of an urbanised South Africa in a magazine, and was so relieved that he wasn't going to "no primitive country," he wore the pages out by showing his friends (ibid.). Ironically, only after being a few hours in Johannesburg, Reeves was mobbed by white Afrikaans fans to the extent that he was left bleeding with torn clothes, a "bunch of barbarians" (as Reeves called them the following day), saying they tried to steal his valuable ring (Jordon, 2011: 407–409). After performing a series of white-only shows, where he sang some songs in Afrikaans, Reeves insists on doing a charity show for Black South Africans, amongst who he also enjoyed a huge fan base, much to the disgust of his Afrikaans hosts. After the show (in which he also sang in Afrikaans), Reeves notes in his diary that they were "a wonderful crowd." Yet despite seeing the levels of segregation across South Africa, Reeves is quoted as saying,

> I love this land and its people a great deal and, outside the US, feel most at home here. Afrikaners are genuine and warm. They say what they mean. You get a clear "yes" or "no" out of them … and they keep their word. Americans are inclined to being vague. You never know where you stand with them. This is the characteristic of Afrikaners I admire and which appeals to me. If there is one other language in the world that I would like to master, it is Afrikaans. Then I could get to know you even better.
>
> *Titlestad, 2014: 503*

After this first visit to South Africa, Reeves returned to the United States and recorded some more songs in Afrikaans, and returned back to South Africa in 1963. He recorded two versions of the album "Yours Sincerely" (released posthumously in 1966), one for South Africa, the other for America and the rest of the world. In the South African version only, he says the following in a spoken-word section:

> I saw a good part of South Africa in my travels and I wish with all my heart that others who speak so loudly against your fine country would go and see it for themselves. You know it's one thing to sit and formulate ideas from hearsay, but it's quite different to go and see things for yourself. Until many critics of your country adopt this policy, they will continue to be guided by ignorance.
>
> *ibid.: 504*

Reeves was born in Texas and continued to live in the South during the Jim Crow era, and would have seen first-hand the oppressive segregation of Black people both in the United States and South Africa. Reeves' widow Mary continued to strenuously deny he was racist up to the time of her own death, to the point of flying from Tennessee to London to demand a documentary was re-edited which she found out made such a claim (ibid.). However, for him to not only be (apparently) blind to the suffering of Black people in both countries, but to also go as far as recording his support for apartheid South Africa in a special released version targeted at the apartheid regime market, is wilful ignorance at best, and at worse, an example of a man who does not want to be seen to hold the racist views he clearly harbours, and thus attempts to glide through life as if the contentious politics of the day do not affect him.

However, the cult status of Reeves amongst his African heritage fans today, for example as seen in the video by YouTuber Harri (2021), is as strong as ever. Recorded in the style of a reaction video, where YouTubers give their immediate responses to songs and videos they have mostly never heard or seen before, or in Harri's case, a song he has not heard for a very long time. In his introduction Harri states,

> I love this man, I think he has one of the most amazing and calming and soothing voices ever, ever, ever, ever, ever.

- MUSIC SEARCH – 'He'll Have To Go *Jim Reeves* – PRESS PLAY

On hearing Reeve's song "He'll Have To Go," for the first time, while watching Harri's reaction video, I find myself agreeing him completely. I think I can feel what my elders first felt when they listen to him. My mum's description of his music as being "really nice" is a significant understatement. For a moment I am transported away from the research task, and become transfixed in Reeve's voice and music, which exudes calm and beauty.

It does not give me any pleasure to burst the bubble of Jim Reeves for his Black audiences. It is sad, exhausting, and to a certain extent, humiliating, to find out that someone you grew with and admired turns out to be racist. As explained by story-teller and artist Inigo Laguda,

> To be Black is also to be perpetually ready for confrontation – of your idols, the nation's idols, your pastimes and treasures … Many people are lucky to never know how profoundly disturbing it is to type a beloved figure's name into Google with the word "racist" next to it and find confirmation that this person, who is idolised by so many, would have hated you on an existential level … I would rather unearth and memorialise the people who were ahead of their time, than commemorate someone who was a product of theirs.
>
> *Laguda, 2019*

To make this judgement call for oneself is entirely appropriate, but to decide to accelerate the research for someone else, and reveal to them an answer to a question that they did not even ask, is a different ethical question entirely, and not one I will be rushing to enact. I love my elders unconditionally and respect the long journey they have been on, and if they find the tones of Reeves soothes them in their twi-light years, who am I to challenge that?

Music as a Meaningful Material Culture

For Black settlers in the UK, the radiogram is both a symbol of the achievement in precarious social contexts, and the attainment of being able to have "nice things" (McMillan, 2009: 147). It is also a social object entwined with our culture's deep connection with music and the pride that associates with a sense of self and the col-lective experience. Through the record player, music communicated the statement of "we are here" subconsciously in visceral ways regardless of what actual record is being played. According to Paul Gilroy (1987: 157),

> [Black creative] cultures, in the form of cultural commodities – books and records – have carried inside them oppositional ideas, ideologies, theologies and philosophies. As black artists have addressed an international audience and blues, gospel, soul and reggae have been consumed in circumstances far removed from those in which they were originally created, new definitions

of "race" have been born. A new structure of cultural exchange has been built up across the imperial networks which once played host to the triangular trade of sugar, slaves and capital. Instead of three nodal points there are now four the Caribbean, the US, Europe and Africa. The cultural and political expressions of new world blacks have been transferred not just to Europe and Africa but between various parts of the new world itself. By these means Rastafari culture has been carried to locations as diverse as Poland and Polynesia, and hip-hop from Stockholm to Southall.

From playing music at home, through to sound system culture, music played "out loud" communicates the arrival of human presence and can galvanise collective experience in ways other media cannot achieve in the same way. Projected cinema can achieve similar collective experience, though it has a reliance on the visual gaze, rather than music which is experienced through the ears, which cannot be closed. Played out loud, recorded music becomes an object phenomenon with a repeatable shape in that space, physically held within the body, recalled through memory. Music theorist Thomas Clifton states that although music is not "factually in the world the way trees and mountains are" (1983: 3), and are "meanings constituted by human beings" (ibid.: 5), he argues there is still a physicality to music that takes on additional dimensions when it comes in meaningful contact with the human senses, by means of engaging with the intellectual mind and touching the visceral body.

> [A] musically behaving person is one whose very being is absorbed in the significance of the sounds being experienced. This significance is not associative, denotative, or otherwise symbolic, but is presented in and by the sounds themselves. It is not altogether accurate to say that this person is listening to the sounds. First, the person is doing more than listening: he is perceiving, interpreting, judging, and feeling. Second, the preposition "to" puts too much stress on the sounds as such. Thus, the musically behaving person experiences musical significance by means of, or through, the sounds.
>
> *Clifton, 1983: 2*

Music has taken on an elevated status in the Black diaspora imagination, with dots being joined from pre-slavery era Africa, through to the plantations in the new world, up to the modern iterations in the form of blues, jazz, soul, gospel, reggae, hip hop, jungle, grime, and all other forms of music of Black origin. Some examples of survey research-studies, which join the dots in the Black music journey, include McGinty (1993), Floyd (1995), Ramsey (1996), O'Brian et al. (1998), Riley (2014), and Boakye (2021). The lines between the joined dots are moments of narrative, the places where stories and memories reside. In Britain, where we now have three and four generations of African heritage families being born in the UK, decades removed from the first wave of Windrush era pioneers that came over in the 1950s and 1960s, it is important we hold onto our stories, and objects can help us transport into that consciousness, into the world of our whole beings, not continually being racialised by the burden of double consciousness, or being defined by struggle.

In 2019, Birmingham-based musician Nicole Justice was a visitor at Fairfield House for the day volunteering with the BEMSCA elders, and together we interviewed Mrs Spalding about what music meant to her throughout different stages of her life, from growing up in Jamaica through to the present day. Quoted here at length, Mrs Spalding demonstrates both the geographic transcendence of music as expressed by Gilroy, and the embodied meaning making described by Clifton.

> I'm Mrs Spalding, I live in Bath. I came to England when I was about 16 years old. I came here and did my training, I did General Nursing then I went into midwifery. I worked in several hospitals over England, and finally settled in the RUH Bath, I worked there for 21 years. I retired from there when I was 60 years old, 19 years ago. I lived in a little village called Dallas Castle in Jamaica, near Kingston. When I was about 15 years old I went to watch a film that had Harry Belafonte, that was the first time I saw the big screen, I was really taken aback, it was wonderful.

> [starts to sing *Island in the Sun* (Belafonte and Burgie, 1957)]

> Oh, island in the sun
> Willed to me by my father's hand
> All my days I will sing in praise
> Of your forest, waters, your shining sand

> Sometimes I listen to Classical music, which I find quite relaxing, and I listen to gospel, yes I love the gospel. [Starts to sing The Lord is my Shepherd].

> The Lord's my shepherd, I'll not want;
> He makes me lie in pastures green.
> He leads me by the still, still waters

> I use music if I'm feeling low, I'd just put the music on and dance around the room, or sing with it. It can take you out of that mood you feel you're in, if you're worried or anything like that, yes. It strengthens you really. Now that I'm worshipping Christ, and give my life to Christ, I just go for Christian music, I try not to wander from that. Pop songs do have a message, like Elvis Presley used to sing pop songs but sometimes he had a bit of religion in it as well, which touches your heart, you know. It says in the Bible to, "Sing unto the Lord a new song", and …"Sing unto Him". The lord loves you to sing to Him. You don't have to sing out, but you can sing within yourself, or meditate within yourself the songs. [Starts to sing Faithful One]

> Faithful one, so unchanging
> Ageless one, you're my rock of peace
> Lord of all I depend on you
> I call out to you
> Again and again
> I call out to you
> Again and again.

In this account Mrs Spalding demonstrates the different roles music can play in our lives – as entertainment (*Island in the Sun*), as a relaxant (classical), form of worship (gospel), a motivator (dancing and singing to music), as inspiration (message in music), adherence to theology as a form of prayer (religious verse), and as an object of focus (meditation). It shows how as a woman navigating places and stages in her life, music has taken on different meanings and stayed close to her wherever she went. Clifton argues that in relation to reflecting upon our musical experiences, that "describing a meaningful experience is itself meaningful" (Clifton, 1983: 6). To appreciate this, it gives us the opportunity to learn from all sides of the music object in 360 degrees, not just by hearing the music experiences of others, but by engaging in a deep learning about others and ourselves. Learning from music does not just involve analysis of the audio, but also through the words used, the context, history, meaning and history of those words, and the bodies of knowledge discourse those words relate to.

> [E]ach person's experience is invisible to other people … We must be willing to reflect on all the possible ramifications of these experiences. [D]escription is meaningful because it involves one in a dialogue with other people. With such dialogue, the description can be revised, supplemented, and refined, thus enlarging the domain of any single experience … We learn then, not only about the self and the world, but about other people, without whose presence in the world the self would not be a self-worth knowing. The task before us then, is the description of musical experience and the objects of such experience.
>
> *ibid.: 6–7*

Reflecting on Mrs Spalding's memories, told more through her life journey than a migration story, I became interested in not only how she carried these memories and stories with her through time and place, but also in how the objects of culture she carries in her body consciousness also contain within them a geography and multiple discourses that can remain (as Clifton says) invisible. The following chart of a thematic discourse analysis of some of Mrs Spalding's words explores this idea further (the analysis it contains is not exhaustive) (Table 6.1).

In relation to Small Anthropology, the style in which this book has been written, what has been embarked on here is a process of "discourse archaeology," exploring the layers of objects of everyday life through the analysis of speech, and the digging

TABLE 6.1 Geographic discourse archaeology of Mrs Spalding's narrative

Reference/Text Quote	Context	Location	Geographic Discourse Archaeology Interpretation
Mrs Spalding "live in Bath"	Residence	Bath	Spalding – "The surname Spalding originated in the place called Spalding, in Lincolnshire … The earliest members of the Spalding family on record were found in Lincolnshire, where they settled on lands granted by William the Conqueror, following the Norman invasion in 1066. The Spalding family rose to prominence in Scotland … The first on record was Gilbert de Spaldingis (Latin form) who held lands here in 1175" (House of Names, 2022)
			Name inherited from enslaved African ancestors in Jamaica via spouse.
			Bath – Place of residence and making home. The idea of home renders static the otherwise physical geographic spaces the body travels through.
Came to England	Arrived when 16	England, Heathrow	Arrival point to a bigger location.
Bath RUH hospital	Worked as midwife	Bath	Place of work, signifier of identity
			One of the first known references to midwifery activities is in ancient Egypt in the Ebers Papyrus, written circa 1560 BC (Flack, 1947: 31).
Lived in Dallas Castle, Jamaica	Previous home	Dallas Castle village, in region of Saint Andrew, Jamaica	"Dallas Castle (which still survives as a district in St. Andrew) was owned by a scion of the family of Dallas, in the state of Alabama, whose descendants played their part in Jamaica history" (Cundall, 1909: 9)
			Dallas Castle is in the Jamaican district of St. Andrews, which is the patron saint of Scotland. Dallas, Moray is an area of Scotland, which also has the remains of a literal Dallas Castle, built in the 1300s. The Dallas name was possibly carried across to Jamaica with, or by, the Scottish-based Spalding family.
			According to UCL Centre for the Study of the Legacies of British Slavery website, the Scottish Spalding family were "slave-owning" and lived in St. Andrews, Jamaica. For example, Dr Helen Spalding (1790–1853) was a "claimant or beneficiary" of compensation when slavery was abolished in 1834 (Legacies of British Slavery database, 2022).

(continued)

TABLE 6.1 Cont.

Reference/Text Quote	Context	Location	Geographic Discourse Archaeology Interpretation
Kingston	Near birthplace	Capital of Jamaica	Dallas Castle is approximately 6 miles from Kingston
Watched the film "Island in the Sun" in a Jamaican cinema	First film watched	"Island in the Sun" was filmed in Barbados, Grenada, and London in 1957.	Film productions often conflate different geographic locations to pass as one, which is then watched as a singular narrative anywhere else in the world.
Harry Belafonte	Star of film "Island in the Sun"	Place of birth, 1927 – Harlem, New York. Lives in NY.	Son of Jamaican parents. Became more famous for acting and singing in "Island in the Sun." As a Black actor his presence and representation on screen had an impact for Black audiences across the diaspora. (Anderson & Dent, 1958: 9)
Classical music	Sometimes listens to, finds relaxing.	Contested	The Oxford Dictionary defines "classical music" as "music written in a Western musical tradition, usually using an established form (e.g. a symphony). Classical music is generally considered to be serious and to have a lasting value" (Pentreath, 2021) Composer Nitin Sawhney challenges the notion that classical is solely a "Western musical tradition, citing examples from Indian music traditions" (Sawhney, 2019)
Lord is my Shepherd Favourite hymn. Multiple writers and composers listed for current version of song.	Written by William Whittingham	Born c. 1525 – Chester, UK Died 1579 – Durham, UK	Hymn based on Psalm 23. Whittingham spent time in Geneva and was one of the translators of the Geneva Bible, which was considered quite anti-monarchist and anti-establishment in tone. England's King James later commissioned his own translation of the Bible partly in response to the Geneva version (McGrath, 2001).
	Written by Francis Rous	Born c. 1581 – Dittisham, Devon, UK Died 1659 – Acton, London	N/A

Composed by Jessie Seymour Irvine	Born 1836 – Dunottar, Kincardineshire, Scotland Died 1887 – Aberdeen	Irvine was one of the few women working as composers at the time. Initially unhappy with her arrangement of "Lord is my Shepherd" (which she had previously titled "Crimond"), she asked David Grant to do some adjustments to the harmony. Subsequently Grant was credited as the only composer of what was later known as "Lord is my Shepherd," until it was challenged by her sister in 1911 (after both Irvine and Grant had died), and Irvine was then credited as a composer of the work for the first time (Devilish, 2022).
Composed by– David Grant	Born and died in Aberdeen – (1833–1893)	St. Clement's East Church, Aberdeen, has a plaque for him. An individual permanently memorialised for contributions to religious culture. There are still claims that Grant was sole author and discrediting the claims made by Irvine's sister (Palmer, 2018).
Harmonisation by	Born and died in Glasgow – (1885–1960)	N/A
Using music to make yourself feel better.	Dancing around the room.	Music as balm, soother, therapy. "[E]ngaging with music is proposed to offer a variety of benefits to health and well-being. For example, music is proposed to reduce stress, and can evoke positive feelings such as joy, relaxation, and empowerment" (Weinberg & Joseph, 2016: 1)

"I use music if I'm feeling low, I'd just put the music on and dance around the room, or sing with it. It can take you out of that mood you feel you're in, if you're worried or anything like that, yes. It strengthens you really."

(continued)

TABLE 6.1 Cont.

Reference/Text Quote	Context	Location	Geographic Discourse Archaeology Interpretation
Elvis Presley	Music with a message	Born 1935 – Tupelo, Mississippi Died 1977 – Memphis, Tennessee	During his lifetime Elvis released approximately 60 gospel songs (Hanson, 2012). Although the dominant perception of Elvis is not as a gospel singer, it is poignant that out of all the artists she could have chosen, she chose Elvis to illustrate her point. On first hearing his name by Mrs Spalding, I thought it was a strange choice, but it now feels wholly appropriate.
"Sing unto the Lord a new song"	Bible reference	N/A	Psalm 96:1
"Sing unto Him"	Bible reference	N/A	Psalm 105:2
"You don't have to sing out, but you can sing within yourself, or meditate within yourself the songs."	Using music as meditation	N/A	Hernandez-Ruiz and Dvorak conducted a thorough research project testing "Non-musician and musician participants in a multisite study evaluated their mindfulness state after listening to four music stimuli, and rated their usefulness and preference" (2020: 1620).
Faithful One, So Unchanging Another favourite hymn	Written by Brian Doerksen, 2002	Born 1965 – British Columbia, Canada	N/A

can go as deep as you are willing to go. The right-hand column gives us the opportunity to visualise and learn from the musical experiences from an otherwise invisible narrative perspective, which in this case has taken us from a journey from
learning something about contemporary Bath, 1930s Ethiopia and Italy, ancient
Egypt, contemporary Jamaica, slavery era Scotland, and other locations, as well as
gaining insights into the squabbles and gendered power dynamics of Aberdeenshire
in the 1800s, music psychology, and Elvis Presley's alternative musical narrative.

Discourse archaeology highlights how multi-culturalism is ingrained and
embodied through consumption of culture, and how both the "foreign other" and
the "parochial local" reside in everyone, with no exceptions, regardless how culturally purist one considers themselves to be. As Black people in predominantly white
spaces in everyday life, our black bodies are often automatically seen as "foreign
other" before we even open our mouths (Du Bois, 1903: 168), yet we know we are
not the only ones.

The Emperor's Radiogram

Having engaged in a form of discourse archaeology, through the analysis of speaking
about music in our lives as inspired by the radiogram, we will now engage in a form
of social history inspired by the same device. To explore this, we will be looking at
an everyday life context in the house of another Black family in the city of Bath –
the home of Emperor Haile Selassie I and Empress Menen Asfaw, while they lived
at Fairfield House.

Mussolini invaded Ethiopia on 3 October 1935, capturing the capital city Addis
Ababa on 5 May 1936. During the initial period of invasion Haile Selassie fought
alongside his troops resisting the Italian invasion (Bowers, 2016: 21–22), though
when Addis Ababa fell, he made the difficult decision to leave his country in exile,
to try and rally for support from world leaders on the international stage. Arriving
in London on 3 June 1936 as a political refugee, the Emperor travelled to Geneva
on 30 June and gave a historic 17-page speech to the League of Nations that
received world-wide coverage (Salazar, 2011: 9). He asked the world leaders to protect small states such as Ethiopia, which, he argued, would have fatal consequences
for the future of the world if they failed to act.

> Apart from the Kingdom of the Lord there is not on this earth any nation
> that is superior to any other. Should it happen that a strong Government finds
> it may with impunity destroy a weak people, then the hour strikes for that
> weak people to appeal to the League of Nations to give its judgement in all
> freedom. God and history will remember your judgement.
>
> *ibid.: 17*

The Emperor goes onto warn the League of Nations that the validity of its very
existence relies on this decision, as it was the principles of the mandate that the
League was founded upon, especially when an aggressor has used chemical warfare

as Italy did, which contravened the League of Nations own Geneva Protocols (Grip & Hart, 2009: 2). This strong stance challenging the world leaders in the West made Haile Selassie "a model of resistance to fascism for all black people [all over] the world" (Abera, 2017: 312).

> The Emperor challenged them saying, "It is the question of collective security of the very existence of the League, of the trust placed by states in international treaties … it is international morality that is at stake … it is us today it will be you tomorrow?"
>
> *ibid.*

Mussolini had not yet publicly sided with Hitler (they did not make their formal "Pact of Friendship and Alliance between Germany and Italy" until 22 May 1939), and no matter how powerful the Emperor's speech was, no action was taken, and the League of Nations ended their sanctions against Italy just four days later (Salazar, 2011: 9). After the second world war, the League of Nations was officially disbanded on 18 April 1946, and many political scientists (even those at the time such as influential United Nations founding consultant Leland Goodrich), cite the League's refusal to support the Emperor's plea as one of its significant failures (Goodrich, 1947).

Returning to London after this dramatic event that had received global attention, the Emperor became an embarrassment to the UK government, as he was so popular with the British people who sympathised with his plight. Being told he would not be allowed to live in London as he had to keep a low profile (Cliffe, 1999), the Emperor first came to Bath in August 1936 for spa water treatment (Bowers, 2016: 13, 87), due to suffering mustard gas burns resulting from Mussolini's use of chemical warfare (Haskins, 1999; Grip & Hart, 2009). Haile Selassie purchased Fairfield House for £3,500 from his own money, and the Ethiopian royal family moved into it during October 1936 (Bowers, 2016: 13, 88–91), at a time of extreme stress for the Emperor for what was happening back in his homeland (King, 1999). The Emperor himself wrote, "Deciding to make Our residence at Bath, We bought a house called Fairfield, and with renewed vigour continued our struggle" (Sellassie, 1999: 6). One of the reasons he may have chosen Fairfield House to be the family's new home was that even at this difficult time, there was a specific quality about the house that was soothing, saying that "the view from its front window always reminded us of the hills of Harar" (ibid.: 36), the area in eastern Ethiopia where he was governor of at the age of 17 (Ullendorff, 1995: 228).

In 1937 Ruth Haskins, a local Bath girl then aged 16 years, was employed at Fairfield House as the nanny to the Emperor and Empress's many children and grandchildren. In 1999 I interviewed Ruth about that time, and this is one of the many memories she shared:

> They had a rather magnificent radiogram, and someone put on a record. Immediately the whole place got into the sounds of, what I presumed, must

be a battle because there was gunfire, there was shouting, there was yelling. It was a tremendous noise and racket. It went on and it went on. I glanced round and everyone looked very solemn. Now the Emperor always sat with his hands on his knees like this. [She places her hands on her knees]. Very relaxed. And on his hands at the back, I'd already noticed were very badly pocked. Because at some point, the children told me, he'd been in a battle and the Italians used mustard gas, and some of it had gone on the back of the Emperor's hands, and so he had these quite sizeable dents. I suddenly realised that there were tears rolling down his face and splashing onto these damaged hands. And although I was only 16, I thought that was terribly sad. But it was of great significance, and I think the memory of the Emperor's tears will always stay with me.

Haskins, 1999

Although the Emperor's use of the radiogram is very different in purpose to how my parents and their peers used it for, after arriving in the UK just over two decades later, it is actually in-keeping with the original intention of the device. According to McLuhan, Thomas Edison's initial vision for his invention (the phonograph) was precisely to be used practically like the telephone, relaying information and having an applied use in business. The idea of it being used for entertainment was apparently not even a consideration (McLuhan, 2008: 302). When Mrs Spalding spoke of listening to music in a meditative way saying, "You don't have to sing out, but you can sing within yourself, or meditate within yourself the songs." – although it appears very different on the surface, the quality that both Mrs Spalding and the Emperor have in common with their listening choices in these examples is the sense of connectedness the audio brought to the listener, and intense focus. Although the sounds of war would, of course, not have been relaxing for the Emperor, the internalising of the war sounds would have triggered his tears in the say way that the soothing music would have soothed Mrs Spalding's soul. The audio object became embodied and extensions of their nervous system. For Clifton the relationship between audio that is pleasurable versus non-pleasurable is a complex tension directly related to subjective choice and practical use. He says,

[It] is entirely possible that, as part of the musical experience, one can feel irritated, depressed, and the like … but it should be clear chat these are experiences which one voluntarily agrees to undergo. If the feeling of oppression is not experienced as ultimately pleasurable and one which we desire to prolong, then we will never understand the difference between an experience whose object is frightful as a matter of fact, and one which is frightful because it gives us pleasure to feel that way.

Clifton, 1983: 4

For the Emperor, this was "an experience whose object is frightful as a matter of fact" – (not pleasurable), but it was an experience he knew he had to undergo to transport his mind from the Bath landscape to the military frontline in Addis Ababa, and focus his attention on the needs of his people – a meditation to focus the mind on purposeful action (Hernandez-Ruiz & Dvorak, 2020: 1621). This distressing utilitarian use of the radiogram at Fairfield House is in stark contrast to Ruth's other memory of the device, which she told to *Adrienne Hack of the Anglo-Ethiopian Society* (Hack, 2005).

> Ruth also recalls a radiogram in the sitting room and Prince Makonnen, the Duke of Harar, singing along to his favourite records.

The prince's favourite record, which he played on repeat all day on the radiogram (much to the dismay of some of the household), was "There's a Small Hotel" by Jack Whiting (Haskins, 1986). As a house that had to serve three key functions – family home, government in exile, and spiritual solace (with an Ethiopian Orthodox chapel and Priests on site), we see from Ruth's memories that the radiogram was being used for at least two, if not all three of those purposes.

End Note – A Man in His Music

On the evening that I finished writing this chapter, I took my dog for a walk in the local park, before it started to rain extremely heavily. As I make my way back home, I can see other people also rushing to get to where they were heading, all caught out by the unexpected downpour. On the edge of the park, I see a Black man by the side of the road, holding plastic bags and containers, stood near a wall. He is hitting the container to a rhythm with a stick, singing in a language I did not recognise. He was not a busker, this was no location for a public performance, he was in his own world. I can only imagine what rhythm he was beating, what song he was singing, what memories he was evoking, and possibly, to what landscape he was transported.

7

(FRONT ROOM) – THE LAST SUPPER

Racially othered in many churches, Caribbean migrants also expressed their religious identities through wall hangings that often included The Last Supper and pictures with homilies, such as "Christ is the head of this home."

McMillan, 2019: 185

In my parents' front room, as in many homes, are signs of religious observance – a souvenir plate with the Lord's Prayer inscribed, a palm cross resting on the mantelpiece, framed Biblical quotes, and more. The two prominent statement pieces of religious art in our front room, one of which is a classic blue-eyed portrait of Jesus which hangs in the corner, blond hair nestled onto his shoulders, stigmata hands raised into view, the other is a picture of The Last Supper (see Figure 7.1).

Most children's responses to close-up portraits, regardless of who they are, is the fascination with how the eyes seem to follow you around the room, and my sister and I were equally fascinated. The portrait slightly spooked us, unnerved by this ever-present form of religious CCTV overlooking an otherwise mostly relaxed family space. Jesus was the only picture of a white person on display in our house, and growing up attending Methodist church with our parents every Sunday, we were fully aware that this was not just a painting of any white person, it was The white person.

According to Emile Durkheim,

Religious representations are collective representations which express collective realities. The rites are a manner of acting which take rise in the midst of assembled groups and which are destined to excite, maintain, or recreate certain mental states in these groups.

1995: 9

DOI: 10.4324/9780367809621-8

FIGURE 7.1 Portrait of Jesus and Dad's The Last Supper picture (© author)

For a sincerely religious person, to display overt religious representation in a home is a statement of intent to both other inhabitants and visitors to the home that, at the very least, there is an intention of values which governs the household, and an aspiration to reach. Public icons in a private space seek to make the house a space which embodies the values of said religion by pure force of visual presence, carrying the hope where to look upon said religious icon is in itself, a declaration of faithfulness, a rite enacted by the eyes, a prayer held within the gaze, and a constant reminder of one's religious service as an example for others. Portraits of Jesus such as this serve to "excite, maintain, or recreate" faithfulness in the onlooker, and the presence of them is a rite in itself, not a passive representation, but an active agent in the space.

Attempting to break the spell of fear of the portrait, aged around 11 or 12, when my parents were not home, I stood on a chair to get a closer look, and took the picture off the wall. By that age I was an enthusiastic artist, and looked for the artist's signature, and any other signs of interest. Holding the picture frame in my hands, I saw how it was not merely a portrait, but actually a contract, authorised by the Pope.

> The sacred heart of Jesus has been solemnly enthroned in this home on the day of 19__ by the consecration of Him of all members of the family, present or absent, living or dead.

Confused by my Methodist parents having a Catholic contract on their wall, which they had not filled in or signed, my intrigue grew looking at the other prominent statement piece of religious art in our front room – The Last Supper (see also Figure 7.1). The composition of Leonardo da Vinci's 1490's depiction, which is painted directly onto the rectory wall of the Santa Maria delle Grazie convent church in Milan, is perhaps one of the most iconic examples of Western art, and the visual reference in our own picture at home is immediately recognisable. The influence of Vinci's composition is now considered sacred in the echelons of Western art canon, even though the seating arrangement in the painting makes no logical sense to how any group of people would actually eat together, it being a mere technical conceit for solving the problem of how to show everyone's faces, which is difficult to do with a round or square table formation. This curious art composition has also inspired its own joke among Art Historians.

Jesus: Table for 26 please.
Waiter: But there's only 13 of you.
Jesus: Yes, but we all want to sit on the same side.

The picture in our front room was unmistakeably da Vinci inspired, but with many unique differences, the most obvious being it was made using a 3D layering technique, with details in the image that altered and shimmered with the different perspective of your eyes. This picture belonged to dad, and he told us it contained a secret, but he never said exactly what it was. The only thing he said about it was, if certain people saw it, they would know something about his theology. The game for us as children became then to get our eyes as close to the picture as possible, moving our heads from side to side searching for the clues, all while trying not to break the surrounding ornaments as we climbed up to see it.

To have an object in your house for the majority of your life that you do not really know anything about, which contains secrets only a minority of people can decipher, is more common than we realise, and is actually the norm for most of the objects that surround us (Highmore, 2011: 58), yet, most often we do not carry on any further personal investment in those objects' origins. Religious objects, however, can take on a different transcendence, particularly when they belong to a past or present family member, as they embody values so deeply connected to the individual that they can feel umbilically linked, to be handled with care when in your possession, even if you did not share the same beliefs. None more so than my dad's Lord's Supper picture. Up to the point of his death in 2018, when I was then in my 40s, he never told us what the visual secret in the picture was. (I reflect now that I am not sure if I ever told dad before he died, that I had found out what the secret was by other investigative means.)

This reflection raises the important question of privacy and ethics, and the warning sign in my parent's hallway (Figure 7.1). My dad is no longer here to consent to me saying more about his Last Supper picture, or to announce the clue it contains. Small Anthropology keeps such trust close to its chest, and is more concerned with the connectedness with what feels right in the field, rather than ensuring neat narratives for the audience. Small Anthropology is also an embracement of the transparent approach to research writing, and the breaking of the fourth wall that comes with an embodied reflexive approach. All bodies of research writing will choose to not tell the reader something, but they do not tend to tell the reader what parts of the information they are withholding. According to Tuhiwai Smith (2006: 139),

> Insider research has to be as ethical and respectful, as reflexive and critical, as outsider research. It also needs to be humble. It needs to be humble because the researcher belongs to the community as a member with a different set of roles and relationships, status and position.

Small Anthropology asks for a humbleness, not only of the researcher, but also of the readers of research. In these pages I walk the tightrope of being a member of academia but also the son of a family in the cultural community I am writing about.

Just Jesus

Andrea Levy's *Small Island* tells the experiences of Caribbean citizens coming to live in the UK after the Second World War, and one of the characters, Gilbert, speaks of some of the experiences he had witnessed and heard. In two sentences

Gilbert expresses the trauma of the contradictions of Christianity on the psyche of Black faithful.

> A devout Christian, Curtis was asked not to return to his local church for his skin was too dark to worship there. The shock rob him of his voice.
>
> *Levy, 2004: 326*

Levy captures the feeling of rejection, at a time when some felt they had no choice but to transform their front rooms into places of worship. Speaking with an elder from the Caribbean who came over in the 1960s, but who wished to remain anonymous, he told me,

> We start hold service in our own homes when we realise the church here didn't want us. Some ignored the stares and stayed in the church, refused to leave, but others of us didn't want to stay where we were not wanted. How could that be a real house of God if they turn away a stranger? I had to do what felt right and safe to me, so I went with others and we worshipped in people's homes. Most of the time it belong to the Pastor, but we sometime moved it around. We could have 30 people squash in a front room, but we were comfortable. We did that until we found some other place that would welcome us, and some set up their own thing. You can praise God anywhere, so where better than your own home?

The relationship between people of African descent and Christianity is complex, with many contradictory and opposing facts being true at the same time. It has been well documented how slavery was initially sanctioned by numerous Popes (Muhammad, 2004: 903), and later how both the Catholic and Anglican churches used Christianity as a tool to subjugate the enslaved, selling the promise of salvation and freedom in the next life (Gerbner, 2018; Thomas, 1997). It is also a fact that Christianity was the ideology that led much of the abolition movement, and enslaved Africans who themselves became Christian, such as Sam Sharpe (Roper, 2013), Harriet Tubman (Humez, 1993), and Sojourner Truth (Truth, 1851; Smiet, 2015), used that theological inspiration to fight for freedom of themselves and others. It is a tradition seen echoed in the contemporary era, particularly in the United States, with Black civil right leaders and being also church leaders, such as Rev Martin Luther King Jr., Rev Jesse Jackson, Rev Al Sharpton, and others. According to Lima (2012: 143),

> Black preachers seized upon the Bible, especially the Old Testament, as grist to their mill; the language, imagery and tales of oppression, of freedom, of promised lands, of salvation to come were ideally suited to a suggestive reinterpretation. Paradoxically, Christianity was both oppressing and liberating by providing the enslaved with such narratives of freedom while demanding that they forget where they came from.

In relation to the expression of one's faith in a home context, this same contradiction can be played out through the plurality of the beliefs of the inhabitants, who may not all share the same view, particularly when considering differing attitudes across generations. Thus, while the home became a place of worship and site of sanctity for some of the early Caribbean arrivals to the UK, in some homes those same spaces became sites of tension in later years, when, at best, their children may develop an indifference to the religious ideology of the parents, or at worst, embracing a different belief system altogether, at odds with the theology of their parents.

If you drew a line from above the dad's Last Supper picture (Figure 7.1), through the ceiling to the room above, you'd get to my teenage bedroom, where my intrigue into how Jesus was represented led me to amass my own collection of religious imagery in dialogue with downstairs. A portrait of a dark-skinned Black Jesus adorning a crown of thorns over his dreadlocks was in direct counter to the blond version discussed above, in addition to a huge poster offering an alternative representation of The Last Supper, which dominated the opposite wall in my bedroom, see Figure 7.2.

Again, immediately recognisable as da Vinci's composition of The Last Supper, the poster is also unmistakable in its overt Rastafari aesthetic, with all the painting's protagonists being Black and wearing long dreadlocks, and with the central figure of Jesus wearing a red, gold, and green robe. Though as upfront as the painting is attempting to be, it does still contain a central detail which would be hidden from anyone who did not already know the cultural reference – that Jesus is depicted using the face and crown of Ethiopian Emperor Haile Selassie I, who is revered by

FIGURE 7.2 The Last Supper, Caleb with Ras Opio

Rastafari as deity. Secrets are obvious to people who already know the answer, but a complete mystery hiding in plain sight to the uninitiated. This is a power of the visual arts, and indeed any form of language, that should never be taken for granted. Most of the time, visual arts are not intended to be secrets at all, they are merely cultural and visual references drawn upon by the artist. The same could be said of my dad's Last Supper picture, now that I know the secret which I cannot tell. The visual cultural reference seems obvious to me now. The problem is, I was told there was a secret in the painting, so I was looking for a secret which did not want to be found. Such sincere gestures can sound alien in a postmodern era with secular sensibilities, where to display religious iconography in the home can be an act of kitsch irony rather than sincere faith. However, when you grow up in a religious household, you know there is no irony in your parents' tastes, which you can either grow to adopt as your own values, respectfully reject, or fervently oppose and revolt against. To the culturally unsympathetic, my Last Supper poster could be dismissed as a postmodern reggae version of this famous Biblical scene, rather than the credible serious version of visual Rastafari theology that it is.

The discussion of the Black versus white Jesus efficiently illustrates the contradictions of how blackness and whiteness is viewed differently in Western society and exposes the fallacy in the liberal refrain of "I don't see colour." When one sees a picture of a white Jesus, it is viewed predominantly as an icon of faith representation, and a statement of spiritual intent. It is not viewed as a statement on race or whiteness. However, when one sees a picture of a Black Jesus, it is viewed as a statement of race in relation to faith, interpreted as a visual essay assumed to be asking the question of what the true ethnicity of Jesus was. Wherever I have lived and hung a Black Jesus in public view, such a picture always draws from the unsuspecting viewer into a debate, either in support, opposition or indifference – "Yes I believe Jesus was Black," or "Was Jesus really Black?," or "Yes, I don't think Jesus would have been white, though I'm not sure he would have been Black either, more Middle *Eastern* …" What has to be understood is that none of these debates were ever asked for. My Black Jesus was not displayed to be a conversation starter about the discourse of Jesus' existential existence or identity. Black Jesus triggers people, and they can't help but make a comment, and we see that they were not colour-blind after all. In the 19 years I lived in my family home, not once do I recall a visitor seeing either picture in Figure 7.1 and starting a conversation about the ethnicity of Jesus. It was "just Jesus," and you choose to ignore it or not. A picture of Black Jesus, however, seems not so easy to be able to ignore. Black Jesus either challenges held assumptions that we have accepted since birth, or it affirms anti-racist arguments about the erasure of Black presence. Seldom can a Black Jesus *just be* Jesus.

With the current challenges to decolonise many aspects of civic society, such as education, museums, the police, and a wide range of services and institutions, has also come the demand to decolonise Christianity. My only response to that is, Christianity was decolonised as far back as 1930, it is called the Rastafari movement. Rastafari (the preferred noun for the Bible-based faith/movement) is predominantly positioned as the spirit of liberation of Africa, and the overthrow of Western colonialism and white supremacy, but it is seldom seen as a fight against dominant acceptance of European aesthetics. The idea of aesthetics is often mistakenly simplified as the surface concern of how something looks, and the preoccupation with beauty and style. However, at the centre of the study of aesthetics is the interest in how power and dominant forces in society can validate or invalidate what gets accepted as standards and taken as the "norm," with any deviation from those standards consigned as deviant, ugly, subversive, and on the edges of acceptable society and even persecuted (Koepnick, 1999). Proponents of European imperialism, transatlantic slavery, and colonisation used justifications of race dominance perpetuated through racist theories developed in eugenics and other sciences, emerging social sciences and humanities, rationale philosophy, and Christian theology to frame European standards of beauty as central to what was considered good in all senses of the term, including in the eyes of God. This binary thinking developed in rationale philosophy, pitched experiential phenomena in opposition, in a code which elevated European male standards above all things and top of the moral and aesthetic hierarchy (Lloyd, 1995).

In a family home, such differences in religious worldviews are classically generational, as well as ideological. In my case, it was when I became Rastafari aged about 17, that I was able to articulate my feelings towards the downstairs Jesus portrait, not through my own words, but through the songs of others, played loud from my teenage bedroom to try and educate the house by osmosis. One song that was played loud for this occasion was *Bald Head Jesus* by Bunny Wailer (Wailer, 1989).

• MUSIC SEARCH – *Bald Head Jesus* Bunny Wailer – PRESS PLAY

The song holds a tacit understanding that Jesus was Black and takes it as a given known fact, to the extent that it is never actually mentioned or even alluded to in the lyrics. The song looks at my Last Supper poster, and argues that the colour of their skin is the least interesting quality of the image. The song is one of the rare examples when a representation of Black Jesus is allowed to *just be*. Bunny Wailer moves beyond colour to instead ask us the central question of the song, "Why [have] you never seen the image of a bald head Jesus yet?" In the lyrics Bunny directly tells us to read Numbers chapter 6 in the Bible, which when studied speaks of the Nazarene vow where "no razor may be used on their head. They must be holy until the period of their dedication to the LORD is over; they must let their hair grow long" (Numbers 6:5).

My teenage research took this study further, to read about the most famous Nazarite in the Bible, Samson, known for having his strength in his hair. The book of Judges, chapter 16 verse 13 and 19 tells us that Samson had (only) seven locks of hair on his head. Aged 18 I started to grow my own dreadlocks, and it is only now, aged 49 writing these words that I realise I may have representations of white Jesus to thank for inadvertently and ironically setting me on this more politicised journey of self-discovery.

Black Jesus has arisen in a range of different spheres of popular culture. What follows is not an exhaustive list, and particularly in music there are plenty more example of references to Black Jesus. At the time of this research, however, I was surprised that that "Color of the Cross" still appeared to be the only depiction of a Black Jesus in a feature film. I am still finding that hard to accept.

Black Jesus in Television

- *Good Times* – American CBS-TV comedy series, 1974, Series 1, Episode 2, titled simply "Black Jesus." The family son J.J. paints a portrait of a local homeless alcoholic man depicted as Jesus. At first the mother is offended, preferring her own portrait, but is convinced by the rest of the family to keep it hung on the wall when the Black Jesus portrait seems to bring the family good luck.
- *Family Guy* – comedy series, Episode – "Jerome is the New Black," Series 8, Episode 7, 2009. Peter befriends a Black man named Jerome, who Peter later finds out used to date his wife Lois 20 years previously, before they met. Peter feels threatened by the (stereotypical) ultra-cool Jerome, and he is depicted as a sexist/offensive character, with short "Black Jesus" audio refrains throughout the episode.
- *Famalam* – comedy series. Sketch – "There is no white Jesus," BBC Three, UK, 2018. A white man in a church is praying desperately to Jesus for help, begging he appears to him or for a sign. A dreadlocked Black Jesus appears out of smoke, bright lights, and orchestral music. The man is surprised of Jesus' appearance and is reluctant to accept his help, and asks if a white Jesus is available instead.
- *Black Jesus* – Comedy series, 2014–2019, Adults Swim Network, USA. Jesus is discovered living in Compton, South Central Los Angeles. The drinking and smoking Jesus has his heart in the right place and attempts to spread joy in the neighbourhood in his own haphazard way.

Black Jesus in Film

- *Color of the Cross* – Directed by Jean-Claude La Marre, 2006. The last days of Jesus are depicted in the first feature length film to cast a Black actor as Christ, where his persecution is related more to how he looks rather than what he is preaching. An often-quoted review in the *Mare New York Times* by Jeannette Catsoulis (2006) argued that "Color of the Cross, a low-budget re-imagining of Christ's final days, makes a big deal out of the relatively tame suggestion that Jesus was black."
- *A Black Jesus* – Directed by Luca Lucchesi, 2020. Feature length documentary set in a small Sicilian town, which has a centuries old tradition of worshipping a Black crucified statue of Jesus. A local Ghanaian man who lives in the town has asked to carry the statue for the annual procession, which has caused some upset among the long-term residents.

Black Jesus in Music Visuals

* *Like a Prayer*, by Madonna, 1989, music video directed by Mary Lambert. Black Jesus is simultaneously represented as a modern day African American for a youth MTV audience, wrongly arrested for murder and as a saintly statue in a church. Causing much controversy at the time, Madonna and Black Jesus share a kiss, and Lambert presents him as a metaphor for the victimisation of African American males in contemporary American society.
* *The Don Killuminati: The 7 Day Theory* – Posthumous album release by Makaveli, aka Tupac Shakur's 1996. The album's front cover image by artist Ronald "Riskie" Brent. The cover shows Tupac as Jesus crucified on the cross, the thorn of crown replaced by his own trademark bandana. The bottom of the image carries the statement, "In no way is this portrait an expression of disrespect for Jesus Christ – Makaveli".

In 2008 Black Jesus stepped out of popular culture and into a church itself, and in the process partly proving Bunny Wailer wrong about hair length. For 10 years, a bald depiction of a Black Jesus was quietly attempting to just be Jesus, represented in a large 12 ft by 3.5 ft alter piece, hanging in a humble church in the English Cotswolds valley in Gloucestershire. St George's Nailsworth church was bequeathed a "substantial sum" of money by a deceased church member,

> on condition that the monies are not used for the general maintenance and repair of the church but for a mural with a religious theme preferably "The Last Supper" on the East wall of the Church behind the high altar.
>
> *Benefice, 2021*

After a word-of-mouth search for an artist, portrait painter Lorna May Wadsworth accepted the commission on three conditions:

1. That she be given artistic freedom to create a painting to the best of her ability.
2. That she be allowed to exhibit the painting in London before it went to Nailsworth.
3. That the model she had in mind for Jesus, Jamaican-born fashion model Tafari Hinds, was Black.

The terms were agreed, and in 2009 Wadsworth's Last Supper painting was unveiled (see Figure 7.3) on St George's Day, 23 April 2009, by members of the departed church member's family, and dedicated by the Bishop of Gloucester.

When contacted for this research, Wadsworth told me,

> I agreed to take on the commission for expenses only. I felt and feel strongly that this inverted the usual power dynamic between commissioner and artist. The church didn't ask for a 12-foot altarpiece – I don't think they knew what

FIGURE 7.3 A Last Supper, Lorna May Wadsworth, 2009 (© the artist)

they wanted or how they would go about honouring this dead congregant's sudden bequest. They had what was a considerable amount of money for a church, but not even a 10% of something that would commission a 12 foot altarpiece which took 9 months to complete. I relished the challenge and the opportunity of making something beautiful for the space, and was crucially very mindful that in doing the painting I may not make any money, but I would have artistic freedom.

Despite a splattering of local press attention, and a debate about the ethnicity of Jesus following the exhibition of the painting in London before it was installed permanently in the church (sources no longer available), here among the Cotswold Hills the painting has hung behind the altar for 10 years, largely without controversy. The painting of a Black Jesus surrounded by 12 white disciples proved to be popular, and responding to requests for its display coming from other churches, in 2019 Wadsworth allowed the image to be scanned, so prints could be sent for display in other locations, and during that time the original painting was also exhibited Sheffield before returning as the permanent St George's altar piece in 2020. It was during the scanning process that Wadsworth noticed damage in the painting (which is painted directly onto aluminium), a dent in Jesus' side, and a ballistics expert confirmed it was a "perfect match" for shot done by an air rifle pellet (BBC News, 2019). It is not known at which point in the preceding (assumed peaceful) 10 years of display at St George's, that the shot was fired. Responding to the discover of the shooting, Wadsworth told the BBC,

> I was always aware that [painting a black Jesus] might be controversial, but I never dreamed that anyone could have a reaction that was so violent.
>
> *ibid.*

Further disruption to Black Jesus just being Jesus came when one of the prints was displayed in St Albans Cathedral, in July 2020, in solidarity with the Black Lives Matter movement. Revered as one of Britain's oldest and most important cathedrals, the world's media took notice of this 11-year-old art work as if it was freshly painted, wrapping into their sub-headlines the previous shooting narrative for added impact. The Jamaican Gleaner newspaper states that Wadsworth was initially "a bit disheartened that nobody seemed to really care about the painting" for the first 10 years, but was now excited by the press attention the St Albans Cathedral display had generated (Peru, 2020).

> When I was commissioned to do this, I asked myself how I would portray Christ. The kind of idea of western artistes painting Jesus in their own image has been uncritically accepted, and I wanted people to think rather than accept the iconoclastic. I cast Jamaican-born model, Tafari Hinds, as my Jesus to make people question the Western myth that he had fair hair and blue eyes. My portrayal of him is just as "accurate" as the received idea that he looked like a Florentine. I knew that there is something in Tafari's countenance that people find deeply empathetic and moving, which is the overriding quality I wanted my Christ to embody.
>
> *ibid.*

The Jamaican Gleaner also interviewed Tafari Hinds himself, talking about how the painting had now reached public consciousness in 2020 due to the Black Lives Matter protests in solidarity with George Floyd. One of his friends shared the anecdote of how a local school in London, where Hinds he now lives, wanted to display a copy of the painting, and "they're now talking about inviting 'Jesus' in to meet the children."

In opposition to the St Albans Cathedral display, a spokesman for the far-right extremist group Britain First filmed himself stood in front of the Last Supper print arguing "This is deeply sacrilegious and offensive to all true Christians, but the politically correct, woke liberals who run the church don't care" (Adams, 2021). According to the article in the Herts Advertiser, the right-wing spokesman tried to start a debate about "race politics" with a member of the St Albans Cathedral ministry. The general embracement of Wadsworth's painting by the British church establishment, and the resistance to it by far-right organisations and anonymous air rifle snipers, is a reversal of events from the past. Previously, any deviation from the "norms" of accepted depictions of Biblical imagery and the endorsed narratives would face fervent resistance and punishment from the established church and state. According to Baucheron and Routex (2013: 11),

> Clerics kept a very close eye on artists, who had little freedom: any hint of originality in treatment or interpretation was seen as revealing an impious tendency to flout the rules of the Church and as demonstrating sympathy for the Reformation. Very few dared tread anything but the most well-worn paths; though, equally, many artists clearly did not feel stifled and zealously depicted and defended their faith in their works. It was not until the Renaissance that artists began to gain greater freedom and confidence.

This greater Renaissance freedom of artists in depicting not only representations of Jesus, but also broader forms of personal religious expression, engendered not only a greater confidence in artists, but also in people in general, to essentially per-sonalise their faith and relate to it in their own image and personality. The Jesus portrait discussed at the start of this chapter is an example of a pre-Renaissance representation, where the mere hanging of the picture was to be accompanied with a consecration ceremony sanctioned by the Pope himself. Alternatively, my dad's Last Supper picture, and more obviously my teenage Last Supper poster, are post-Renaissance representations, encoded with details that would speak to certain contemporary viewers with shared sets of values.

In Nailsworth I arrange with one of the church wardens to see Wadsworth's painting on a weekday, and I drive up with my eldest daughter, who herself is an artist (and designed the cover image of this book). We are both surprised by the scale and impressed by the spectacle when we see it for the first time, "Wow! This is so cool!" was the exact reaction from both of us. The representations of the fig-ures are life-size, and the painting creates a commanding presence behind the alter nearly spanning the width of the wall. I talk with the church warden about the piece, and what the reaction has been.

> Everyone in the town is very accepting of it, hasn't caused any controversy. We don't have many Black people who live in the town, but everyone has been very supportive of us putting this painting here. None knew what Jesus looked like, but he definitely wasn't fair skinned, blonde and blue eyed. When the artist discussed her plans, we said fair enough. I don't think of this being a progressive painting. It's the Last Supper, how much more traditional can you get? We don't make a big noise about the painting being here. We're a small community, and it's nice just to have it here, we don't need attention for it. It did get damaged by an air rifle, we noticed damage to a window, but didn't see the damage on the painting until years later. The artist wrote an explan-ation of why Jesus was Black, but after a few months we thought, "what's the point of displaying that?" It didn't feel right, and it wasn't needed. It was like over explaining. Just allow Jesus to be, it doesn't need explaining.

Jesus to Just Be

Although my dad and I had different views relating to who Jesus was and what he stood for, it was not an important enough day-to-day concern to get in the way of our relationship. In his last days, which were spent in a hospital bed, I used my phone to share some of our favourite music. The song played most often was Aretha Franklin's *What a Friend We Have in Jesus*. Neither of us asked which Jesus Aretha was singing about.

8

(FRONT ROOM) – SOUVENIRS AND ORNAMENTS

A big generalisation about the homes of many of the arrivals from the Caribbean in the post-war period, is that every surface in the front rooms and living rooms is full of souvenirs and ornaments. It is a gross and crass generalisation, and the second quality of Small Anthropology methodology (as described in the Introduction) is to "not make any grand narratives or universal claims." That said, as a child of that generation, from my personal observations, I concede the generalisation is largely true ("Reflexivity of the Researcher" tick box also checked).

What are souvenirs and ornaments, and why do we have them? This chapter works to the general acknowledgment that a souvenir is a keepsake from a particular place, and an ornament is a decorative object with the prime purpose of being aesthetically pleasing. "Practical Philosopher" Danielle LaSusa (2007) tracked the meanings of souvenirs, working through a range of ideas locating them in definitions such as "a thing that is kept as a reminder of a person, place or event" (ibid.: 274), through to arguing that the collecting of them "should be considered important in the illumination of various elements of the modern and postmodern state of being-in-the-world. It gives insight into the contemporary person's relationship to identity" (ibid.: 271). This chapter is not primarily concerned with the difference between souvenirs and ornaments, though as previously stated, it does acknowledge there is a difference in emphasis. However, depending on what the thing is, there is a gradual spectrum of what might constitute a souvenir and what is an ornament, and will thus use the terms interchangeably.

The front room of my parent's house is full of souvenirs, and as I look around me in my own home office as I type these words, I see that I am also not immune to the collection of things. In my mother's souvenirs (99.9% of them are mum's) I see geography – ceramic plates, quote souvenirs, tea towels, map pictures, ceramic spoons, keyrings, and many other Barbados-marked items somewhere in every room of the house. There are also singular objects labelled with other locations, such as

DOI: 10.4324/9780367809621-9

London, New York, Snowdonia, Paris, Illinois, Weymouth, Ghana, Totnes, Cyprus, Switzerland, Abergavenny, Barcelona, Barry Island, Cymru, Dunster, Southsea – some places I know my parents have visited, and other places I know they have not.

I know a bit about the story behind a few of the objects (especially if I bought it for them) but most of them I do not know anything about (in that respect, souvenirs are much like some of the photos on display in our parent's/grandparent's homes that we know nothing about – see Chapter 2). The one thing I know for certain about many of the ornaments is that some have been there for as long as I can remember.

Alternatively, looking around my own house where I now live, there are not so many overt mentions of different places written on objects (like traditional souvenirs), but there are definitely things I have here that were bought when I visited a particular place as a memento. The difference is many of my souvenirs tend to speak more towards what the thing is, rather than mainly pointing towards where I bought it from. For example, I have a small collection of bracelets of various designs all without wording, however, the references they speak of are no less clear, as all my bracelets feature the Rastafari colours green, yellow, and red. Further looking around my own home, I see handmade and bought objects from my daughters, also African carvings, Rastafari pendants, badges, rings, Buddhist figurines, small versions of African musical instruments, my teenage hip hop "DASH" belt buckle (my old "street name"), and my most recent charity shop acquisition – a decorative African style carved pot. Whereas in my mum's objects I saw a clear cross-cultural written geography, in my own I sense a more predominant idea of signifiers of a cultural identity. However, that said, my writing here may simply be betraying my own bias, as I am selecting what I tell you I see. I look around me again as I type this (I avoid mentioning functional things like staplers, computer memory sticks, etc.) – I also see a Rubik's Cube, a Father's Day mug written in Welsh, a star of David wooden necklace, my childhood St Christopher pendant, pebbles and shells, and a couple of things that belong to my partner – a cloth owl, and a cloth rabbit wearing a cardigan. The attachment of souvenirs is not rational, and perhaps the study of it belongs more in the realm of storytelling, than it does in psychology. According to Csikszentmihalyi and Rochberg-Halton (1981: 17),

> One can argue that the home contains the most special objects: those that were selected by the person to attend to regularly and have close at hand, that create permanence in the intimate life of a person, and therefore that are most involved in making up his or her identity. The objects of the household represents, at least potentially, the endogenous being of the owner. Although one has little control over the things encountered outside the home, household objects are chosen and could be freely discarded if they produced too much conflict within the self.

There is something in common that all souvenirs and ornaments have in relation to the person who own them – it provides something to hold onto. This is not going to be an attempt to psychoanalyse a whole generation of Caribbean elders as to why they collect so many souvenirs, or an analysis of taste, as that would be disingenuous, unethical, and unfair. What I am interested in, however, is in the generational difference in the tone of the souvenirs, and ask why that may have come about. When I look back at my mother's souvenirs, and those of her generation, a certain sense of aesthetic and cultural freedom can be seen that I do not see in my own or many of my peers. Besides the aforementioned multiple souvenirs labelled with the countries of their birth, the objects of my parents are mostly politically and ideologically benign, such as figurines of cats, Edwardian characters, glass fish, ceramic boots, and rabbits. This is in contrast with my own self-conscious laden aesthetic (and some of my second-generation born peers), which are often dominated with more overt figurative and symbolic references to our cultural heritage – nods to Africa and a visual embracement of our cultural heritage. A generational difference in using domestic decoration as an extension of their (our) cultural identity, an expectation that our elders were seemingly free from. My mother's ornaments are displayed because she simply likes the look of them, whereas many of my objects on display are because I feel they *mean* something.

I become jealous of the lightness of my mother's unburdened domestic curation policy, and constrained by how my own analysis of my identity has seemingly limited my willingness to display anything I simply like the look of. It is a project of attempting to transform the arbitrary into rationality, the criteria of decorative ornamentation to reach the standard of being read as meaningful cultural signifiers. This is not a constraint that limits my own appreciation of art and culture in the external world, just what I choose to display overtly in the home. This self-conscious intentionality of domestic display could be critiqued as a self-imposed cultural straightjacket, or alternatively, it could be celebrated as an awareness of self and cultural identity to be encouraged. As with all binary oppositions, this is in some sense a false dichotomy, as nuance exists in all cases. However, the forcefulness of how much the values of the domestic displays are manifested in our wider lives is reflected in our views of the relationship between culture and identity, and what role our bodies play in the perpetuation of culture in the face of challenges to our existence. Our argument that our culture is under threat saw us embark on a project of survival that is reflected in our aesthetic preferences and forms of expression. For some of us that meant changing our names, our hairstyles, the clothes we wore, the words we spoke, the food we ate, the relationships we formed, the God we prayed to, and invariably, the objects we chose to surround ourselves with. Quoted in Franz Fanon's *The Wretched of the Earth*, Guinean President Ahmed Sékou Touré argues for the need for the embodied solidarity with Africa for all who support the anti-colonialist and anti-racist struggle towards the empowerment of the continent and its people.

> In order to achieve real action, you must yourself be a living part of Africa and of her thought; you must be an element of that popular energy which is entirely called forth for the freeing, the progress and the happiness of Africa.

There is no place outside that fight for the artist or for the intellectual who is not himself concerned with and completely at one with the people in the great battle of Africa and of suffering humanity.

Fanon, 1962: 166

In this context, with such high expectations of how one carries oneself in society in the cause of the anti-colonial and anti-racist struggles and other activist causes, the space for joy, leisure, frivolity, and the "lighter" aspects of life seem like a luxury of time that we can seldom afford. Though, of course, joy, leisure, and laughter in life are a necessity and are highly important (and I argue that so confidently, I refuse to include a reference citation for this plain fact). During chairing an event on Creative Arts as Activism, I asked *Museum of Colour* Director Samenua Sesher about this tension, in how the struggle can become embodied to the extent it begins to define our identities and existence.

> Our need to correct the narrative, yes I understand that, and that is abso-lutely valid and necessary – it is a <u>real</u> thing. But part of the correction of that narrative is the absence of our joy. We are extraordinarily some of the most joyful people in the face of pain, and yet if I'm living that pain, if I'm living that struggle, I'm living those challenges on a day-to-day basis, when I come off my work beat and flick on my TV, or I want to hear podcast or whatever, I don't want to hear more pain! … So, it's important to me that even though the correction of the narrative is a deep part of my practice, is that I must find ways to express the joy as well.
>
> *Sesher, 2021*

I ask my mum what drove her decisions to buy some of the ornaments she had. It felt like a stupid question at the time, but as with all things academic, having it articulated can also prove useful. Her immediate response was to just laugh.

> Well … if I see something I like, I buy it, if I can afford it that is. It's good to surround yourself with things that make you smile. I don't look for happiness in objects, but if you have pretty things around the place, what's wrong with that?

One of the souvenirs in the family front room is a small ceramic cat resting on a ball that changes colour in different weathers and temperatures, stamped with the label "Weymouth" (see Figure 8.1). It was one of my fascinations as a child, realising that different temperatures could affect the look of an inanimate object. Compared with my own (apparently serious) adult ornaments, such as a brass dish with carved Egyptian sphinx and pyramids (also in Figure 8.1), I realise now that the cat is as valid a form of cultural expression as the Egyptian dish – the makers just had different themes they wanted to creatively express. Both these objects ori-ginate from my childhood (I acquired the Egyptian dish at some point when I was

FIGURE 8.1 Weymouth weather cat and Egypt decorated brass dish (© author)

a teenager), but it is the only one of the two objects that came with me during my transition to adulthood when I left home, by then already politicised and embracing my African heritage.

These objects are not mutually exclusive, and even though I can own and enjoy both, they are separated by 13 miles of distance between my current and childhood homes. Seeing the cat ornament makes me smile, but only the dish buys into a teenage-nurtured politicised sense of self, built upon an ethos of awareness raising and nation building, but neither object is intrinsically "good" or "bad," and the Egyptian dish is in fact as ideologically benign and objectively as arbitrary as the cat. The meaning of either object only resides in the narrative afforded to it by the viewer and is highly subjective (Berger, 1982: 47). To me, the Egyptian dish could represent the longevity of an ancient African society, but for others it could just a nice picture of some old buildings. Likewise, the cat with ball could easily be dismissed as a kitsch novelty souvenir with a visual effect, but for someone else it inspires the creative innovation of science and the possibilities of reactive materials. The very reason I was so fascinated by the cat ornament when I was a child is precisely because of the awe of the playful and fun innovation of science. It certainly made (and makes) me smile more than the Egyptian dish. I was about to follow this by stating, however, that the dish made me think more, but I realise that it was not necessarily the case either, so I will not make that claim. Both of these objects contain different forms of cultural value, and as previously stated, it just depends on which questions we want to ask of them. The souvenirs and ornaments of my mother and her generation speak of an unhindered visceral immediacy, representing a certain un-self-conscious freedom. I now see joy, and a freedom of mind that I admit I do not readily possess. I lament in a reflective melancholia, as I know it is a joy and freedom which I cannot access nor share.

To understand this melancholia, and the persistent drive for the embodied reclaiming of African heritage, we need to explore the meaning of the Ghanaian Adinkra symbols, particularly looking at the concept of Sankofa (which was briefly explained at the beginning of Chapter 4, and will be explained further in this chapter). The Adinkra symbols are a series of approximately 60 visual aphorisms which originate from the area now known as Ghana, with scholars offering different dates of their origin, ranging from the pre-historic/pre-slavery era (Kuwornu-Adjaottor et al., 2015: 25) through to the 1600–1800s (Adom et al., 2016: 43–44). Whichever the case, the Adinkra symbols are accepted as indigenous forms of visual communication that acts as "tools that convey the thoughts, beliefs and values of the Asante people" (ibid.: 42). Endorsed by President Kwame Nkrumah after Ghanaian independence (Jørgensen, 2001: 123), the Adinkra symbols, and particularly that of Sankofa, experienced a revival which epitomised the anti-colonial struggles and the fight towards independence across the African continent. According to Jørgensen (ibid.),

> Nkrumah revived the old Akan symbol, Sankofa, which is accompanied by the mottos: "Go back to your culture" or "Go back and take it." Hereby he stressed the interrelatedness of past, present and future. Nkrumah's ultimate vision was African unity, and re-building Ghana as a black nation was the first important step in this direction.

The Sankofa symbol is represented by a bird reaching back to gather a seed into its beak (see Figure 8.2). The aphorism of Sankofa is – "there is no shame to go back and fetch that which you have forgotten." It is widely interpreted as meaning to reclaim and embrace your history, heritage, and culture, and using a re-aligned past as a firm basis of knowledge to move forwards.

Kuwornu-Adjaottor et al. (2015: 26) describe the philosophical lesson of Sankofa as:

> The symbol teaches the wisdom in learning from the past to help improve the future. It also teaches people to cherish and value their culture and avoid its negative adulteration. This is the symbol of positive reversion and revival.

The Adinkra symbols are still widely used by Ghanaians to the present day, and due to this message of reconnecting with the past to move forward confidently as a people, Sankofa is now arguably the most popular and recognisable Adinkra symbol across the African diaspora (Mullings, Sobers and Thomas, 2021: 415), due to its narrative speaking directly to the experience of cultural displacement and the strategy towards re-alignment. Christel Temple, Professor of Africana Studies at the University of Pittsburgh, charts how the notion of Sankofa became a phenomenon that inspired millions of African Americans (Temple, 2010), and the African diaspora worldwide, who felt cut adrift from their African heritage due to their forced displacement due to slavery. She states:

> It is empowering to acknowledge and bear witness to the fact that the popular emergence of a Diasporan Sankofa practice did not evolve from a single organizational push for Diasporan communities to unite in the name of this

concept. Instead, behaving as intuitive African selves, Diasporan communities simultaneously favor this concept in practical applications, responding to an internal desire for cultural definition and reacting to cultural casualties sustained in the experience of being involuntarily immersed in Western culture.

ibid.: 128

Temple goes onto argue that the Adinkra system should be referred to as *communicators* rather than symbols, which she states is a reductive term that does not fully appreciate the complexity of the visual aphorisms and a language system, and "another example of the European-inspired oversimplification of African culture" (ibid.: 130). As a language and discourse, the notion of Sankofa presents a powerful framework for the values of personal expression, especially when you are a Black body in a Westernised space which marginalises your contributions, and your full identity as a human being with a cultural history. Quoted in Temple (ibid.: 140), influential Black Studies scholar Maulana Karenga states:

Sankofa contains three basic elements and processes:

(1) an ongoing quest for knowledge, that is to say, a continuing search for truth and meaning in history and the world;

(2) a return to the source, to one's history and culture for grounding and models in one's unique cultural way of being human in the world;

(3) a critical retrieval and reclaiming of the past, especially the hidden, denied and undiscovered truths of the African initiative and experience in the world.

Of course, collecting African-centred objects is not as important as any of the above responsibilities Karenga describes, and if Adinkra is indeed a fully encompassing language communicator, then the collection of objects which reflect those sensibilities is a mere symbol, as is changing our names, clothes, hair, and any other outward form of expression, and more important is how you live and what you do. As an analogy, however, it would seem strange to walk into a church and not be surrounded by related Christian religious imagery and paraphernalia, likewise, our homes become personal temples of cultural resilience, signifying both the joy of survival and the narrative of that surviving.

Using photography, I produced a self-portrait in the form of a Sankofa sculpture (see Figure 8.2). My culturally significant objects placed onto an A-zero-sized sculpture led on the floor, captured from above. I am the bird, made up of things that reminded me of who I am – music, books, carvings, pendants, flags, nature … The beak that I use to "go back and fetch" is made from a multi-coloured plastic heart that was made for me by my daughters, and the seed the beak it picking up is made from a pile of rice. There is my joy (Chapter 10 expands on this).

Looking further into the communicators, I produce another photographed Adinkra symbol, this time of "Denkyem," which represents the theme of adaptability

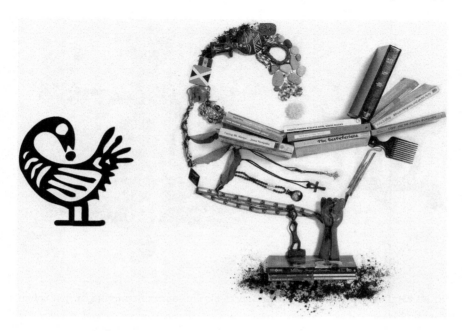

FIGURE 8.2 Sankofa Adinkra symbol and Sankofa self-portrait (© author)

(see Figure 8.3). The visual icon itself is a depiction of a dwarf crocodile, a species found on the west coast of Africa. Descriptions of the Denkyem symbol include the attribute to be able to adapt effectively to different circumstances, the example given being that the crocodile can live in the water and also breathe air (Adinkra, 2007). The crocodile is considered clever for its adaptation qualities that is looked upon favourably by others (Symbolikon, 2001), and has an "ingenuity coupled with formidability and mystery ... that embodies superhuman traits" (Adinkra Symbols, 2020).

The meaning of Denkyem makes me think of my parents and their peers, which now gets labelled as the Windrush Generation. Their bravery leaving their homelands of the Caribbean to arrive in the UK in the post-war period when many were still teenagers and in their 20s. Their strength of character in the face of racist hostility, and the solidarity they showed each other, and the genuine friendship bonds they formed with allies. Their navigation skills making sense of the new terrain they found themselves in, making lives for themselves and security for the families they created. Their skills that went unrecognised, their achievements that went uncelebrated, and the legacies that went undocumented. The descriptors of "ability, cleverness and superhuman traits" are apt, and in the Denkyem sculpture I carefully lay my mother's ornaments in place in tribute (see Figure 8.3).

The ornaments here represent and celebrate the adaptability of people in flux, who even when stationary and settled are still aware of their movements and how travel features as a defining aspect of their life narratives. People in movement have

FIGURE 8.3 Denkyem Adinkra symbol and Denkyem souvenir sculpture, Shawn Sobers (© author)

to adapt to new customs, laws, languages, foods, weather, norms, values, beliefs, politics, fashions, expectations, practices, and more. Some of the things collected along the way are held onto and put on display. Whether the object is strictly speaking a souvenir or an ornament, the thing takes up physical space and presents itself as "I am here," proud in the Front Room.

I Am Here.

As We Are.

9

(KITCHEN) – DUTCH POT

In 2007, with my colleagues Rob Mitchell and Louise Lynas, we arranged for the elders from BEMSCA to visit the National Trust property Dyrham Park, on the outskirts of Bath. The visit was for our project *Re:Interpretation*, which was exploring the financial connections between certain National Trust properties in the South West and the trafficking and enslavement of African people. During the tour of the house in one of the large plush rooms of the main house, Mrs Ottway, one of the group of elders, got visibly upset at the realisation that the Braithwaite family were able to trace their ancestors back to 1571. Previously Mrs Ottway, who was born in Barbados, had attempted to research aspects of her family history, but she hit a block in the official records going back just a few decades. Seeing her looking upset, I asked her if she was ok – her feelings started to pour out …

"We don't know who we belong to. It's like we are non-entities, we are nothing, we don't count for anything."

This is diametrically opposite to when the house tour took us below-stairs to the kitchen and other areas of labour. The group became animated and much more talkative, and clearly more relaxed than in any other more luxurious spaces in the house. When I asked them about this, they said they could relate to the below-stairs areas more "as this is where work happened and where 'real people' lived." I have previously written about this moment (in Mitchell & Sobers, 2013: 136) describing it thus.

> The BEMSCA group largely assumed the property had a connection with the slave trade without finding much need to explore or question it further. The subject proved to be of less interest to them than objects in the house that reminded them of their own past. The elders, who were mostly [Caribbean born] women, pro-actively "found" their reflections and representations in Dyrham Park, though not by looking at the paintings or speculating about

DOI: 10.4324/9780367809621-10

the house's connection with slavery, but by using objects and scenes in the house to trigger their own memories. Members of the group became inspired by the kitchens and the utensils that were similar to those they had used when back in their homelands. The Dutch Pot particularly was seen as an object that had travelled through the slavery and colonial eras, firstly with the Empire builders and subsequently being adopted across the Caribbean and the Americas (and also in Britain via the colonies) as an effective method of slow cooking … A note acknowledging the symbolic importance of the Dutch Pot was thus included in the interactive exhibit produced as part of the Re:Interpretation project [see Figure 9.1].

BEMSCA elders became clearly excited at the sight of a Dutch Pot at Dyrham Park, laughing and sharing stories about using the pots "back home." Objects in the kitchen and working spaces sparked their imaginations and got them interested and engaged, and it was the first time during the visit when they started to relax and feel less self-conscious. This asserts Attfield's argument that "objects mediate emotions, relationships and identities" (Attfield, 2000: 121).

Although it is present throughout the Caribbean (with other names, such as the Buck Pot in Barbados), the Dutch Pot has become particularly synonymous with Jamaican cooking, accompanied with often-heard (parody) culturally essentialist in-jokes, such as "if you don't have one of these pots in your house, you're probably not a Jamaican!" (SouFLoTV, 2015), and presenter Emprezz Golding saying on Smile Jamaica TV – "What's more Jamaican than having a Dutch pot, aka a Dutchie? If you are Jamaican and you don't own one, something wrong wid you!" (Golding, 2017).

FIGURE 9.1 Dutch Pot at Dyrham Park, in Re:Interpretation interactive exhibit. Firstborn Creatives, 2007

The cooking technique of making pudding in a Dutchie was discussed by the BEMSCA elders - that the pot has the ability of adding heat at the top through the lid, as well as from below as normal. This technique comes with its own well-known Jamaican jingle, celebrating the uniqueness of the Dutch Pot in producing the finest food results, "Hell a top, hell a bottom, hallelujah inna di middle," which some elders have remembered since childhood (Smith, 2019). Most famously perhaps in 1982 Black British reggae group Musical Youth released "Pass the Dutchie," which reached number 1 in the singles charts in the UK and top ten in the US, which contained the lyrical refrain between each line of the verses – "How does it feel when you've got no food?" The close association of the Dutch Pot with Jamaica, and that with the Caribbean more generally, is further strengthened by many independent Caribbean restaurants, take-aways, and catering businesses being called The Dutch Pot, in many places in the Caribbean, United States, UK, and Europe. According to "The Dutch Pot Jamaican Restaurant" website in Florida, "The Dutch Pot is the only way to do authentic Jamaican cooking. It is because of The Dutch Pot that the heat and temperature is always consistent" (The Dutch Pot, 2016).

Despite the visibility of Dutch Pot references in popular conversation and culture, there is no substantial independent or academic research of the history of the Dutch Pot, in relation to its connection with the Caribbean, yet produced. The significant documented mentions being in cook books, oral history accounts in YouTube videos, in blogs, and in the websites of Caribbean restaurants and Dutch Pot sales companies. Yet, in contrast, the history of the Dutch Oven (as this object is known in the rest of the world) is thoroughly documented, and its connection with Europe and the United States enjoys a much wider body of research, both academic and independent. This disparity is symbolic of how epistemologies that are widely familiar in Black heritage cultures can be side-lined in the shadow of a more established research cultures (i.e. European narratives), where the Black experience aspect is a mere footnote, if mentioned at all. When searching for sources, I mention this apparent lack of research on Caribbean Dutch Pots, to Oklahoma-based Dutch Oven expert and state educator Luann Sewell Waters. She confirms the lack of research, and laments on the precariousness of the documentation of valuable local knowledge of this kind of everyday life material culture. She also helpfully reaffirms for me, the motivation and confidence I needed to finish writing this book. She said, "So often, the things used every day aren't 'seen' by most people. The items are so common, no one stops to think that in 100 or more years into the future, someone might want to know their history." Writing this chapter has perhaps surprised me the most. I expected to be flooded by choice of research about the Dutch Pot and was surprised to find very little. It was an urgent reminder that with each member of the older generation that dies, we lose another chapter in our oral history knowledge base.

In a YouTube video on the Kenny GoodVibes TV channel, posted August 2021, the cameraman Kenroy McDonald interviewed Reagall Wolfe, the inherited owner of a Dutch Pot manufacturing business and shop in St Mary, Jamaica (McDonald,

2021). In the process of the interview, Wolfe talks us through a selection of the 68 different Dutch Pots styles that he has displayed on the wall for sale, each with different names. For example – "The Six Flat," "The Belly Mumma," "The Roaster," and "The Choppy." The latter is named in tribute to his Rastafari father Zacariah "Choppy" Wolfe, who ran the business from 1982 until his death in May 2021. Zacariah inherited the business from his own father who founded it in 1973. Reagall is the latest proprietor in a family-run business that had so far lasted 48 years, over three generations.

While conducting more research, I find that Zacariah himself was interviewed in Jamaica's The Star newspaper in February 2021, just three months before he died. He was lamenting to the reporter Simone Morgan-Lindo that he had not sold a single Dutch Pot that day due to the Covid pandemic, where usually he would have sold at least five minimum, and he said it was the worst business he had faced in over 30 years.

> People rather buy food now than a pot. Mi stand up on mi foot until dem all start swell up … [but] People still like a good Dutch pot so mi a go always make dem because no matter how the kitchen full a fancy pots and pans, there is always a good Dutch pot somewhere.
>
> *Morgan-Lindo, 2021*

In the interview, Zacariah speaks with pride about having learnt to make Dutch Pots. He also talks about his children, saying he hopes they take on the business after he is gone, as even though making the pots can be messy, they can make good money. When I re-watch his son Reagall's interview on YouTube, it is poignant to see that he is holding a wooden photo-plaque tribute to his father throughout the 15-minute video. Behind the camera, we hear McDonald say he knew Reagall's father as "Uncle Choppy" (although they were not blood related). At the beginning of the video, we see that McDonald's own young daughter is in the car joining him to interview Reagall, and we find out that Zacariah had made the pots that McDonald himself still uses. I am fascinated by how the dynamics around this one object, the Dutch Pot, has been the mainstay in the everyday life of the Caribbean (in this specific case, Jamaica), and has been a constant thread in this family for nearly 50 years, and how it has overlapped with at least two generations (that we know about) in McDonald's family. With his daughter, McDonald is now joining the dots in their interconnected social, cultural, personal narratives, by making the effort to stop and talk to Reagall, the man in the pot shop they usually just drive past on the busy main road.

Dutchie History

Contrary to popular belief, it was possibly not the Dutch who brought the Dutch Oven to Jamaica and other Caribbean islands governed by the British, evidence suggests it likely by the British themselves through the personality and influence of an English Quaker named Abraham Darby. Darby copied the technique of the original Dutch makers and managed to patent the process for himself. Historian Rebecca Sharpless describes the introduction of Dutch Ovens into the enslavement plantations in the Southern states of America (2017: 114).

> First invented in the early eighteenth century, the Dutch oven remained the pot of choice … for well over two hundred years. After seeing them made in the Netherlands (hence the origin of the name), English Quaker Abraham Darby patented the process of casting iron pots in sand and began cranking out cookware from his Shropshire foundry in 1708. Just prior to the American Revolution, colonial merchants imported them, along with lots of other kitchen goods, from London and Bristol [where Darby later manufactured them] … Southerners took quickly to the pots. While few African Americans, if any, could choose their own work tools, they adeptly used the pots that their owners provided to cook their own families' meals as well as their owners'. When an enslaved man named Sam ran away from his owner, Gabriel Jones, in 1775, he took an "iron pot" with him. In 1780, Lawrence Thompson, the overseer of River Plantation near Falmouth, Virginia, purchased "One dutch oven" for People's [enslaved Africans] use.

Dutch Oven historian John Ragsdale also describes Darby's copying the technique from the original makers in Holland and goes onto describe adoption in the British-governed colonial territories (Ragsdale, 1991: 4).

> In 1708 he received a patent for the process and soon thereafter began producing a large number of pots at his furnace in Coalbrookdale. By the mid-eighteenth century, these pots were being shipped to the Colonies and throughout the world markets (Tyler, 1971: 29). It is possible that the adaptation of this Dutch system for this patent may have led to some colloquial or even later reference to the Dutch pots. This is possibly the root for later references to Dutch ovens.

It became routine on many slaving plantations for overseers to distribute kitchen objects such as cooking pots and cutlery to enslaved people for their domestic use and also to cook food for other plantation workers (Delle & Fellows, 2021: 1004). Even though the Dutch element of the name has been retained, the manufacture of the pots became an enterprise, which the Africans took on themselves, and much in the same vein as Abraham Darby, in Jamaica they built their own foundries using recycled metals as source materials, and developed the skills for metal production which has passed down generations and still exists as thriving businesses today (McDonald, 2021; Sinclair, 2017; Sweetness, 2019). The Dutch Pot is another example of how West African descendants, through enslavement, took ownership of things given to them by the overseers and wholly made it their own, far eclipsing its original intent and vision. This phenomenon is a particular example of a form of modernity and transformative sense of cultural expression resulting from what Gilroy termed the 'Black Atlantic'.

> New traditions have been invented in the jaws of modern experience and new conceptions of modernity produced in the long shadow of our enduring traditions – the African ones and the ones forged from the slave experience which the black vernacular so powerfully and actively remembers.
>
> *Gilroy, 1999: 101*

Gilroy argues against an essentialist quest for an authentic African-ness. He sympathises with the motivation, though critiques that such searches for a "true" un-interfered-with sense of cultural identity (which bypasses the years of enslavement to focus on a pre-slavery era) actually continues to assert the dominance of white supremacy by centring and reacting against it, and turning our backs to vernacular forms of modernity that we created (ibid.: 193–194). It is a challenging but persuasive argument, as to reject all the aspects that came through the experiences of slavery, rejects the very existence, struggles and lessons in survival that our ancestors embodied and conquered. To reject the Dutch Pot because it came through slavery would be to deny a significant manifestation of African creativity and transformation, and the ability to use resources and opportunities at hand that made life better for them and their communities. Mintz describes it at thus.

> Within the plantation, life was supposed to be lived as the master ordered, and to a large extent, this was the case. But we have amassed evidence to demonstrate that the patterns of cultivation and marketing developed largely outside the formal demands of the plantation regime, either with the overt and explicit cooperation of the planter class or, in some cases, without it. Most interesting, perhaps, the remarkable economic performance of Jamaican slaves made their [the planter] society dependent on the slave group in ways that no early planter could have predicted – or might have been willing to concede.
>
> *Mintz, 1989: 211*

It is a bittersweet reflection to hear about the efficiency of the enslaved. The want is to hear about their rebellion, and how their trickster-ism made life as difficult as possible for the overseers and their kin. To hear about their hardworking nature, and how their productivity was so high that it helped to maintain the wider slaving system of everyday life itself, is a challenge to our values and sense of what it feels right to celebrate.

In *Capitalism and Slavery*, Eric Williams (1945) reminds us that origins of slavery by Europeans in the New World was economic rather than racial, and subsequent racist ideologies were used to justify the enslavement of Africans after the servitude of Native Americans, Caribs, Arawaks, Irish, and poor white English, proved not to be as profitable. The assertion was that this difference in work-power across cultural groups was due to the physical endurance and ability of Africans to work longer hours in the hot plantation conditions (ibid.: 7). According to Williams,

"The Spaniards discovered that one Negro was worth four Indians" (ibid.: 9). Still nothing to celebrate here, perhaps until we try and reframe the question. The relentless project of European Empire expansion, and the pursuit of the early iterations of capitalism, saw them put their own people into servitude, and the forced labour of natives of the lands of their conquests, before settling on the brutal and systematic form of chattel slavery on the "inexhaustible" supply of African labour (ibid.). As Williams argues, Europeans "would have gone to the moon, if necessary, for labor. Africa was nearer than the moon" (ibid.: 20). Faced with this organised machine of captivity, the enslaved Africans also become relentless and systematic in their endeavour to survive, adapted the landscape, resources and languages to make them their own. When I see the endurance of the Dutch Pot, and how it has now become synonymous with the culture of the Caribbean, I do allow myself a smile at the audacity of boldly claiming an item that has a different nationality in its label. Perhaps that is the trickster factor to notice and applaud.

Casual Hero

In July 2020, after the first Coronavirus lockdown in England, one of my photography students, Naomi Williams, produced a photo series about her granddad in Nottingham (Williams, 2020). Among the sensitive depictions of her granddad house, close-up details of some of his items, and a peaceful portrait of him sat in his kitchen, another image from the series caught my eye. A beautifully lit photograph of her granddad's sink and draining board, there basking in the sunlight is the lid of a Dutch Pot (see Figure 9.2).

FIGURE 9.2 Granddad, Naomi Williams, 2020 (© Naomi Williams)

The photograph is a pictorial appreciation of everyday life and the mundane, unselfconscious in a raw documentary style. By position of the light, the Dutchie lid is the casual accidental hero of the image. Objects of utility tend to blend into the background and are called upon to be reliable as air. Functional objects tend not to be on gallery walls and celebrated (Duchamp's "Fountain" is an early pioneer exception). Statues of everyday objects tend not to be placed on plinths in our cities, and the sight of them do not usually become tourist attractions. I think back to the BEMSCA elders going around the National Trust's Dyrham Park, and how they got excited seeing the Dutch Pot in the below-stairs kitchen, declaring "I've got one of those." Such moments are key signifiers in the forging of a sense of belonging. Seeing the potential for a sense of self in foreign places.

10

(KITCHEN) – RICE

Occasionally on Sunday mornings, when I was maybe 10 or 11, if I'd escaped having to go to church, one of my parents would ask me to help pick the rice for the day's meal. While sat watching television, I had a tray next to me on the sofa and pick through the large pile of uncooked rice, one grain at a time, moving each good grain to the other side of the tray, and dropping any bad grains into a bowl at my feet. An hour or so later the pile would have moved to the other end of the tray, and in the bowl was a small assortment of rogue entities. Although it did not happen every week, this was a home ritual that I strangely enjoyed whenever I was asked. Such was my long-standing relationship and love of rice that I was prepared to undergo this arduous process with seemingly little protest. Would I have undertaken the same task with a tray of split peas, which I did not like? I am not so sure. One of my oldest friends, Andy, often reminds me with amusement of a conversation we had when we were teenagers in the 1980s, when I told him that rice was my favourite food.

What do you mean? Rice?
Yes, rice.
Really? Why?

Now in 2022, I asked Andy about why that memory has stayed with both of us approximately 35 years later.

Well, it's such a bizarre answer, it just sounded so practical, rather than a luxury. It's like choosing a potato rather than wedges with some flavour to it. Rice has little nutritional value, and the first time you eat it it's boring, so I just couldn't understand it.

DOI: 10.4324/9780367809621-11

We are both laughing as he gives the explanation. He asks me if the practical element was behind the answer, and the truth is much more primal rather than intellectual – I simply like rice. I'm reminded of another moment in the early 1990s. While at college, me and my classmate M went to town during lunch. In the food court of the shopping centre, he stared at my plate of white rice and Indian curry asking, "What is that?".

> It's rice.
> What's rice?
> Rice is rice. You've never had rice?
> Nope, but I think I've heard of it.

I may well have spat out my food with laughter hearing that.

Rice was so normal for me throughout my entire life, to conceptualise a meal I'd start with the rice and try to picture what other foods would surround it, whereas for M and Andy, rice would not only be the last thing they would think of, but it would not enter their list at all. (For reference, both Andy and M are white English, but I am not reducing this as a white/black disparity, as that is a far too simplistic generalisation.) The absurdity of these memories highlights how differences in such small and seemingly insignificant life practices can open a door to glimpse the life experiences and values of those otherwise close to you, and how the bonds that can bring people together outside of the domestic space can be at odds with the taken for granted ritual practices that happen behind doors (such as rice picking). When it transcends outside of the domestic space, food particularly is a medium that provides visibility to differences in cultural practices (Fischler, 1988: 275), but the preparation and consumption of food inside the domestic space is such an intimate and private practice that external representation of food cultures, such as in form of restaurants and other commercial food ventures, will not replicate the intricacies of what that food means to the culture itself. According to Fischler (ibid.),

> Food is central to our sense of identity. The way any given human group eats helps it assert its diversity, hierarchy and organisation, but also, at the same time, both its oneness and the otherness of whoever eats differently. Food is also central to individual identity, in that any given human individual is constructed, biologically, psychologically and socially by the foods he/she choses to incorporate.

Food, by nature, is an embodied medium in the narratives of our everyday lives (Barthes, 2009: 69; Stajcic, 2013; Zhang, 2013). It is both taken for granted and valued as a privilege. Expectations placed upon our food choices is relational to the places in which the food is prepared and served. As an everyday life medium, food is a part of everyday discourse, and forms part of the commentary on the other forms of media we consume. During the 2021 series of ITV's *I'm A Celebrity… Get Me Out of Here!*, the default no-frills diet and punishment was having to eat rice and beans. In Caribbean, rice and peas is the common name for what is actually rice and kidney beans (it is not green peas!). As we watched the celebrities almost in tears at the thought of that basic food combination, many of the Black people in my household, and also some vocal on social media, were unanimous in their response,

> What's wrong with rice and beans?
> All it needs is a knob of butter and salt.

These conversations about rice and beans were all humorous and light-hearted, and as is well known about social media, it has enabled people to share their views across time and space and test opinions that were previously unarticulated in the public arena, previously unsure of collective consensus. The proliferation of Black context experience and knowledge exchange has become deeply impactful, and an influential presence on Twitter particularly, and the key characteristic of what has become collectively known as "Black Twitter." It is characterised as an unapologetic and unadulterated discourse space, ranging from the urgent to the irreverent (Graham & Smith, 2016; Brock, 2012; Florini, 2014). To publicly share that the "poor meal" of rice and beans is in fact valued as "good food" for many is to casually make an intangible aspect of culture visible, and to add into dominant narratives (in this case emitting from primetime mainstream television) that there are alternative viewpoints held by cultural groups different from the voice of the production entity. The Twitter rice conversations were just witty observations rather than a serious criticism of the TV show, however, when analysed as a body of social knowledge, it visualises a parallel meta-narrative that was previously absent from the public domain. The social media writers and onlookers can take comfort in realising they had shared ideas, and no matter how commonplace the basis, a sense of belonging (Gruzd et al., 2011; Graham & Smith, 2016: 439; Anderson, 2006).

The tension between rice being a "poor food" of "little nutritional value" and a food stuff that is popular and feel affectionate towards is historically situated. As one of the world's oldest foods (Sweeny & McCouch, 2017), rice has now become the staple food for over half the world's population, is the largest consumed food in Asia, and fast becoming a relied upon food source across Africa and Latin America.

> Rice provides up to 50% of the dietary caloric supply for millions living in poverty in Asia and is, therefore, critical for food security … However, rice remains one of the most protected food commodities in world trade. Rice is a poor source of vitamins and minerals, and losses occur during the milling process. Populations that subsist on rice are at high risk of vitamin and mineral deficiency.
>
> *Muthayya et al., 2014: 7*

Rice, as a mainstay of Caribbean and African heritage cuisine, is both a truism and a stereotype. Rice is not native to the Caribbean region, and its presence there is a result of the transatlantic trafficking and enslavement of African people. It was widely assumed that rice was solely brought to the Americas and Caribbean by the European colonisers and plantation owners (Gewin, 2017). However, that assumption started to shift with research emerging slowly over a period of four decades, by historians Peter Wood (Wood, 1974), Daniel Littlefield (Littlefield, 1981), and Judith Carney (Carney, 1998), culminating in the 2002 book by Carney (inspired by the research of Wood and Littlefield) titled *Black Rice*. What Wood, Littlefield, and Carney argued was,

> "People and plants together migrated," and it was people who brought with them knowledge of how to plant seeds, cultivate crops, and process, store, and cook what they harvested. Since "the only people in South Carolina" possessing knowledge of how to grow rice in wetlands were West Africans, one must look to them "for adapting the crop to challenging New World conditions."
>
> *Hawthorne, 2010: 153; Quotations from Carney, 2002: 6–8, 81–82*

These bodies of research, which tells the story of the agency and ingenuity of African people despite their enslaved status, is now known within academic historian discourse and the *Black Rice Thesis* (Eltis, Morgan, & Richardson, 2007: 1332), taking inspiration from Carney's book title. Carney continued to build on this research with knowledge from the oral traditions of African heritage people from Brazil (Carney, 2004), arguing that enslaved African women smuggled rice seeds in their hair across the treacherous Atlantic journey, and on the plantations developed the farming and cooking techniques they brought with them from West Africa. These innovations by African women saw rice thrive as a crop in the new world and take such a hold on the region that has now lasted centuries. Carney traced specific types of rice and cultivating techniques to specific areas of West Africa (Carney, 2006: 101), and the arguments have proven to be both compelling and controversial (Hawthorne, 2010: 152). Detractors, such as Eltis, Morgan, and Richardson, argue there is a lack of convincing evidence and paint the work as a product of a revisionist re-writing of history. They state,

> [T]he emphasis on African agency resonates with histories from the bottom up and with subaltern studies in general. That [the new world's] rice industry was built not just on slave labor, but also on the slaves' agricultural and technological knowledge, is an exciting and appealing revelation. In a multicultural world, it is reassuring to realize that the black contribution to American life involved more than just backbreaking muscle power. The development of American rice culture, the claim goes, marked the transatlantic migration not only of an important crop but of an "entire cultural system." It was a major African accomplishment.
>
> *Eltis, Morgan, & Richardson, 2007: 1332–1333*

With the *Black Rice Thesis* and the narrative's critics, the history of rice in the new world has become a cultural battleground, upon which values, ideologies, hopes, and cynicism can be projected. The labour of enslaved Africans in the cultivation of rice is undisputed, and whether we accept or not that their farming skills developed rice growing techniques could be argued to be a moot point, when those techniques would ultimately have made the plantation owners rich, and especially when the extreme violent nature of life on slavery plantations is considered. The rice crops were also used to feed the enslaved Africans on the plantation, as it is considered relatively cheap and is mass produced. As an embodied medium that has been cultivated and consumed over generations through hundreds of years, with the life of enslaved ancestors literally depending on it, the inherited properties of rice are layers of biological, social, and cultural, a physical embodiment of the Black Atlantic. Such is the paradoxical and complex relationship between pride and poverty. In 1831, when she was a free woman, abolitionist campaigner Mary Prince wrote about her experiences of being born into enslavement on a plantation in Bermuda. She recounts the memory of when the need for sustenance in the form of rice got one of her peers tortured twice, and saw the overseers asserting their dominance over the minor transgression.

> Mr D– had another slave called Ben. He being very hungry, stole a little rice one night after he came in from work, and cooked it for his supper. But his master soon discovered the theft; locked him up all night; and kept him without food till one o'clock the next day. He then hung Ben up by his hands, and beat him from time to time till the slaves came in at night. We found the poor creature hung up when we came home; with a pool of blood beneath him, and our master still licking him. But this was not the worst. My master's son was in the habit of stealing the rice and rum. Ben had seen him do this, and thought he might do the same, and when master found out that Ben had stolen the rice and swore to punish him, he tried to excuse himself by saying that Master Dickey did the same. thing every night. The lad denied it to his father, and was so angry with Ben for informing against him, that out of revenge he ran and got a bayonet, and whilst the poor wretch was suspended by his hands and writhing under his wounds, he run it quite through his foot. I was not by when he did it, but I saw the wound when I came home, and heard Ben tell the manner in which it was done.
>
> *Prince, 2004: 21–22*

I would like to think in some way that my Sunday morning ritual of picking rice was attention to detail, inherited through generations from my ancestors, and the suffers they endured. We tell ourselves stories to make sense of things, and imagination takes over where facts do not reach. Perhaps, rather than me choosing rice, rice chose me.

Singing for Supper

Jamaican reggae singer Roman Stewart wanted to use his music to escape poverty, and in 1976 he wore his heart on his sleeve and put that aspiration on vinyl, recording *Hit Song (aka Natty Sings Hit Songs)* (Stewart, 1976), and used the proceeds to move to New York in the same year to try and escape the poverty he was singing about (O'Brien Chang & Chen, 1998: 55).

- MUSIC SEARCH – *Hit Song Roman Stewart* – PRESS PLAY

Written and recorded at the age of 19, the lyrics are an appeal to the world from the perspective of a young man, coming to terms with the fact that he does not have what he sees others having. He tells us he is using singing, the one skill he feels he has to change his circumstance of birth locked in poverty. There is also the hint in the lyrics that with poverty can come the spiral of criminality and bad choices, and it is clear that is a road he does not want to go down. "I'd be a better man if I had money in my hand, Help me oh JAH, I want to come on strong, I want to sing a hit song." Three years later, still based in New York, Roman reflected on the theme of poverty once again, recorded the song *Rice and Peas* (Stewart, 1979), which he became well known for. Rather than the theme of escaping poverty, instead he reflected on the lived experience of growing up in poverty, and specifically, how that limited your food choices, and in parallel, how your food choices can be a signifier of social class.

- MUSIC SEARCH – *Rice and Peas Roman Stewart* – PRESS PLAY

Roman sings about how he was born poor in the ghetto in a family of four, and how his mother would send him to the shop to buy a coconut, so she could make rice and peas for the whole family. He calls rice and peas a "sufferers feed," and tells how poor people all over the world are eating it, and name checks Jamaica, America, Canada, and Europe as examples. Now living outside of Jamaica in that earlier calculated move to the US, Roman saw that poverty was everywhere. He saw how the signs of being poor, such as recognisable patterns of food consumption, was repeated across cultural and national boundaries. In his lyrics we see how food is a medium which speaks to an aspect of lived experience regardless of geographic proximity or ethnic demographic. The song is a celebration of how rice and peas, as a staple food of necessity, has sustained a global community who are unified by their experience of financial struggle and survival. It is both a lament and a love song.

Roman Stewart continued to live in New York, releasing songs and performing regularly, sometimes for free at the gigs of his friends (Upsetter, 2022). Not quite reaching the heights that his talent was destined for, and seemingly still locked within the magnetic force on the fringes of poverty, the spiral he warned about in his early record *Hit Song (aka Natty Sing Hit Songs)* had sadly become visible in the form of self-harm, with the heavy use of drugs and alcohol.

[T]he harsh lifestyle eventually took its toll. He died in January 2004 in New York after a heart attack. True to his tune "Natty Sing Hit Songs", he was on stage singing one of his hits when he suddenly cut his performance short, complaining of chest pains. Roman Stewart died of heart failure the next day.

ibid.

Reflecting upon Roman Stewart's life and work has created a significant shift in my own thinking, which affects the remainder of this chapter. The methodology of Small Anthropology, which this book is an exploration of, is one of encouraging transparency of methodology where appropriate or poignant in the final outcome – conflating process and product. This approach makes visible the nuances and unexpected twists and turns of the research process, and to present to the reader a reflective and perhaps tentative learning experience, which sees the writer learning in real time alongside revelations revealed to the reader. Usually when reading academic texts, it is as if the writer's head was full of all the knowledge from page one, and simply uploaded that knowledge onto the blank pages for the reader's digestion. Small Anthropology admits that the writer is in a mode of discovery even at the point of writing and promotes a vulnerable position (Behar, 1997), asking myself the question – "how do I know what I think until I see what I write?".

I make this statement at this point, as I have come to a personal realisation in the moment of the writing process. This chapter about rice was always going to include an analysis of the controversy regarding Chef Jamie Oliver's release of his brand of Jerk Rice in 2018, when he was accused of cultural appropriation. Lots of my good friends were publicly part of the criticism, but at that time I was not of the same mind, and saw the whole thing as an overreaction (Charles, 2020), and I argued that there were more important issues to be vocal about. I saw the Jamie Oliver episode as a challenge for Black businesses to establish their own brands, and dismissed the outrage as a distraction from the more urgent issues of the day. But now, having written through the Roman Stewart narrative above, it has made me reflect differently about the Jamie Oliver situation, and subsequently relate more to the criticism that Oliver faced. Rice has been entwined with the life and survival of Black people in the areas of West Africa long **before** the beginning of transatlantic slavery in 16th century (Sweeny & McCouch, 2017: 952). Whether you subscribe to the *Black Rice Thesis* or not, it is undisputed that the sweat equity of the enslaved was used to maintain the growing and cultivation of rice, the success of which was the basis of their own survival, and likewise their survival depended on the growth of rice. The brutal experiences that the enslaved faced during life on plantations has been well documented and communicated in many areas of research, mass media and popular culture, and shall not be repeated here. To state that the lives of enslaved African people depended on the success of their free labour is no understatement or hyperbole. To see the modern-day Jamaican iteration of rice commodified and packaged, with no reparatory measures to acknowledge the source of what Oliver's company will now profit from, is an insult indeed.

With the abolition of slavery in 1834, the slavery system gave way to the colonisation era and the "Scramble for Africa". The Berlin Conference in 1884 saw African lands being captured by European forces, rather than the direct capturing of the people – (though of course, they captured the land and ruled the people), slavery under a different guise of policy and strategy. According to Walter Rodney in his ground-breaking work "How Europe Underdeveloped Africa" (1988: 145),

> When European capitalism took the form of imperialism and started to subjugate Africa politically, the normal political conflicts of the pre-capitalist African situation were transformed into weakness which allowed the Europeans to set up their colonial domination.

With colonisation and the expansion of European empire building on a global scale, the majority of black and brown skinned people worldwide were now either

1. Living in extreme poverty in the new world, as a result of having been "freed" from slavery with no compensation, so forced to continue working for their former "slave masters" for a mere pittance just to survive, the circumstances of their existence barely changed.

Or

2. Continuing to live in their homelands of Africa, Asia, and South America, which were now occupied and ruled by European coloniser forces and made into a financial underclass with limited rights in their own countries by the ruling elite.

In the United States, segregation and Jim Crow laws became established in its southern states during the 1870s, while the UK and the rest of Europe tried to maintain the façade of tolerance of others on their home soil, while "abroad" they wielded human rights atrocities in the countries they colonised across Africa, Asia, and South America.

It is a sober reflection to make that from the 16th century onwards through to the present day, rice has been used by the poor in all areas of the world as a staple part of their diet (Sweeny & McCouch, 2017; Muthayya et al., 2014), and the reality of how "global conditions began to change in the sixteenth century" (Beaudoin, 2007: 12) has exacerbated and entrenched the huge levels of poverty that we see in the world today (ibid.: 35–47), which are still very much rooted in the former European colonies across Africa, Asia, and South America. As clearly argued by environmental activist Vandana Shiva (2005),

> The poor are not those who have been "left behind"; they are the ones who have been robbed. The riches accumulated by Europe are based on riches taken from Asia, Africa and Latin America. Without the destruction of India's

rich textile industry, without the takeover of the spice trade, without the genocide of the native American tribes, without Africa's slavery, the Industrial Revolution would not have led to new riches for Europe or the US. It was this violent takeover of Third World resources and markets that created wealth in the North and poverty in the South.

This is the energy with which Roman Stewart sang. Lest we forget.

11

(BATHROOM) – AFRO COMB

This chapter is symbolically positioning the bathroom as a place of privacy and grooming. Locked in, looking into the mirror as you do your hair, brushing your teeth, getting ready to go out. Much has been written about the politics of Black hair (Blake-Hannah, 2022), so this chapter will not repeat those discussions here, and instead conduct a polemical analysis of the afro comb itself. We hear of things being described as "design classics," which according to Ideal Home magazine website includes the Anglepoise lamp, Frtiz Hansen's series 7 chair, the Alessie lemon squeezer, and the Falcon enamel pie dish (Ebert, 2018). For me, the red, black, and green folding afro comb is a design classic and should be acknowledged as such. It is both a functional and symbolic object, its connection with the physicality of Black hair being just one part of a chain of interlocking narrative ideas contained in this one piece of design (Figure 11.1).

Design Narratives

To look at the comb design in a purely descriptive manner, the body of the comb is black, with long metal prongs to detangle the hair. Each of the two folding handles are red and green, respectively (see front cover of this book for the colour version). However, when we look at the comb through the lens of critical semiotics, things get more interesting (Genosko, 2016). Red, black, and green is the flag of the Universal Negro Improvement Association and African Communities League (UNIA-ACL), founded by Marcus Mosiah Garvey, Jamaican cultural and political leader, philosopher, entrepreneur, and activist. Garvey was one of the first to publicly campaign and remind Black people in the Caribbean and across the United States that they were not just Black, that they were African. In 1919 he set up the Black Star Line shipping company, with the aim to repatriate all consenting Africans in the diaspora back to the African continent. Present day Ghana's black

DOI: 10.4324/9780367809621-12

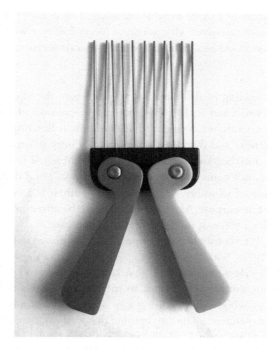

FIGURE 11.1 Red, black, and green folding afro comb

star in the middle of their flag is in honour of the Black Star Line requested to be placed there by Ghana's first President Kwame Nkrumah when the country became independent in 1957 (Dodoo, 2011: 68). This was 17 years after Garvey himself had died, such is the influence of the man. Red, black, and green became the flag colours of Pan-Africanism, an ideological site rather than physical landmass, representing people of African-decent wherever they were around the globe, a flag unifying, in Garvey's words, "Africa for the Africans at home and abroad" (Garvey, 1923: 35). The influence of Garvey's flag can still be seen in many of the national flag designs across Africa and the Caribbean, combined with the yellow influenced from the flag of Ethiopia, the other galvaniser of a unified pan-African identity.

Red symbolises the blood that flows through all human beings that should unite us all, and it also symbolises the sacrifices that have been made by our ancestors that should not be never forgotten. Black represents African people at home and abroad, and the struggles for survival that enabled any of us alive today to have breath, a reminder of who we are and where we came from, a colour to salute the ancestors, and to salute yourself. Green is for the natural resources, richness, and beauty of Africa, and the landmass that birthed civilisation. For Garvey, the idea of nature took on a theosophical dimension (Garvey, 1983: 433), with nature having a transcendent consciousness and parental interest in the fortunes of the African people it birthed.

God and Nature first made us what we are, and then out of our own created
genius we make ourselves what we want to be. Follow always that great law.
Let the sky and God be our limit and Eternity our measurement.

Garvey, 1925: 2

In context of this reading of the visual representation of the afro comb object, it
has a history, a rhetoric, and an ideology that can be considered, appreciated, and
deconstructed long before we even get to analyse how it functions practically as a
comb. It has an identity and discourse as a noun, not only when it is enacted as a
verb – it does not only become a comb when it is combing, it is already an object
with even when it's not being used. Such is the power of good design. It contains
an existence outside of its utility. As a functional comb, it is a synchronic (static)
object in service of its purpose. As a symbolic object, the afro comb is a diachronic
(dynamic) storytelling piece of media which communicates.

The afro hairstyle famously become popular and politicised in the United States
in the 1960s and 1970s, with the wave of rising Black consciousness and the fight
for civil rights. The style rapidly crossed the Atlantic to inspire us UK-based cousins,
with the stench of colonialism still thick in the air across lands of Africa and the
Caribbean, some of whom were gaining new sense of identities in the time of
promise of state independence. The afro became the outward manifestation of Black
pride and was called the "natural," idealising an embodied sense of pride, informing
both the way you looked and the values you inhabit. Yet the afro did not come
with a manifesto of how to behave or what to believe – it was a fashion statement
inspired by politics, rather than the signifying hairstyle of a political movement.
However, it was a statement with a very specific meaningful purpose – to say to
anyone who cared to look, listen, and understand that you are not subscribing to
dominant Western standards of beauty, and privileging an Africanised aesthetic of a
"natural" state of African hair. Free from the use of straighteners or chemical perm
products – becoming the first line of defence of your soul identity as an individual
who was both Black and proud, in the face of a state apparatus that challenged
your existence. The afro was not the hairstyle of Garvey's movement, but his forth-
right words from nearly 40 years previously were again evoked, "Do not remove
the kinks from your hair – remove them from your brain" (Garvey quoted in
Patten: 2006: 29), as a rallying cry for Africans to "know thyself" (Garvey, 1923: 37),
to "have a new race, we would have a nation, an empire, resurrected, not from the
will of others to see us rise – but from our own determination to rise, irrespective
of what the world thinks" (ibid.: 38).

The patent for the folding afro comb was issued to Arthur Rogovin of Yonkers,
New York, on 12 January 1971 (Shujaa & Shujaa, 2015: 85), and soon became
iconic on both sides of the Atlantic. Museum curator Sally-Ann Ashton, who has
researched the history of the afro comb and led a community project on the topic,
reports that in the UK in the 1970s and 1980s, the prevalence of police stopping
and searching Black people saw their combs with metal teeth being confiscated
"viewed as potential weapons" (Ashton: 2014).

Considering an everyday object such as a (seemingly benign) comb, for the uninitiated, the green, black, and red style would assume to be interchangeable with any other colours on the spectrum. Such is the way that knowledge discourse works (Foucault, 2002) and the invisible narratives that lie behind most pieces of design.

Colour Codes

At the time of writing in 2022, we are seeing the colours of blue and yellow all over social media, on ribbons and badges worn by people on our TV screens, flags in house windows, and even coordinated whole blue and yellow outfits worn to work or school or by celebrities at award shows. Yet, before Vladmir Putin invaded Ukraine, the public display of wearing blue and yellow would have seemed as inconsequential as the colour of laces in our shoes. Yet blue and yellow in the context of spring 2022, has taken on a significant symbolism and new meaning for new sets of people, who had previously not given the country a second thought.

When we pay attention to such social codes, the language becomes recognisable and such subtleties subjectively adopt new understanding, though what has changed is not the social codes, but the receiver. Blue and yellow has been the official flag of Ukraine since 28 January 1992, likewise, red, black, and green has been the Pan-African flag since 13 August 1920, yet for some that information has always been known, for others that knowledge came in being at different points in their life. As a Black person, the colours red, black, and green, and in parallel the Ethiopian colours of green, yellow, and red, have long been part of the tacit knowledge of my existence. On seeing the colours even as a child, I would know they are a shorthand to represent, in the crudest term – Black people. The sets of colours exist in those combinations in different meanings, narrative understanding of symbols is reliant upon contextual reading which foments understanding in that discourse of knowledge. When we learn the meaning of symbols in relation to specific contexts, what is being communicated by such symbols renders into focus and becomes clear. We become conscious, privy to a body of knowledge not previously accessible for us. This demonstrates how what Pierre Bourdieu called Habitus works – how bodies of knowledge are incrementally built around different social spheres of interaction and consensus (Bourdieu, 2005: 44). According to anthropologist Daniel Miller,

> [T]he main process of socialization into becoming a member of any given society was the everyday association with practical taxonomies embodied in the order of material culture. From Bourdieu we learnt how individuals become a typical Kwakiutl, Trobriand Islander or New Yorker through habits and expectations fostered in our everyday object world. Through catching salmon or catching taxis.
>
> *Miller, 2009: 4*

The everyday habits of a society are coupled with the language symbols of those social groupings and become naturalised and soaked into the consciousness, in alignment with your peers. Such practices and languages are not fixed, though at given moments they become collectively understood and safely considered "norms" within shared social space. In 1973, musician Roy Ayres released an album titled *Ubiquity*, which contained the song *Red Black & Green* as its fourth track. The song teases the influence of such shared language symbols on the collective conscious in the African diaspora. The repetitive style of the song lyrics takes on a circular quality like a meditative chant, "Red black and green, if you think about it, you know what I mean" (Ayres, 1973).

• MUSIC SEARCH – *Red Black & Green Roy Ayres* – PRESS PLAY

Aged 33 at the time of the song's release, Ayres is reaching into the levels of tacit knowledge, imploring us to trust in the feeling of the invisible wisdom – "*Red Black & Green. If you think about it you know what I mean*" – the hope of the discourse of pan-Africanism as an invisible scaffold that holds us up without us even realising. However, messy reality brings complexity to such cultural idealism. Symbols that had much political depth for some are now worn by different generations and across cultural demographics and rendered as kitsch fashion, fancy dress, or pure style without the political awareness or interest in what it represents. Good design is an awareness of the context of how the object will be used, and for the aesthetic style to find a balance with the core function and not inhibit the intended use. Good design can enhance the experience of owning an object, not just using it. Good design transforms a mere functional object into something we enjoy, covet, treasure, and keep safe.

Beyond function and aesthetics, the third layer of good design, which does not get spoken about often beyond design school classrooms and funding applications, is narrative. Ideas that inform design are an auratic attribute, which connects the designer with the object owner and sympathetic onlookers. In the case of the Garvey-inspired afro comb, it speaks a narrative of cultural resonance where an African aesthetic can be celebrated unhindered by the burden of double conscious-ness (Du Bois, 1903: 168). Although when I look at the design of this comb it makes me smile, however, there is also a melancholia. The real-world complexity of this analysis is the fact that when buying these combs today, they are made in China. The symbology is seemingly divorced from the politics which informs the look. Soon after Barbados signed to become a Republic on 30 November 2021, a move Marcus Garvey would have undoubtedly applauded, much analysis was published about the growing relationship between the two countries. Headlines in the West's press included – The Express with "Barbados warned over ditching Queen as China 'gifts' £400m 'No such thing as free lunch'" (Scarsi, 2021), The Diplomat's header, "Barbados' New Republic: A Win for China?" (Mwai & Ashmore, 2022), and Bloomberg's "Barbados Splits from the Queen, Trading One Empire for Another" (Ivens, 2001). The "watching brief" that the United States had on China's rela-tionship with the governments of America's neighbouring Caribbean islands has taken on an added urgency (Semple, 2020). In an interview with BBC journalist

Zeinab Badawi, Barbados Prime Minister Mia Motley defended against this scrutiny of her country's links, highlighting the hypocrisy of the charges from countries who themselves have strong and long-lasting business dealings with the Chinese government.

> [T]o focus on the Caribbean or Africa with China, without recognising the role that China is playing in Europe or in the North Atlantic countries, is a bit disingenuous and really reflects more that we are seen as pawns, regrettably, rather than countries with equal capacity to determine our destiny and to be part and parcel of that global conversation to fight the global issues of the day like climate and a pandemic.
>
> *Motley, 2021*

To see an African-heritage Caribbean country declare themselves a Republic and negotiate as equals on the global stage is one point towards a Pan-African vision, but in real terms it is one small step amongst many more needed. The questions arise of will the other Caribbean countries drop their former colonial masters as their Heads of State and work together as a union of islands instead of each island-nation having to negotiate alone? That would be the second step towards a Pan-African ideal. The third crucial step would be for partnerships being drawn between the newly autonomous Caribbean and the different nations across Africa, with the same energy that they are queuing to sign up with China. The final step of the Pan-African aim is for the nation states across the continent to erode the colonial borders of the Berlin conference, and no longer define themselves according to the boundaries carved out by the European expansionists. That is the point at when the true Pan-African conversation begins, its aim fulfilled, and the beginning of the next journey.

The humble red, black, and green comb is but a reminder of the much work to do, heightened by where that object is now made. It metaphorically connects the personal body with the individual negotiation within the state body politic. Ideological and political strategy needs also to have a design and an aesthetic value. Design for how to build the formation of the overall vision, to see how the strategy object can be put to use as a functional tool for practical and inspirational purpose. The continual evoking of the symbols, whether that be in hair, clothes, language, and other codes, can connect with the inner values of our motivation and purpose, which for many of us need re-igniting and re-inspiring from time to time.

12

(BATHROOM) – SICKLE CELL ANAEMIA MEDICATION

Children's author Ursula Vernon (2015) describes the sanctity that a bathroom affords and the illusion it overcomes to create that feeling of a safe environment.

> There is something about a bathroom that feels like a fortress. A closed bathroom door may only be about two inches of plywood, but it feels like an iron bar.

The bathroom is the most private space in the house, and the wall cabinet is a double confidential zone containing items the owners want hidden from view, contents which can speak to some of the most secluded parts of ourselves. However, the cabinet represents a precarious state of privacy, housed within a semi-public space albeit within the private home. What we perceive to be the contents of other people's cabinets is largely informed on how we use our own (Sadlier, 2019) – toothpaste, creams, plasters, medication, and other discrete possibilities. For this chapter we use medication as the object of material culture as the starting point to explore medical illness through the lens of Black experience of sickle cell disease.

In truth, any room in the house could have been used to explore the narrative of illness and sickle cell disease, as the reality of the condition and the related stories far extend beyond the boundaries of that one space. However, subjectively, the bathroom is representative of the idea of medical themes, think of how the bathroom cabinet is also commonly known as the medicine cabinet. According to Wan (1999),

> The medicine cabinet is traditionally a bathroom fixture for a reason: the bathroom is a highly frequented quarter where many daily personal care activities already take place.

DOI: 10.4324/9780367809621-13

To conceptually place the idea of medical illness in the bathroom, rather than for example a bedroom, is to suggest the person with the condition could have been any member of the family, rather than in one of the bedrooms, which would be specifically owned. However, the point of this book, as hopefully the reader will have realised by now, is not to artificially keep the narratives within the confines of the room, and for the focused-on objects in the room to be a launch point, and the stories to be allowed to take us anywhere – such is the way with memory and historical narrative underpinnings, they are not confined by time or space, and serve only the function of explanation of a phenomenon in any shape that takes (Deleuze & Guattari, 2001: 21).

A persistent mythology of physical illness is the perception that it is a cultural leveller that medical conditions affect all people the same regardless of ethnicity, class, and other dynamics. However, as clearly argued by Psoinos et al. (2011: 3) (as well as articulated by many other medical researchers and cultural commentators),

> It is a well-known fact that the incidence, prevalence, and mortality of many diseases may vary by ethnic group; these variations are regularly linked to well-documented disparities in access to prevention, treatment, and palliative healthcare services based on ethnic group.

Kate's Story

Illness is a mostly private phenomenon with degrees of public/social awareness and interaction. Even within the family home, talking with a close relative about their illness can be taboo, perceived to "keep families in illness" (Arestedt et al., 2014: 32), and the default, based on an approach of love and care rather than neglect, becomes not to talk about it at all. This was the experience of Kate, born in the UK to parents from the Caribbean in 1963 with sickle cell anaemia. (Kate's name has been changed and Caribbean island concealed to protect identity.) Sickle cell is a condition which predominantly affects Black people of African and Caribbean heritage (although according to research, such as Nietert et al., 2002: 358, the illness also exists among native communities in countries such as Italy, Greece, India, Pakistan, China, and other locations). Kate speaks about how her condition has given her a very specific set of memories about the family bathroom and reflects on what this meant to her in relation to her quality of childhood and sense of herself. Having been ill since she was born, some of Kate's earliest memories were of being sick in the cold outside toilet (which were the norm for working class terraced houses, Highmore, 2014: 140; Scott, 2008: 105; Faire, 1998: 43), before an inside bathroom was built upstairs in the 1970s.

> I spent a lot of time in the bathroom when I was a teenager, either in excruciating pain, and sometimes throwing up. I'd have to get my mum or sister to get my tablets out of the bathroom cabinet as I couldn't reach. Having sickle cell meant I was shorter and skinnier than the other children, I didn't

go through puberty until I was about 15. The meds I needed were antibiotics and folic acid tablets every day, though I often didn't take them, as I didn't want to be different from my siblings.

Kate was officially diagnosed with sickle cell relatively early at 2 years old, at a time when testing for the disease was rare. Admitted to hospital in relentless pain, by chance the attending doctor said he thought he recognised Kate's symptoms from what he saw during his time working in Africa, and following that thread of an educated guess, that is the precarious circumstance which led to Kate being diagnosed. That was the first time either of her parents had heard about the disease.

> I'm thankful that the doctor had chosen to travel to Africa to see the experiences of different cultures. It was purely by chance that he was there when I was taken in, otherwise goodness knows what might have happened. Back in the day before routine testing, some people didn't get diagnosed until they were much older.

As haphazard, precarious and fortuitous as this circumstance sounds, this "by-chance" and anecdotal route to diagnosis was surprisingly common. This is reflected in a 2019 episode of BBC's *Call the Midwife*, set in 1964, just a year before Kate was diagnosed. Spotting recognisable signs in a new mother's symptoms, the midwife tells the baffled doctor she had seen similar during her time working in South Africa. The doctor goes onto educate himself about the disease, while criticising the medical information and training he has access to for not being up to date with the changing cultural demographics that Britain was experiencing at that time (BBC One, 2019).

According to Chakravorty and Williams (2014: 48), "significant process" started to occur with improving the life chances of those living with sickle cell disease from the 1970s onwards, "before which very few affected subjects survived beyond 10 years" (ibid.). Learning from innovations happening in research and clinical innovations in the United States, in England routine sickle cell tests were eventually offered to parents for babies within two weeks of birth in 2006 (Streetly et al., 2018: 648).

Within post-colonial discourse, particularly in the 1960s in the era of growing independence movements across Africa and the Caribbean, the reliance of African descendants on medical knowledge gained from working trips to Africa by Europeans could be viewed as a form of cognitive dissonance – that knowledge gained from charitable support missions as a result of underdevelopment, is now proving to have positive effects across the continent and diaspora. This is **not** a reductive argument of stating "it was all worth it then," but merely a transparent reflection on the complexity and entanglement of colonial legacies (Knudsen et al., 2022: 266), and how individual agency and sincere motivations can contradict the more problematic overarching political and academic theories and ideologies that individuals operate within. There is no neat summary of what this cognitive dissonance means in this context (Seltzer & Bender, 2003), and Paul Gilroy's exploration of the notion of the Black Atlantic shows how the holding up of two contradictory or contested realities at the same time – of new cultural forms born out of troubling circumstances – can produce results to celebrate, in spite of knowing the antecedent colonial contexts that gave rise to that knowledge and forms of cultural expression (Gilroy, 1999). As Gilroy states, "racial subordination is integral to the processes of development and social and technological progress known as modernisation. It can therefore propel into modernity some of the very people it helps to dominate" (ibid.: 163).

Here Gilroy was not referring to the medical arena, and I have used his words to try and illuminate this discussion in relation to the topic of this chapter with regards treatment of sickle cell. Used in this way, these are no doubt controversial thoughts to articulate out loud, in context with African heritage people who have benefited from such advancements that were problematically situated in colonial frameworks. However, the pain associated with sickle cell disease and the relief that appropriate medication brings sufferers of the illnesses cut through the pretensions of my academic musings with a disdain that it possibly deserves. That does still not invalidate highlighting the complexity of knowledge acquisition and the colonial project and the realisation that people of the world have to move forward in their entangled states. What also needs highlighting, however, is that advancements in the treatment of sickle cell have not been left solely at the mercy of former colonial European countries, most notably the United States, as progress at an institutional and state levels have been largely propelled as the result of Black-led activism and advocacy groups that have been successful in pushing sickle cell concerns to the forefront of the medical agenda to be regarded as a priority. As argued by Siddiqi et al. (2013: 245),

> The transformation of sickle cell disease (SCD) from obscurity in Africa to visibility in America over the past 100 years is intertwined with politics and race relations unique to America. Parallel to the development of a conventional scientific understanding of the disease and the evolution of disease control strategies, SCD also developed socio-politically. Initially thought to be a disease exclusively affecting a minority group, it was brought on the political agenda through concerted efforts made primarily by the community that identified closely with the people who suffered from it. The socio-political development that propelled investments in research into the disease's origins, treatment, and models of care resulted in considerable improvements in life expectancy of people with SCD over the past nine decades.

Such are layers of the colonial legacy entanglement in the "new world" for the African diaspora, building upon any positive advancements that have been made in any arena. Not settling for the satisfaction of merely being seen and nestling uncomfortably in a state of cognitive dissonance, but being prepared to demand equal treatment and resources for the benefit of not only ourselves but for future generations – as has been the case with routine screenings versus the circumstance of "by chance" diagnosis. The sobering reflection that individuals such as Kate will invariably have also helped such medical advancement by sheer unwitting use of their own Black bodies in those moments of severe pain. Sufferers of sickle cell did not ask to be activists, but the screams and cries from their painful bodies were heard and echoed down the hospital corridors.

For Kate, her fragmented memories of childhood shift between time spent in hospital over long periods, through to specific moments and general feelings of what life was like in the family home. She remembers waving her siblings off as they went to visit the zoo on a day trip, not understanding why she was not going with them. Kate was aware that she was the only child she knew of that had to take lots of medication, that had to be regularly hospitalised and attend a hospital school, that was in constant pain – and other noticeable differences growing up. I wondered what impact that these traumatic experiences can have on a person so young at the time. To explore this further, I ask Kate if she ever felt a sense of self-pity or resentfulness, that she was the only child among her siblings to have inherited the full sickle cell condition, and if that has affected her confidence and sense of her own identity. I offered a preamble to this question, saying it was a sensitive topic and for her only to answer if she felt comfortable. She describes it in the following way:

> Oh no, I felt pleased I was the only one to have it, as I didn't want anyone else in a million years to have to go through what I was going through. Even though I didn't always understand what it was, I never felt resentful or self-pity to that extent. Though I did decide not to have children, as I could not bear the thought of a child of mine experiencing the unrelating pain and trauma this illness brings.

Kate maintained a philosophical acceptance of the responsibility of having the disease, rather than bitterness, resentment, or self-pity. She makes a joke of the memory that she was always made to be the school sports team's mascot, as the teachers knew she would not be able to participate in the games themselves. She does admit it was an extremely lonely childhood, even though she was one of many children. She spent her time reading books, and being lost in her own imagination. She recalls times when she was laid in bed in agony at home, saying to her family she would be alright in a bit. Her sister would often just call an ambulance, and Kate would subsequently spend the next two weeks in hospital. By her own admission, Kate initially had a self-denial attitude towards her condition, and as a child reluctantly made the conceptual connection between going out and playing with friends without a cardigan on, and being hospitalised for weeks afterwards, a result of her body entering a sickle cell crisis due to effects of being cold. Such realisations are difficult for a child to have to reconcile, and she said that even today aged in her 50s, the idea of centring herself as a person with sickle cell is still an evolving and complicated process. (Kate admitted to me that she never thought she would reach the age that she has.) The presence of sickle cell disease is a constant reality of her everyday life, even as I was speaking to her, she explained her elbow was in pain "sickling," as was her knee, and she grew hot and cold continuously adding and removing the same layers within intervals of minutes. (Kate humorously added that her hot and cold state could also be caused by menopause.) Such was Kate's everyday way of coping with severe pain, I would not have suspected she was in any pain in that moment, and she would not have told me if I had not asked. One of the sad ironies about pain associated with chronic illness is that the need to function in an everyday life capacity means the pain threshold is raised so high in the mind of the sufferer that the pain can then be rendered invisible and mistakenly non-present in the eyes of the people surrounding them. Unless the pain is articulated, it does not exist. As explained by Jackson (2005: 342),

> [P]eople tend to view the stoic as mentally sound and morally upright; however, the problem remains that people interacting with individuals who "suffer with dignity" must have some way of finding out about the status of the sufferer's pain. As already noted, the problem with the stiff-upper-lip approach is that most people find it hard to believe someone is experiencing severe pain unless reminded of it intermittently.

An aspect of medical illness will always remain in the realm of the private self, as no one can fully relate to what it is like to live with circumstances that affects another person's body, even with mass amounts of communication and self-narrative transparency about the experiences of living with a condition. Likewise, Kate argues that there are as many sickle cell anaemia conditions as there are people who carry the illness, with no two life-experiences being the same. Even after being diagnosed, Kate had no contextual references to compare her own experiences with, as she described it, "I thought I was the only person in the world to be going through this." It was not until the age of 36 that Kate first knowingly spoke to another person that had sickle cell and shared their life experiences. Such comparable representation is a powerful motivator and vehicle for piecing together an understanding of what a person themselves might be going through.

Sickle Cell on Screen

The representation of sickle cell anaemia in film and television is (perhaps unsurprisingly) scant. More representations may have helped people like Kate realise they are not alone in experiencing this disease. According to a combination of IMDb, BFI, and other database searches and archives, the first documented reference to sickle cell in moving image media was a 1972 TV film starring and produced by Bill Cosby, and the most recent (at the time of writing) in 2022 was an animated short. According to the databases, in the 50 years between those years and including those two productions, a total of 39 titles with sickle cell anaemia (or variants of) as a keyword were produced. They comprise:

Three feature films
Three TV movies
Two feature docs
Four short films
Ten TV drama episodes
Ten TV factual episodes
One TV advert appeal
Six corporate/independent videos

While this number may initially sound higher than expected, what must to be considered is many of these productions had sickle cell as brief mentions in the narrative rather than being the main focus, and some were unreleased or limited release independent videos. Also, when considered these works are spread across all international territories, 39 starts to sound rather meagre. It is acknowledged, however, these archives will invariably contain gaps and be generally westernised, especially of films made in the African continent, although some were included in the databases. What will now follow is an analysis of the first and last films in this list, using these two examples as a heuristic device to explore common themes and differences in how sickle cell narratives are represented.

One of the first media representations of sickle cell disease on screen was the TV movie *To All My Friends on the Shore* from 1972, broadcast in the United States. The 70-minute film was written by and stars a 35-year-old Bill Cosby, playing the main character Blue. (Cosby also wrote the screen music.) The film co-stars Gloria Foster as Blue's wife Serena, and follows their journey as they try to find the best way to raise and support their pre-teen son Vandy, who we learn sometimes experiences feeling "feverish," which the mum rationalises as being "probably just growing pains." The audience very much walk alongside the Blue and Serena as they try to understand Vandy and what he is going through. They (and the audience) are very much in the dark about his sickle cell condition until he is diagnosed at the near end of the film, when his symptoms are recognised by a Black doctor and subsequently put through a series of tests. Preceding that, the main hour of the film is an exploration of the Black family dynamic, and the perceived expectations of masculinity that Blue places on himself and the impact on his wife and son. Seeing himself as the main income generator (Serena is a cleaner while training to be a nurse), Blue works four jobs and places huge pressure on himself to relentlessly save for a better life for his family, planning to buy a derelict house, which he regularly visits in a nearby "nicer" suburb, which he plans to renovate.

Blue's ultra-focused approach renders him as an emotionally unavailable father, to the detriment of quality time spent with Serena and Vandy. Throughout the film Blue is portrayed as an honest and hardworking man with good intentions, but as a flawed father and husband due lack of communication, and the tension of him embodying the fears he sees as the hopeless life that lies ahead of them. At one point in the film Blue states, "Vandy's sickness is he was born Black and poor." Not until Vandy is eventually diagnosed with sickle cell does Blue re-evaluate his approach as a father, and the final scene of the film is the first time we see them having fun together. During the film we hear of Vandy being ill and in pain, but the audience does not witness it for themselves. Vandy's vulnerable body and psychological state is an underlining constant thread throughout, the latter portrayed through the tensions he has with his father. In one scene, Blue refuses to allow Vandy to go on a day trip with his friends and their father, saying he has chores to do in the house. Blue's refusal is due to a fear that Vandy will likely get ill during the outing, but does not articulate this, instead choosing to portray himself as a tough cold father with no explanation, resulting in Vandy shouting that he hates his father. Privately Serena takes Vandy's side and castigates Blue, but never in front of Vandy, leaving him feeling like he has no ally and very much alone.

At the point of diagnosis Serena and Blue learn about sickle cell disease, a condition they had not heard about before. After a moment of tears and sadness about what Vandy's survival chances might be, they are seemingly able to focus on the emotional needs of their son for the first time. Vandy's illness is like a fourth unnamed character in the film, to the point where, before the official diagnosis at the end, the audience were not sure whether it is indeed real or a fabrication of Vandy's mind. However, the effects of the invisible fourth character – in how Blue and Serena respond to it – are very real and visible to see. In case of Blue, a detached tough love approach which backfires, and with Serena, an overprotectiveness over Vandy which he himself gets irritated by. The film demonstrates how an invisible and unknown illness in the family can affect the relationships of the whole household, and only when it is revealed and addressed directly can all the individuals really see themselves for the first time and take each other into consideration.

At the end of the film we see the family having fun on a tiny new boat that Blue bought. Abandoning his stringent plans for the future of buying the derelict house, Blue instead spends the money for the family to enjoy in that moment. The words of Vandy, from earlier in the film, are seemingly ringing in Blue's ears – "How come everything has to be someday, how come there's never anything good right now?" Importantly, Vandy is the one in control in that final scene, steering the boat and his parents out of the harbour into the bigger waters.

The title of the film *To All My Friends on the Shore* becomes relevant in this end scene, and is directly drawn from a line in the poem "My Bed Is a Boat" by Robert Louis Stevenson (1924). The poem evokes the story of an ill child dreaming of sailing in a peaceful sleep, helped onto the bed-boat by a nurse. In the second verse the boy tells us, "At night I go on board and say, good-night to all my friends on shore." By the end of the fourth verse, the child wakes up back in their bed, safe and satisfied, confident for the day ahead. Stevenson himself experienced many illnesses as a child (Furnas, 1952: 25), and thus the poem can be read as autobiographical in tone. Being evoked at the end of Cosby's film, it is a testament to the scriptwriting for such a sensitive portrayal of the Black family to be represented in such a nuanced way, rarely seen on screen, then, or now. The great sadness of the story of *To All My Friends on the Shore* is that due to the real-world controversies of Cosby himself, being accused and imprisoned (and later released) for sexual assault on multiple women. In the face of such controversy, it is doubtful whether the film will ever again be seen by large audiences. Its message lost in the shadow of a more dominant representation of a sexually deviant Black man.

At the time of writing, 50 years after *To All My Friends on the Shore*, the most recent documented media release on the topic of sickle cell anaemia is the 2022 short animated film *The Park Bench*, written and directed by African American writer Rob Edwards, whose other screen credits include writing *The Princess and the Frog* and *Treasure Planet* feature film animations for Walt Disney, both of which were Oscar nominated. At 4 minutes 50 seconds in length, *The Park Bench*, in narrative terms (rather than in actuality), could be considered a continuum of *To All My Friends on the Shore* – in the old film the young boy has sickle cell disease, in the new film set in the present day, the character with the condition is a man with a family. The film opens with dramatic tension, a close-up of medicine being administered via a hypodermic needle, the man rolling around in agony on a hospital bed, and his wife looking worried stood next to him. We see a girl child stood watching from the door, and the woman (the girl's mother) shuts the door in her face, to spare the child witnessing her father in such a traumatic state. Cut to seeing a mother on the phone in the family home kitchen, in the foreground is a book titled *Coping with Sickle Cell Disease* (in a glimpse so swift I missed it the first time watching). In *To All My Friends on the Shore*, the fourth character (the disease) is not named until the very end. In *The Park Bench* the disease is established (with this glimpse of the book) at the beginning, and thereafter never named again. It is rendered back into the shadows of the narrative as the underlining subtext, and we see the world through the young girl's eyes.

With her father in hospital, the girl sits on a bench near her home and finds a surrogate entity to fill the void in her heart, in the persona of a duck with a wounded wing, which she nurses back to health. The girl and mother coexist with the duck as their new temporary housemate as a distraction from their father/husband being in hospital. When the day arrives for him to return home (fragile on crutches), it coincides with the day the duck is ready to fly back into the wild and re-join its family. As the human family bond back together, the duck flying with its flock overhead drops a feather onto the bench as a gift of thanks for the girl.

It is humorous, quirky, bright, and fast paced, but the serious subtext is one of showing the impacts of a parent's illness on children, the reverse of *To All My Friends on the Shore*, which focused on the impact on parents. In neither of the films do we see a similar focus on the actual individual with the illness, or see the impacts it has on them. The representation of illnesses on screen from these two examples presents an opposition to the statement above that "medical illness will always remain in the realm of the private self," in dramatic representations illness can be seen to belong to the people around that person, with a shift away from the individual struggle and towards a social phenomenon. However, there is no universal claim being made here on all representations of sickle cell on screen, and it is beyond the scope of this book to carry out a full analysis of all 50 years' worth of the 39 film and television productions listed.

Kate herself has written a book about sickle cell, which is yet to be published. She has her own platform to make her voice and experiences fully heard, in a way that I have only teased in this chapter, mediating her life experience through my own narrative agenda. I offer to Kate that once I have finished writing this book, that I will help her with hers.

"I may well take you up on that. I really might!"

I am pleased, and hope she does.

13

(PARENT'S BEDROOM) – SUITCASE/ GRIP (PART 1)

When I was promoted Professor in January 2022, I felt the urge to make an artwork to mark the occasion. Some of the key words of my thought process were (in no particular order):

Journey
Achievement
Pride
Representation
Responsibility
Life
Imposter syndrome
Child
Scary
Learning

Instinctively, the starting point for the artwork became the suitcase my dad brought with him from Barbados in 1960. I had seen it (again) in my mum's bedroom a few weeks before, and it was on the forefront of my mind to do something with at a future opportune moment – so this felt like a good time to experiment. The front of the suitcase still carries my dad's name "Mr T. Sobers" written in white paint, now extremely faint. I took the suitcase downstairs to the living room, set my camera phone to a self-timer, and standing next to the photo wall (from Chapter 2), held it up in front of my face. In post-production I erased the room behind me, leaving some of photo wall, and superimposed my mum sat on her bed holding a bouquet of birthday flowers. With dad no longer alive, the suitcase represents him (see Figure 13.1).

DOI: 10.4324/9780367809621-14

FIGURE 13.1 Upon the shoulders, 2022 (© author)

Before taking the photograph mum asked if she should take out the nasal cannula, which she needs to use to receive oxygen, and I advised not, as that is now part of her and nothing to be ashamed of. Due to her health problems, a large part of this book has been written in her house while I have been caring for her. This is apt, as that is the house I grew up in, and which inspired the concept of the initial proposal and the book's format from the very beginning. Re-finding dad's suitcase, I was not sure if I had noticed his name on the front of it before. With my sister at the time, we both had a collective "wow" moment, and wondered aloud about the things the suitcase may have seen. In the image the suitcase is held out in front of me, a metaphor for the ancestors guiding my footsteps. This positionality of the ancestors in front of me, rather than according to the dominant chronology that history is behind us, is inspired by the philosophical work of John S. Mbiti. In his study "African Religions and Philosophy" (1969), Mbiti argued that according to certain African traditions, the ontology of time is opposite to that of the West, and we move towards history, rather than away from it. Those who have died are therefore in front of us, and remain "living-dead" as long as their names are mentioned, only truly dead when their names are no longer evoked in spoken word or memory (Mbiti, 1969: 15–28).

The suitcase (also known as a "grip") is a carrier of the tools that will be needed to negotiate and navigate the terrains ahead. In his work on analysing old photographs from the "West Indian Front Room," Michael McMillan reflects on the clothes that would have been in the suitcases of those who arrived in Britain from the Caribbean in the 1940s and the following four decades, and how those clothes are essential tools in maintaining the values and aspirations of that generation.

> [T]hey had dignity and respectability packed deep in their suitcases, and they were formally dressed as a sign of self-respect – with dresses pressed and hats at an angle in a "universally jaunty cocky" style, in preparation for whatever was to happen next. These immigrants, coming from the colonies, saw themselves as British citizens, and through education sometimes knew more about English culture than the English themselves. They inherited a puritanical Victorian ethos ... where first impressions mattered. To wear the best garments on special occasions, such as attending church, was part of this sartorial principle, and traveling to a distant foreign land was no exception ... Style, self-respect, and respectability were inscribed in one's appearance.
>
> *McMillan, 2009: 140–141*

Like the passport, a suitcase feels like a particular type of witness to historical occasions. Hats, coats, shoes, etc., have also been places and can evoke nostalgia and reflection, though there is something about a suitcase which carries with it a certain aura of not only being witness, but co-participant in events of the past. Perhaps this is due to the role it plays in not only being present in places, but also an instigator in bringing other things along that journey, each with their own bodies of memory, knowledge, history, and specific roles to play in the future. The suitcase, like a passport, is an active participant in plans of travel, not a passive bystander. This was reflected in an interview by The Gleaner with Jamaican sculptor Basil Watson, after his design (see Figure 13.2) was chosen in a UK government-supported public consultation in 2021, for a statue commemorating the "Windrush Generation" to be installed at London's Waterloo station.

According to Watson, the suitcase is an active agent in the experiences and fortunes of the Caribbean family migrants, and intertwined with how the family is represented.

> Windrush is a personal journey, as well as representing the journey of immigrants throughout history, immigrants throughout the Windrush generation, [and] immigrants in general. I tried to see and create an understanding of what it feels like, and I've experienced it too, as I'm an immigrant here in the United States. I packed my suitcases and my belongings, and I came here looking for a better life, looking to extend myself, you know, so, this is what I tried to express. I used the family – the father, mother, a child and created that connection of the family being important. It's a family movement [that] is not just an individual, but family and the suitcases that [they] stand on [represents]

FIGURE 13.2 National Windrush Monument, Basil Watson. Waterloo Station, London, 2022

their culture, represents all that they have valued and their foundation that they will use as a springboard to move ahead in their new environment.

Watson, 2021

Together the family stand on top of the pile of suitcases as if they are rocks on the top of a mountain, their chins raised upwards as they scan their eyes across the new British landscape that will become their homes. The sculpture is reminiscent in composition to the 1818 painting by German romantic artist Caspar David Friedrich titled "Wanderer above the Sea of Fog," in which a solitary male figure is standing on a rock surrounding by a rough sea (see Figure 13.3).

The sense of adventure, drama, and anticipation of a possible future are present in both works of art. Though where Friedrich's painting has been interpreted as patriarchal and colonialist in representation and tone – of a sole heroic white male figure in a confident astride pose conquering new lands (Smith, 2018: 181) – Watson's sculpture could be said to be a response image directly challenging that ideological romanticised view of the colonial era. In Watson's representation, the family stands together holding hands, and their body language suggests less confidence than Friedrich's figure, they are leant back into each other, the child has her

FIGURE 13.3 Wanderer above the Sea of Fog, Caspar David Friedrich, 1818. Hamburger Kunsthalle museum, Hamburg

arm across her chest, and looks of caution are visible on their faces. Watson's family suggests a humble and cautious arrival into a new territory, as opposed to Friedrich's unapologetic confrontation. Like the dramatic foundations of Friedrich's landscape on which his hero stands, in Watson's sculpture, the suitcases, filled with the immediate essentials for new life in a new land, is the stable foundation on which the family stand and gather their strength. To try and get into the minds of Watson's family, I revert to the interview I conducted with my own parents in 1998 about this very moment in their own lives, and what thoughts it brought up for them. In the year of this interview my dad had been living in England for 38 years (since 1960), and for my mum 36 years (arriving in 1962).

Dad:

> My parents encouraged me to come to England, but at the same time they didn't want to see you go. But they took it alright. For most of us, including myself, the plan was five years. Back then five years was a long time. Ten at the very most. Did we plan to stay here indefinitely? No. Sometimes, of course you do reflect back, but you will never know. I can't say I've ever regretted it. There were times in the past when things weren't going to well for you,

but then as the years go by you get commitments, and ten years has passed by before you even think about it. I know that a lot of people who stayed in Barbados are now doing very, very well for themselves. As a matter of fact, I would say better that many of us are doing over here. But I can't say that I would have been one of those, that's the trouble with trying to look into the past or the future – you just don't know.

Mum:

> My friends were leaving and moving to England, but I didn't know anyone else on the flight. I got talking to the other passengers and by the time we landed we were like a close family, because for everybody, it was their first-time leaving home. I was 21 at the time, because in those days you had to be 21 before you could sign any documents or anything. My birthday was in March and right after that my Dad helped me pay for my flight and I came over. I was met at Gatwick Airport by my cousin, and I was quite amazed. I kept looking out for the nice houses and pretty gardens which I thought England would be full of, but as I was travelling, I just saw the backs of houses and little chimneys on top of buildings. I wondered if they were a whole lot of little factories because in Barbados, the only time you would see a chimney poking up into the sky, was on top of a factory which was grinding canes, you know, or engineering work. So actually, it was a very good experience – travelling, I haven't regretted it, really … With God's help, we would like to go back some time in the future.

Mum later told me she has a little cry in the car at the sight of all those (what she thought was) factories. It is clear, however, from the literature and narratives of the "Windrush generation" travellers that their psychology on travel and initial arrival was generally one of optimism. This hope was in response to the pull factors of enticement, such as reported better job opportunities, higher wages, life opportunities, and standards of living (Parkins, 2010: 11–12; Ramachandran, 2006: 3). After arriving in England for the first time, it was 10 years before mum went back to visit Barbados, with my elder sister and me as a new-born, in 1972. It would be 15 years before dad went back for a visit, in 1975. The only time they were able to travel back to Barbados together as a couple was in 1998 for my sister's wedding, which was the first time we were all there as a family together, and as children our first time there with dad. As a couple they travelled there once more together in 2001. Other times it was too expensive for us all to go at the same time, and the other parent would always stay behind and keep working. Dad died in 2018, and mum is no longer well enough to travel. Their suitcases are still in their bedroom, now consigned on top of the wardrobe, largely redundant, but as secure in the house as any fixture.

The physicality and assured presence of the suitcase, and its agency as a witness of the experiences of post-war Caribbean arrivals, is the interest of UK photographer

Wendy Leocque, who I spoke to for this chapter. In an ongoing series of work, she has used the suitcases that both her Jamaican gran and mother brought with them from "back home," her gran arrived in 1956, and her mum was "sent for" in 1960 aged 9 years, when her gran could afford to bring her daughter over. For as long as Leocque can remember she had attached herself to her grandmother's suitcase.

> I think I've always had it, and the first time I moved house I was in my twenties, I definitely had the suitcase then. And when I moved to Bristol [from Birmingham], I also had it with me. I've always had it. Even when my nan was alive, I had her suitcase. It was just something that just travelled with me everywhere, and I don't even think I was using it to store things in it, I just had hold of it.

Leocque says in those early years she did not particularly think of the suitcase as a historic object in relation to her gran's journey from Jamaica, she just knew it had a sentimental attachment for her, simply as she loved her gran. At the time Leocque was not thinking she was going to do anything with it creatively, the thought had not entered her mind.

> Though when nan passed away 12 years ago, I think it took on more sig-nificance. It came out of the loft at that point, and I started photographing it, and just thinking, what do I want to do with it? I started thinking about her arriving here, holding this handle, and I can hold the same handle that she held when she arrived here as a 20-something year old woman all by herself, and in that suitcase was everything that she ever owned. It's almost kind of like her hopes and dreams are in that suitcase. When you look at it, it's not real leather, it's cardboard and completely battered. She's got a part on it where she scratched her initials in there. You know, this thing is well worn, and it holds stories as well. The lock is broken, and she told me the story about this lock and why it was broken, but I'm not going to share that. I'll hold onto that.

The suitcase accompanied Leocque's gran on the three-week boat journey from Jamaica to England. In keeping with the slowness of the journey and the idea of the suitcase as a witness, after conducting some initial photography of the suitcase as an object, Leocque turned the suitcase itself into a pinhole camera, placing the photographic paper inside to capture what it sees.

> When I'm thinking about the images that I'm doing, I'm thinking about my nan – about what she would have said, what she would have done, the things that she liked, what she would have thought of what I'm doing. I don't need a reason to think about my nan or to mention her, but this is a thing that connects us. Whenever I now take this pinhole camera out, I'm holding that

handle. It's taking me on another journey of discovery in so many different ways. I do like the slowness of it. I don't think it would work in any other medium for me, because it works so perfectly as a pinhole camera, and it works so perfectly as this kind of space where I can reflect, always with my nan at the forefront of my mind with it. The sense of meditation is an important part of the process for me, almost like she's guiding me really.

For the first image Leocque made with the adapted grip, she sat the suitcase-camera upright against the headboard on her nan's bed, and exposed the pinhole she made on the front for an 18-minute exposure of the bedroom (see Figure 13.4). During the last few months of Leocque's nan's life, she had become housebound and spent much of it in this bed sat upright against the headboard facing the window, "confined to her room, that was her view."

On a later visit to Birmingham with the suitcase-camera, Leocque's mum mentioned the suitcase that she herself had brought with her from Jamaica aged 9. (The story of "sent for children" is explored further in Chapter 15.) Leocque herself had never seen her mother's suitcase, and did not know it had been kept. Figure 13.5 "Grip to Grip" shows the next pinhole photograph Leocque made that morning when her mum had gone to church. Taking the pinhole camera

FIGURE 13.4 Grip (© Wendy Leocque, 2022)

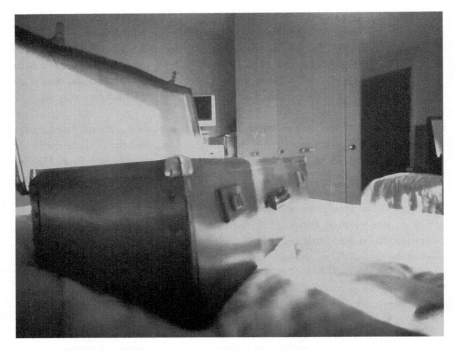

FIGURE 13.5 Grip to Grip (© Wendy Leocque, 2022)

she previously made from her gran's suitcase, and using it to capture a shot of her mother's childhood suitcase in a 3-minute exposure,

> When I took the pinhole photo of my nan's bedroom, I was like, "I wonder if anything came out," because you've got to wait to see the image. It teaches you patience. We're so used to seeing everything immediately and having everything now. You have to wait until you get to a darkroom, and even then, you're asking, "Has it worked?". But I do quite like to wait and see if something has worked out. I literally got the image of my mum's suitcase taken with nan's pinole suitcase camera, and I phoned my mum as soon as I developed the image, to tell her it worked. Mum now has ideas for more images using the suitcases. It's turning into a collaboration with my mum, which is great. It's that kind of importance that comes with making images like this. It's not just the actual pictures, it's everything else around making them as well.

The basis of this work sees Leocque occupying two interlocking intergenerational and transnational spaces – that of being a daughter/grand-daughter learning the narratives of her direct elders, and a first-generation born Black British woman finding her cultural and politicised voice through creative means. Through her pinhole suitcases project, and another project she was working on with photographer Garfield McKenzie of portraits of Caribbean British elders, Leocque acknowledged that cultural and political politics was entering her creative practice for the first time. She also states how the personal connection with this theme, in relation to the experiences of her nan, mum, and other members of her family, had brought with it a renewed motivation to use her photography to address themes relating to racism and the "hostile environment" ushered in by the British government, and an awareness of her own personal development.

> I'm reading a lot about Windrush now. I'm realising, there's a lot of things that my family didn't talk about. I wasn't aware of the level of hostility. They never came home and showed that to us, of what they were going through. I think maybe when I was older my nan told me certain things about her first job, when she was employed as a machinist in a factory, and they wanted her to clean the toilets, and she had to tell them she was there to sew not clean! Both of my parents are from Jamaica, and that made me really angry about the Windrush scandal thing in general, again you have to fight for that acknowledgement. All of these people that came from the Caribbean to fill jobs in the hospital, on transport and everything else, crossing oceans to care for other people, leaving their own children behind, that's not a light thing. But it just doesn't seem to be recognised or appreciated. They now want to deport them back to the Caribbean. So now making this work with my nan's and mum's suitcases, it feels like the first time my creative voice was coming through, I feel connected with the work. Even though I did a photography degree years ago, this work feels completely different and personal to anything else I've done.

The "Windrush scandal" that Leocque speaks of "refers to the callous mistreatment of British citizens, notably those born in the Caribbean" (Wallace et al., 2020: 2), when the Conservative UK government attempted to deport people who had arrived in Britain as children before 1973. Like Leocque's mum, Paulette Wilson was a "sent for child," arriving aged 10 from Jamaica in 1968. Paulette hit the headlines in the British press in 2017, for sharing with Guardian journalist Amelia Gentleman her experiences of being detained by the UK government and threatened with deportation to Jamaica, even though she had not been there since the day she left 50 years previously (Gentleman, 2017). Paulette Wilson became a prominent campaigner fighting for justice for victims of the Windrush Scandal, but died suddenly in July 2020 aged 64, a month after submitting a petition to Parliament.

The government argued those targeted by these harsh "Hostile Environment Policy" measures (brought in by the then Home Secretary Theresa May MP in 2012) did not have the appropriate paperwork to prove they were legal citizens, even though they were British citizens at the time of their arrival, and spent their whole lives in the UK, going through education, having full-time jobs, paying taxes, and had British passports. Some of those caught up in the situation lost their jobs were wrongfully arrested, had their passports taken away, and lost access to NHS healthcare and other rights as a UK citizen, which was the only citizenship they had known (Gentleman, 2019). Due to heavy criticism and legal challenges, the Conservative government dropped the policy and included the resignation of Home Secretary Amber Rudd in 2018, at which point Theresa May was the UK Prime Minister. According to Wardle and Obermuller (2019: 81),

> When it became known that many longstanding British citizens with a West Indian background were caught up in the "hostile environment" policy drive, the term "Windrush generation" acquired a new meaning. What had seemed to be settled facts concerning the status of the Caribbean community in Britain were suddenly being violently disrupted. At the same time there was growing awareness that racist preoccupations, seemingly dormant in immigration debates over recent decades, were reappearing and gaining legitimacy and even government sanction.

Whereas in 1997, writer Myriam Chancy argued that attention on how elders and young people have been affected by racism and the legacy of colonialism exposed a "rupture of cross-generational bonds" in African-Caribbean life in Britain (Chancy, 1997: 63), the Windrush scandal reignited that attention and inspired a cross-generational solidarity of political concerns (Vernon, 2018). With Leocque, what we see – with the familial physicality connections and tactile-ness of her time-based working processes – is the processing of not only the photographic image, but also of intergenerational political discourse. Through the work she is revisiting the moment of arrival with the affordance of knowledge of the present day, and enacting a personalised form of slow and quiet activism, a form of politicised creative practice that activist scholar Dr Liz Crow describes as being activated "through connectedness and dialogue, transforming the encounter to a dynamic site of meaning-making and influence" (Crow, 2022: 170). The encounters in the context of Leocque's work are those moments where audiences come in contact with both her work and her own presence talking the narrative through, whether that be on Instagram, in the community centre where she has run a photography darkroom, or other spaces where she shares her work. The connected narrative cannot be separated from the form. The suitcase-camera is simultaneously and seamlessly the methodology, technology, story, and style. Whatever Leocque points the suitcase's pinhole lens at will became part of the Caribbean/Black British traveller's narrative.

In the context of Caribbean expectants arriving in the "new world" of post-war Britain, the suitcase represents a moment of hope for the future and anticipation of what adventures lay ahead, their "grips" tightly packed with what they felt was necessary to accompany them on their literal and metaphorical journey. However, for those targeted by the draconian Hostile Environment policy, such as Paulette Wilson, the childhood suitcase of her 10-year-old self loses its innocence and is transformed into a site of retreat, defensiveness, and the necessaries for harsh survival. Post-colonial scholar Bill Schwarz visions the tragic scenario of Paulette's suitcase by her side as she learns or her fate (2021: 294–295).

> [Paulette] received a letter from the Home Office headed by the ominous words "Notice of Immigration Decision." This is how she learned that she was to be "removed." According to Amelia Gentleman, it shook "her sense of who she was." [Gentleman, 2019: 19]. Or in Paulette's own words, "It made me feel like I didn't exist" [ibid.]. We can imagine her retreating, like many before her, to a private sanctuary – her suitcase packed, her destiny sealed – and reflecting on the fate her black skin caused her.

In hopeful scenarios, the suitcase represents the journey of the recipient of a "pull factor" motivation for travel, "better wages and employment conditions" (Parkins, 2010: 12) and generally positive reasons for wanting to move from one place to another. Alternatively, "push factors" are negative reasons people feel forced to move from a place regardless of their own wishes, such as "crime and violence, an unstable economy" (ibid.) and also life challenges, such as fleeing abuse, or moving from a house due to the break-up of a relationship. As we can see from the experiences of the "Windrush Generation," they experienced a continual colonial tug of war with their senses, to the extent that, for some, the pull factors of leaving the Caribbean very quickly morphed into push factors being told they were not welcome here as the criteria changed. This sense of push and pull, of whether or not we belong and are welcomed in the UK, is a sensation that has persisted through to the younger generations today, still grappling with the conundrum faced by our elders since the 1940s.

Suitcases and the Recovery of Apartheid Memory

As seen, the Hostile Environment policy in the UK saw the government attempting to use and adapt the law to forcibly remove legal British citizens such as Paulette Wilson, and it was largely the loud protests from public opinion that has seen some of those policies overturned. Apartheid era South Africa saw racism transformed from inter-personal relations into the overt structure and rationale of the entire state apparatus of the country. For Black people, notions of belonging were not left to individual musing, it became the governing framework of your entire existence – you were told where you did and did not belong by law and state-sanctioned violence. In this climate, the residents of the District Six community in Cape Town were subjected to some of the most brutal policy decisions of the regime. In 1966, at the stroke of a pen, it was decided that District Six was to become a "white only area," and over the following years approximately 60,000 Black residents were forcibly evicted, and their homes demolished. Push factors at an extreme level.

In 2019 I visited the District Six Museum, where former residents of the area are the tour guides, telling their stories first hand of the traumatic experiences they and their families lived through. I was struck how the symbolism of the suitcase had

FIGURE 13.6 District Six Museum, Cape Town, 2019 (© author)

come to represent such brutal events, and evoke the feelings of being ripped away from their homes, forever embedded in their collective memory. I asked the (now former) Director of the museum Dr Bonita Bennett about the suitcase exhibit I saw at the museum (see Figure 13.6), what thoughts it evoked for her. She sent me the following account for this book.

Suitcases in the District Six Museum
Dr Bonita Bennett

District Six was an inner-city neighbourhood in Cape Town which was razed to the ground as part of legally sanctioned forced removals under apartheid. The area was declared "whites only" in 1966, and as the majority of the area was occupied by Black people, their homes were destroyed and they were forced to move to areas constructed for the racial category into which they were divided under apartheid (i.e. African, coloured, or Indian). The museum's formation was prompted by the twin issues of land rights and memory of the land.

A few years ago, the District Six Museum started a "suit-case project" with one of the outputs of the project being the installation of a suitcase in its main gallery.

Suitcases are used symbolically in this project. The circumstances that resulted in people moving from District Six under apartheid were not conducive to having the opportunity to neatly pack a suitcase. Oral accounts refer to the chaos of forced removals which often meant that people stuffed their belongings into any containers that they had at hand: pillowcases, plastic packets, boxes, and if they had them, suitcases. They packed what they could but often had to leave some things behind.

The suitcase in the context of the exhibition is a universal visual signifier of movement from one place to another. Visitors who enter the space, even those who have little or no background to the story told by District Six Museum, immediately have a clue that part of the story centres around movement. As they engage the exhibition further, they get the broader picture of how people were displaced under apartheid, and what the impact of such displacement was. They get a sense of the racially constructed areas of residence where the suitcases and their owners were forced to live after their communities were destroyed.

District Six Museum's permanent exhibition is named *Digging Deeper*. It refers to the methodology of working with the unfinished story of District Six (and South Africa) and suggests a constant layering of new meanings into the exhibition space. The suitcase installation is part of such layering.

However, the project's intention was not solely to add onto the existing exhibition. Essentially, it formed part of the Museum's healing work which includes the recovery of memory, and a piecing-back together of the shattered lives of people whose homes were destroyed. It is an intergenerational project in which former residents of the area were invited to work with young people who interviewed them about their lives, and co-curated suitcases as memory boxes which would represent their lives in some measure. They were invited to imagine what, if they had been given the choice, to take along in a single suitcase which they could pack before leaving their homes for the last time, what they would select as being most precious and meaningful to them. Alternatively, they were asked to select objects that would give whoever was to look into the suitcase, a good picture of who the suitcase owner was. The contents of the suitcases are a combination of the owner/storyteller's own memorabilia, or replicas that were sourced or fabricated if they no longer had the precious object in their possession.

For Small Anthropology methodology it is important I include Bennett's words verbatim. I could have paraphrased her words and selected choice quotes to include, but after ten days of being in Cape Town, whereas Bennett has been there her whole life, I do not claim an affordance of knowledge on the topic over hers, and any words I paraphrased would have been building on her insights. Therefore, collaboration in this small way felt like the appropriate method to present that narrative. It is also a humble gesture towards the pan-African ideal of equality and collegiate partnership across the diaspora, Africans at home and abroad (Garvey, 1923: 35).

Returning to the Moment of Leaving

The other signifier of the suitcase, especially in a Western context, is as the represen-tation of holidays. As children we were fully aware these holidays "back home" were not solely leisure time, they were a combination of obligations to visit and spend time with family and their friends, with the occasional day off to do some-thing touristy, such as visit the beach. These visits for us children to Barbados were approximately once every 7–10 years. With a few exceptions, growing up we tended not to have holidays in the years in-between, instead going on various day trips during our six weeks summer breaks from school. This personal reflection is a common memory of many of my peers, and also concurs with the findings of one of the few research studies in this area of Black British life experience, not-ably *"Holidays and the UK Afro-Caribbean Community"* by Stephenson and Hughes (1995: 430). In Ramachandran's (2006) study, he explores the notion of "Visiting Friends and Relatives (VFR)," the specific field of study in leisure and tourism of the returnee tourist market. He cites the various factors at play that feature in the motivation of returnee holiday visits which may limit choice, such as pur-pose of visit, occasion or event, budget, also the availability of rooms when staying with family and friends (as opposed to staying in hotels like unconnected tourists) (ibid.: 2–4). Other studies, such as Dennis Conway's (2007) *"Caribbean Transnational Migration Behaviour: Reconceptualising Its Strategic Flexibility,"* look at the integrated international networks that are implicitly entwined within the Caribbean migrant family, and the negotiation of those networks, relationship building, and communi-cation over geographic lines and time zones.

Transnational geographies at the micro- and meso-scales of the family and the community provide the relational contextual spaces within which migrants, their families and friends and community associates live out their transnational lives, across borders and within social networks, while maintaining social linkages and managing to find ways to make the best of their multi-local worlds. "Homes" and "homes away from home" provide the micro-geographical "roots" of migrants' transnational existence, of their experiences, identities and degrees of national and transnational consciousness.

Conway, 2007: 418

This transnational negotiation of identity and the maintenance of relationships related to a question I asked my parents, in the interview I conducted with them in 1998, about how they kept in touch with their families back home. About how they felt whenever they went back to Barbados for a visit, and if they still felt part of that culture (Sobers, 1998a).

Dad:

> I always kept in contact with my family and wrote every week … It was nice when I first got back and I wondered why I left it so long – everyone was glad to see you, more than glad! Familiar faces, new faces, additions to families you never knew before – it was great … In some ways, you've been living in another country for so long you find you have different habits and your culture fades a bit – I'm not saying it completely goes, but you've got to say you change a bit – living in another country for more than half your life. Once you get back to Barbados though, it doesn't take long for your birth culture to come back to you.

Mum:

> Oh yes, we never lose contact with family. Always write very often and was always promising to go back … [When I do go back there] it feels as if you're thawing out of a deep freeze. You don't have the time to get used to it though because work will only let you have a certain amount of time off, and it's never enough. Once you're over there though, you get into a few sea baths and you feel really happy!

It is an obvious point to make, though it is still worth noting that these transnational networks and communications were being maintained a long time before the internet and mobile phones were invented, and all the ease of communication that the digital era brings. I am in awe of my parents and their generation, which how dedicated they were to maintaining their friendships and strong bonds with other Caribbean friends and family locally, nationally, and internationally – almost every weekend it felt like were going to London from Bath to visit someone, or staying local and visiting one of their friends. As a child I used to somewhat resent having to go to these places, but now as an adult, I fully appreciate the fact that my upbringing had a dual and somewhat parallel cultural consciousness – a Black Caribbean cultural upbringing within the largely white geography of Bath. It is a balance of cultural discourses that I feel has equipped me for negotiating the space I now frequent in both my professional and personal lives. In today's terminology it is called "code switching." Growing up, it was simply the method for living.

14

(TEENAGE BEDROOM) – STUFF (PHOTO ESSAY)

How much do the objects we own really say something about us? The BBC programme "Through the Keyhole" used to have Lloyd Grossman (and subsequent presenters) look through the houses of anonymous celebrities, and the panel had to guess from the clues Lloyd flagged up who the house belonged to. The key clue was often the bookcase. Certain book titles were focused as clues towards the owner's interests and personality. If any of us looked at our bookcases and record collections, I am sure we would find examples which would defy the common assumptions about our identities and be surprising for others, and that kind of diversity of taste is surely a healthy approach to the consumption of culture. We would also own items that we would not welcome to be used as "clues" in a reductionist way to ascertain what our identities might be. For example, I own a copy of a biography of Benito Mussolini, not because I like him as an individual or anything he stood for, and the presence of the book can easily be explained in relation to other areas of research I have conducted. Though taken out of context, the book choice can look disturbing as if it is a signifier of glorification, but it would be absurd for me to feel the need to discard the book in fear of such misrepresentation.

Contrary to attempts of traditional ethnographic studies, this book has attempted to avoid making universal claims about a whole set of people. As individuals we are all complex and defy easy categorising, and certainly cannot be reduced to being defined by material objects. The aim of this book has been to use objects as a way to explore collective narrative, as opposed to a reductionist defining of identities, though I acknowledge it is a fine line that is walked. It has been a heuristic device to cherry pick different objects to represent different rooms as a vehicle through which to explore story and memory, however, even in a generalised sense, how do you go about choosing an object to represent a child's/teenager's bedroom? The teenager's bedroom, it feels to me, is the space where more than any other

DOI: 10.4324/9780367809621-15

room, is the place where individual identity is (at least partly) formed. As Highmore (2014: 197) states,

> Today the stereotypically denigrated teenager can be imagined festering in a miasma of hormones and whiffy socks while listening to loud, mournful music and contemplating the failure of the adult world to understand them. Generally, they are imagined in a room of their own.

Possibly the only single object which could get close to representing the teenage bedroom would be the door itself, or more specifically, a lock (if there was one), or the classic teenage "Keep Out!" sign. With the transparency that Small Anthropology methodology encourages, I could not conceptualise this chapter to work in the same way as the others and needed a different, interdisciplinary approach.

Therefore, this chapter speaks directly to the Small Anthropology quality of "Mixed methods in research approaches and output style," as highlighted in the Introduction. It is presented in the form of a photo essay with minimal words to try and encapsulate the randomness, eclecticism, and developmental nature of both the mind and physical space of teenagers. I asked some people I know the question, "What did you have in your bedroom when you were a teenager in the 1980s and 90s?" This photo essay presents the possibilities of the diversity of the Black imagination, in this instance, of a demographic now aged approximately 45+. This diversity and eclecticism never leave us, though it is seldom seen except by close loved ones.

Chimamanda Ngozi Adichie tells a story which illustrates this well, in her now famous 2009 TED talk "The danger of a single story" (Adichie, 2009) (which at the time of writing has amassed over 11 million views on YouTube).

> ... I left Nigeria to go to university in the United States. I was 19. My American roommate was shocked by me. She asked where I had learned to speak English so well, and was confused when I said that Nigeria happened to have English as its official language. She asked if she could listen to what she called my "tribal music," and was consequently very disappointed when I produced my tape of Mariah Carey (Audience laughter). She assumed that I did not know how to use a stove.

In symbolic terms, the teenage bedroom represents the non-essentialist nature of Black people, when we are often presented as beings of "Single Stories." The world is still surprised to see a Black person that can play classical music, sing opera, recite Shakespeare, or any other activity deemed to be the preserve of the upper classes. Even when levelling the assumed class categories, the sight of a Black punk, gothic, heavy metal fan, etc., can gain the same reaction and looks of suspicion and curiosity. By not subscribing to the narrow myths of what Black people are supposed to like and do, we can attract the accusation of not being Black enough, of acting white, of selling out, of not knowing our culture, of overstepping our boundaries, of getting above our station, of trying to be something we are not.

The innocence of our childhood imaginations, and the (hopeful) safe space of the child and teenage bedroom, is the place where we get to explore what we like in the sanctity of our own selves with no external judgement. Whether that be the music we listen to, books we read, politics we identify with, people we are sexually attracted to, or any other metric. Teenage years are often notoriously the time when those confusing and conflicting messages navigate around our minds and bodies at frightening speed. Little wonder the teenage years are often deemed to be ripe time of experimentation, risk taking, and other forms of self-expression (both wholesome and problematic). Unfortunately, the innocence of our childhood selves gets less as we become more self-aware, and in a supposed streetwise move, we hide certain things we like and do, in favour to show other things which are deemed more in keeping with "people like us."

By presenting the remainder of this chapter in purely visual form, in the context of a visual essay comprising four compilation images (Figures 14.1, 14.2, 14.3, and 14.4), I invite you to read the images slowly. Take notice of what you initially clearly see, and consequently, take notice of what your eyes skipped past and did not register or remember. Some of the visual references may "pop out" with instant familiarity, and others may fade back into negative space and be rendered near invisible or indifferent. The invitation is to slow down your eyes and focus on each of the elements, and reflect on your own eclecticism of interests, and what that might look like mapped out in a similar transparent way. How might that look like if it was guaranteed to always remain private, alternatively, would it look the same if you had to make it public? Any differences in those two mapped versions automatically generate the question "why?".

FIGURE 14.1 Teenage stuff 1. A full inventory of this montage is provided at www.smallanthropology.wordpress.com

FIGURE 14.2 Teenage stuff 2. A full inventory of this montage is provided at www.smallanthropology.wordpress.com

FIGURE 14.3 Teenage stuff 3. A full inventory of this montage is provided at www.smallanthropology.wordpress.com

FIGURE 14.4 Teenage stuff 4. A full inventory of this montage is provided at www.smallanthropology.wordpress.com

15

('SENT FOR CHILD'S' BEDROOM) – SUITCASE/GRIP (PART 2)

I remember seeing the suitcase when I got to Heathrow (aged six years old). I remember when the couple who travelled with me on the plane, who I didn't even know, handed me over to my dad in the car park, along with my suitcase. It looked like a small brown briefcase, and I saw my name painted on the front in capital letters in white paint. I don't know who wrote it on there. I remember it also had an address under my name, also in capitals in white paint. I didn't know what the address was then, but I soon found out it was where my mum and dad lived. My mum would have unpacked it when I got to their house. It only had about three or four items of clothes in there, and I only had summer clothes as that's all we needed in the Caribbean, but I arrived in England in the winter. My mum had to take me out shopping to get some winter clothes, the thickest thing I had was a cardigan. I don't remember seeing the suitcase again after that day I arrived.

These are the words of Veronica (not her real name), who was born in the Caribbean (exact country will not be disclosed), who remained living there with her gran when her parents left for England, eventually joining them in the UK when she was 7, discovering three younger siblings.

In academic writing, we are not very good at listening without interrupting. We inject our own descriptions and interpretations, add reference citations and footnotes, we bring in the voices of others, and add selected quotes from celebrated thinkers. Even when we are advocates of participatory methodologies and approaches, academics seldom allow people to just speak for themselves. For this reason, italics have not been used in this chapter to denote a quote, and Veronica's words are presented as the main body text.

Here I am going to break the mould and challenge conventional academic writing, and present an interview transcript as the main text of this chapter. It is by

DOI: 10.4324/9780367809621-16

no means 100% verbatim, or a pure unedited transcript, and it has been edited to fit and flow. However, what it does aim to do is challenge the academic tradition that the academic knows best, and that the respondent's words are only there to be tested, interpreted, triangulated, counted, and become representative of some form of cohort or community.

It is important to note in this case Veronica's story is not representative of the experiences of all "sent for" children, as none would ever be. Veronica's narrative, however, is one that needs to be heard (of course, in my opinion). It is important also to note that I did not know Veronica's story before the moment of the interview, and I did not know what direction it was going to take. So therefore, Veronica was not sought out to tell this specific type of narrative, and not to represent any particular angle of the "sent for children" experience and documented history.

Some readers may get upset with Veronica's story being published in this book, as it does not present some of our Caribbean elders in a good or positive light. I know if I was the reader, likewise I would probably be equally uncomfortable and possibly even disappointed. However, in the spirit of transparency and also vulnerability that Small Anthropology methodology encourages (and also just plain academic honesty and integrity), it is important that Veronica's story is not omitted just because it makes us uncomfortable. Some readers will say I should have included the stories of other "sent for children" who had more positive experiences, to balance the representation out (and that approach has been taken elsewhere in this book), but Small Anthropology methodology does not attempt to make the research accounts representative of a whole cohort or community. So rather than trying to achieve a representative soup of data, over the next few pages will be presented a single narrative with no interruption, with all of the hard lessons that it contains. It is no longer about Veronica's physical suitcase, but everything about what that suitcase represents for her in the arch of her life, from that day of arrival in the 1960s, to the moment of this retelling in 2022, which was the first time she had ever told her full experience. Some of the details of Veronica's words have been edited to protect her identity, such as place names and exact dates and years.

Veronica's Story

"Mum came over to Britain when I was six months old in the 1960s. Dad had already come to Britain earlier, and then he sent for mum. I was left in the Caribbean with my gran, and I would say I had a good childhood. I was spoilt, and I got a lot of beating but, to be fair, I was quite naughty growing up, but I was still shown a lot of love.

I always thought that my grandma was my mum. I didn't know no different, there wasn't any pictures in the house to say "that is your mum and that's your dad." I just knew that, like, twice a year or something like that, a big barrel will come down and ma said to me, "This came from your mum," but her telling me it came from my mum didn't make no sense to me because I was only about three, four years old, so I didn't understand. She'd take all these nice dresses out, and shoes and toys. Nobody ever sits you down and said, "Your mum has going to England, you're left with us." I just thought my grandmother was my mother. We just went on with life, and at four I went to school, and I was never in the bottom class as I was bright, I was always the top class. I enjoyed going, and had a fun childhood.

One day I just heard crying, crying, crying, I thought someone died. Ma said, "You're going to England." I said, "England?" She said, "Yeah, you're going to your mum and your dad," and I was like "who are they?" In all that seven years mum's never been back to the Caribbean, so there was no one I could put a face to. Then all of a sudden I'm leaving all the people that I know and feel secure around. I remember leaving my grandmother and holding onto her and bawling and saying, "No, I'm not going." I opened my suitcase and I put all these stones in it, and she was like, "What are you doing?" I said, "I don't know if they've got stones over there." So I was putting all these rocks in my suitcase and my grandmother was taking them out. She was like, "You can't take them over there. They have rocks over there too," and I said, "No, but I want my rocks!"

I remember my grandmother couldn't even come to the airport because she was so distraught. My aunties were like, "You can't go to the airport, ma, because if you go, she's not going to get on that plane." I wouldn't have got there. Years later, my aunts told me that for weeks afterwards ma didn't eat because she missed me so much. I came to Britain with strangers. It was my dad's friend and his wife. I didn't even know these people, I had never seen them until I met them at the airport. But they were a nice couple. On the plane they really looked after me and made sure I was okay, but to me it just felt strange.

When we landed and got off the plane it was so cold, everywhere was foggy. I had just left hot sun and here I was shivering, I didn't even have a coat. I remember the man's wife wrapping her coat around me. Obviously, they took me through customs and things and then handed me to this man I'd never seen before and said, "This is your dad." I just looked at him and was like "who's my dad?" All the way driving from Heathrow to the house, he did not say a single word to me. He did not ask if I had a good flight, or if I was cold or hungry, nothing. We drove in silence. When we got to the house, I walked in and I remember the smell of a paraffin heater. A woman mum came out from the back and was like, "Oh, hello Veronica. You all right? I'm your mum." That was my greeting. There was no hugging. There was no affection to say, "I'm glad you're here," you know, "I love you." Nothing. She said she was out the back washing clothes and said, "Oh, sit down there. I'll come back in a minute."

I sat there with this little suitcase and I was cold, and I'm just ready to go back through the door. In my head I was like, "I'm not staying here!" I'm thinking you can get on a bus and go back. It's not in your head. You're not thinking you just came here on a plane. I found it very traumatising, I came to strangers and when you come you didn't feel that warmth and that embrace. Then all of a sudden, this little boy and little girl appear out of nowhere and staring at you like you're something in a zoo, and there was also a younger brother. Every time they asked me something and I answered they would be like, "She talks funny. What did she say?"

So it's almost like you became a clown. That carried on, so when mum and dad weren't looking, I hit them, and mum ask them why they're crying, "But she just hit me," and mum was like, "What happened?" I was like, "Oh, well, they were laughing at me," and then mum was like, "Well, that's not a reason for you to slap them." You expect her to say, "Well, this is your sister or your big sister or whatever, you don't mock her," nothing. It was like, just saying to me "You shouldn't be hitting them." They already had that bond with mum, I had nowhere to fit in. I didn't even know they existed until that day. Two of them were already at school, so it's not like I was arriving here to babies, and they've never been apart, and they've never been left, so they've got that bond with mum and dad. Sometimes you will find mum reading you a story and my brothers and sister will be either side of her, and I'm at the bottom of the bed, no attempt made to bring me closer.

When I first came, if I wanted something, I would never go and say, "Mum, can I have this or that ..." I will say to my brothers and sister, "Go and ask your mother if I can have an apple. Go and ask your mother if I can have a drink." It was always go and ask your mother ... One day mum heard me say it, and she went ballistic. She was like, "What do you mean ask your mother? So, what I'm not your mother too?" In my head it was like, well no, you're not. I couldn't say that out loud, and they never asked to find out how you feel.

Every time I did something wrong mum will say, "I send you back to the Caribbean to ma. I'll send you back," so the more she said that and because I wanted to go, obviously the more and more I became naughty because I really wanted to go back and then one day she'd look at me and said, "Oh, if you think when you keep doing all these things that you're going back to ma, you're not going nowhere. You're staying here. I'm your mother, not ma." That thing really scared me for a long time. In my head I'm thinking, "But you are ungrateful because you left me at six months." Ma raised me to six and a half years old. When I come here, I could do everything for myself. You didn't do nothing for me. You know, you weren't there when I fell down and grazed my knees. You weren't there when I had a headache or stomach-ache. So, for her to turn around and say I wasn't going to be going back, it was like my whole world collapsed. I was totally devastated.

Then you go to school and back in those times they feel that because you come from the West Indies, they think you're dumb. They think that you're not educated. So they put me in the bottom class for everything, and the work that they were doing I already did like in infant school. They don't care how bright you are, you remained in the bottom class and they never move you. You find that a lot of children that come from the West Indies, they come here really bright, and they end up getting like nowhere in life because you spend half your time messing around because they're not catering for your needs. If you can't do work, you're bored in the class because there's nothing for you to do. I mean, the lessons that they were teaching, I could have taught that class myself. When I came here, I knew all my times tables, but at the school here they're still teaching two times tables to the class they put me in. You knew how to write your sentences, and they're telling you things like "the cat sat on the mat," and you're thinking what is this? So you become disinterested. That's a real thing that I think a lot of us went through coming from the West Indies.

It's very hard to get out of it unless you had parents that would go and fight your corner. My mum and dad never went to the school. The only time my dad ever went to the school was when I got into fights. My dad or mum would just go to the school and they don't ask me what happened, but whatever the teacher said was what happened, they went along with. I remember one time, when I was about 14, getting into trouble at school and it wasn't my fault, and my dad was like to the headmaster, "Oh, you think if she was in the Caribbean, that she could do this? She would be caned," and the headmaster said, "We can't cane children now," and dad said, "I'm giving you the permission to cane her." I remember I got into trouble the next day and the headmaster came over and said, "You know your dad say that you can be caned?" I looked at him and said to him, "Listen, my dad said I can be caned, so seeing as he's given you that permission you go and cane him, but you're not caning me." I walked right out of his office, no way!

I remember doing my exams and coming home and I said to mum, "I got a one in English, two in maths, then I had three in something else and then I had a five in geography," because I didn't like history, so I got a six in history. Mum said, "What do you mean to say you failed all the exams and only passed two?" So I said, "Huh." So she said, "Well, the four, the five and the six." To this day I still laugh at it because they never had no contact with the school, so she didn't realise that one was the highest mark and I literally only failed geography and history. And you know I got to the stage where I couldn't even be bothered to correct her, as they wouldn't understand or listen or think I was lying, so what was the point? Up to this day I laugh about that.

At home, I just got to a stage where I just didn't care because there was no inter-action. They didn't ask what type of food you liked, everything is just put in front of you, there's just no affection. It's like they grow up in a stage where their parents never said, "I love you," or their parents … it was just children must be seen and not heard and so therefore they're bringing up in that same way, but then when you looked at my brothers and sister it was different with them. People used to come to the house and say to mum, "Is she adopted?" Mum would be like, "No, she's my first child." You will come and brothers and sister with mum and dad on one side, and will be at the other end of the room, I was always reading a book, and as I got older, I spent most of the time in my bedroom.

I joined the church when I was in my 20s, got married a few years later, and my husband was also born in the Caribbean and sent for when he was a child, so we can relate on that level, which has been good, I think has stabilised me as well. I think church helps a lot because I think you draw on your faith. You don't forget but you learn how to forgive. I think sometimes why some people end up with nervous breakdowns in our age group is because you spend so much time trying to suppress something but it only takes one thing to happen and it explodes. If your mind can't cope with it, you end up on antidepressants. There are so many people that I know that can't get over their past, and their life is just in a mess because they can't let go of it and move on when you have the experiences that we've had. I think I learnt that because through my own faith and my own stubbornness and my own determination, that's why you always say not everybody's as strong as you or everybody deals with things in a different way.

I always just felt that if I had stayed in the West Indies with my grandmother things would have been so … but then if I had stayed there, I most probably wouldn't be married today and have my kids. So, what do you say? Things are meant to be and I think some experiences that you go through, it helps you to be a better person as well and it helps you to understand other people because perhaps if you don't … if I never went through this, when somebody now is telling me what it feels like to be distanced from their parents, you would never understand because your life was rosy.

There's a lot of things that my kids will say to me, "Why are you like this? Why are you like that?" But because you don't want to tarnish that respect or that love they have for their grandparents, you don't sit down and say to them, "Well, this is what happened to me. This is how I was treated." They just see mum and dad as loving grandparents. My children would say, "Grandma, I love you. Grandad, I love you." They have that relationship with them. Why would I rip that away? I don't feel that I have that right.

Some of our parents, they did it out of ignorance, some did it because they couldn't be bothered, and some were just not cut out to be parents, and some did it because they thought they were doing the best for you. Some did it because they felt that was what was expected of them, and some were just wicked. Out of those categories, where would I put my mum and my dad? I would just say they were ignorant. You know, it's like what we would call a generational issue. My parents never sat down and talked to me. We as the younger ones now, we need to learn how to break that cycle. My children can come to me and hug me and say, "Mummy I love you." I can say to my sister, "I love you. I'm so proud of you," and things like that. We've learnt how to be survivors and some of us are able to overcome our past, and some can't, and that's where it's become sad. You need to know how to talk it out and free yourself from it."

Postscript

Veronica does not hold any animosity or resentment towards her parents, and has fully forgiven them. She loves her siblings, and has tried not to let the experiences of her past affect her present or future. As I sit and listen to her speak, tears well up in my eyes and I am humbled by her strength and capacity for love. There is nothing I can say expect thanking her for sharing. I could only listen.

16

(GARDEN) – SOIL

It has been well documented and publicised how the Covid-19 pandemic lockdowns saw an increase in the amount of people taking up gardening (White et al., 2021 and Egerer et al., 2022), with Black people being no exception to that general growing trend (Tolliver-Jackson, 2020; Reed, 2020; Hutton, 2021). As a relatively new allotment holder, I also became counted in such statistics and featured in some of the articles and films produced about the phenomenon (Pipe, 2020; Columbia, 2021; Hoare, 2021; Maunganidze & Menter, 2021). As unorthodox as it may be, before this chapter gets into its main area of discussion, I first encourage conducting online searches for phrases such as the following:

> black british gardeners / gardening
> black gardening covid
> black gardening increase
> black allotment growers

One will find a wide range of covid-inspired articles discussing gardening in context with wider cultural issues, such as Gal Dem's excellent article written by Aimée Grant Cumberbatch titled "The history of Black British gardeners is one of resistance," which discusses the context of gardening during slavery times and how cultivating the land essentially kept them enslaved (Cumberbatch, 2020). The narrative context echoes the history of rice cultivation that was explored in Chapter 10 of this book, that the enslaved Africans brought growing and farming skills with them from Africa which far exceeded the knowledges and capabilities of the overseers. According to Cumberbatch,

DOI: 10.4324/9780367809621-17

Gardening was also used by enslaved people as a means of resisting and surviving. Gardens were a place they could grow food to supplement the deliberately meagre and malnutritious diet slavers allowed them.

The article goes onto discuss the significance of the early Black gardeners in the UK in the 1800s through to 2020, and how the resurgence of Black growers and growing initiatives "help Black people understand their connection to the land as ancestral" (ibid.), and is a continuation of a practice, tradition, and way of life that has been ever present in Black/African cultural life even when not visible or documented.

Again, by conducting such online searches, another article which surfaces is a report from the Office of National Statistics (ONS, 2020). The report looks into the important issue of how Black people were disproportionally affected by the Covid-19 lockdowns in relation to lack of access to gardens and open spaces, carrying the headline – "The percentage of homes without a garden is higher among ethnic minorities, with Black people in England nearly four times as likely as White people to have no outdoor space at home." According to Natural England data (quoted in the ONS report), 37% of Black people having no access to a private or shared garden, patio or balcony, compared with 10% of white people with no access to similar spaces.

Attention is brought to those online searches as they are all important topics to explore and learn from, and if they had not been previously written, that may have been the type of content that would have filled this very chapter. However, as those articles have been written, the content will not be repeated here, and this chapter will take a different direction for its main narrative. The history of the connection to the land of African ancestry and the present day was not the justification of my experience or motivation to take up gardening and get an allotment, and this chapter will take a more personal line of enquiry to explore this newfound relationship to the natural world. As with some other chapters of this book, some sections will be deeply autoethnographic, but the discussion will not remain in the personal and connect into broader areas of related discourse. It is necessary to start in the one of the most personal touchstone moments – the time of death of a parent.

Nature and the Grieving Process

After a long illness, Dad died in 2018. I found that an effective way for me to deal with the grieving process was to pay closer attention to nature, probably as a distraction. On a practical level, I had the tasks of dealing with the paperwork that follows the death of a close loved one and organising the funeral, but in the quiet moments, when I was answerable to no one else but myself, I found tuning into different aspects of the natural world helped calm my mind and emotions. Initially this was not gardening in a practical sense as I was not green fingered at all, but first through observing nature, mostly by photographing it, I started to pay attention to my surroundings in a different way, taking notice of things that I might usually have passed by. For example, connected back directly with the death of dad, I noticed that every single one of the many sympathy cards in mum's house had a representation of nature on the front image. They ALL depicted flowers in some way, even as abstracts, and in addition many also included butterflies or birds. I started to conduct close-up photography of all the cards and thought about why representations of nature seemed to automatically equate to comfort and emotional forms of healing.

In one of the few research studies on the topic of nature themed images on greetings cards, communications scholar Diana Rehling describes a series of different images on specific occasion cards in relation to the text found inside – including a Thanksgiving card featuring an autumnal scene full of orange leaves; an Easter card with rabbits on a lush green grass; a Christmas card with a snow-covered mountain, pine trees, and a deer bathed in bright moonlight; a sympathy card featuring a peaceful green valley, pond, daffodils, and butterflies; and a general motivation themed card featuring waves breaking over rocky shore with a rainbow in the background (Rehling, 2002: 17–18).

> In all of the above examples, nature provides the tone or inspiration for the verbal expression. This type of turning to nature happens particularly with the expression of sentiments that relate to spiritual matters, such as celebrating religious holidays, grieving a death, or seeking encouragement during difficult times (a kind of turning to nature for what cannot be found in commercialized society). And with comfortable familiarity, the irony that such communication comes in the form of manipulated images of nature commodified in the form of mass-produced greeting cards fades from view.
>
> *ibid.: 18*

The final line in Rehling's quote suggests a critical analysis of the commodification of sincere sentiments as commercial merchandise, whilst at the same time acknowledging that they can bring genuine comfort for the receiver. Another way of describing that criticality is that, even though we recognise such cards, images, and text sentiments to be a cliché, it has become an effective cliché that can be worth perpetuating at the appropriate times when required.

One of my favourite and most quoted lines from literature is "The only Zen you find on tops of mountains is the Zen you bring there," from Robert Pirsig's hailed classic *Zen and the Art of Motorcycle Maintenance* (Pirsig, 2004: 220), which I read as a teenager in the late 1980s. I now re-evaluate those words. While I do still believe that the ultimate state of peace is embodied in the mind, and therefore a state of calm can be found in a busy city car park as much as in a lush green meadow. I do concede, however, that to deny the tranquillity and escape from the urban rush of living that those romanticised rural spaces can provide is to throw the baby out with the bath water. I accept this is an urban-biased interpretation of the text, though as a lifetime city dweller, fully consumed in the rush of work with little respite, in my middle age I now fully embrace the clichés of the rural. Give me all the picturesque mountains and golden sunsets you can muster. Zen is in the car park, but it is hard to find through noise of engines, seen through smog, or heard over the ping of smartphones. The mountain tops might be a cliché, but it is a great one that is hard to argue with.

While on compassionate leave I started to recognise a shift in my usual work-aholic tendencies, away from the screen and towards the soil. In-between planning the funeral (which was happening over a month after dad died) to occupy myself I pledged to tidy the back garden of my terrace house, which although tiny, had overgrown to become a jungle. I found the process of cutting down and tidying away the tall grasses, weeds, bushes, and random debris cathartic, and it gave me a confidence to not only clear away, but also to try and keep the space maintained at this new level where it could be used and enjoyed. For the first time in my life I bought some (Covid lockdown 'essential items') gardening tools, and put a selec-tion of random plants in the soil around the garden and tried to keep them alive. Tending for plant life has never been something I have been knowledgeable about or comfortable with, but secretly I wanted to be. Soon afterwards I met my friend Ruth for lunch, and after telling her about my new emerging hobby, as an allotment holder she persuaded me to sign up for a plot at her site. After just over a year on the waiting list (during which time my close cousin Sharon also died, and thus the grieving process reignited), in October 2019 I was offered an allotment plot, which I promptly covered with tarpaulin and forgot about for the next seven months, though the tending of the back garden and gaining confidence in growing plants continued.

If I had the benefit of premonition of the arrival coronavirus pandemic and the first lockdown in 2020, I would have seen myself operating in the mode of photojournalist, roving around the city with my camera, interviewing people at a social distance, attempting to make sense of the strange world we found ourselves in. However, I surprised myself when lockdown happened, that I did not have the motivation to behave in that way at all. At the first opportunity after finishing assessing student work leading up to the spring break, rather than picking up my camera, I picked up the gardening tools and headed to my allotment plot for the first time on 6 April 2020, the first day of the Easter holiday. I worked on it every day, all day, for the next three weeks, and became obsessed with it up until the winter, proudly producing much vegetables as a result. Growing up I paid little attention or interest to the gardening my parents did in their back and front garden (it was only recently that I found out dad grew peas and potatoes in the back garden), and in 2020, my mum, sister, and children were visiting me (at a social dis-tance) on my allotment as if I had always been there.

Thus, my entry to the world of tending plant life and appreciation of the soil had nothing to do with my Blackness or through a discourse of cultural politics, but had emerged from "being physically active [as] a form of expressive distraction and a conscious way of diverting from thoughts of grief and despair" (De los Santos et al., 2022: 14), and through "the practice of gardening in the time of COVID-19, where it has been identified as one of the positive coping behaviours and produced affective benefits" (ibid.). However, in Black everyday life, the rupture and reminder of racism and the legacy of enslavement and colonialism can quell the peace both expected and unexpected ways. As described by a journalist for Columba Global Reports (Columbia, 2021),

> When the statue of British slave trader Edward Colston was toppled and dumped into Bristol Harbor on June 7 [2020] by Black Lives Matter activists, Shawn Sobers was watering his allotment, avoiding the crowds. It wasn't until later that evening that Sobers, an associate professor at the University of the West of England, walked down to take a look. By 7pm, the growing twilight was charring the blue sky grey. Then, he saw it – the empty plinth. Sobers felt disoriented. "My head was spinning," he told me.

For the next year of my life, immersed into the new patterns of working life, and as a member of the newly formed *We Are Bristol History Commission* (which was set up by Bristol Elected Mayor Marvin Rees as a result of the Colston statue toppling), I worked directly with Bristol museum curators to put the statue on display surrounded by wider context about the slave trade, which opened almost a year to the day of its toppling. However (at the time of writing), my allotment has now still not been as cared for as much as during that initial approximate eight-month period before the first winter began. I was spending time tending to the re-telling of the slave trader Colston story, rather than tending to the soil and growing sweetcorn, carrots, and peas to eat with my rice. I'm reminded of the much quoted (and personally loved) sentiments of Toni Morrison (1975), about how racism is a distraction, how it cajoles you to have to spend all the time justifying your existence, and distracts you from the core aim and goal of whatever else tasks you should have been doing in your life instead. My eventual and anticipated re-engagement with the allotment and immersion of my fingers back in the soil, will be different to the first time in April 2020. Re-motivated by the warning words of Morrison, this time it will invariably be fuelled by my Blackness through the discourse of cultural politics, and the reclaiming of my Black body to spend more time in a place of personal nourishment, rather than an existence of commodified labour.

The reunification of the mind/body split in the Black body was the interest of bell hooks, in her beautiful essay *Touching the Earth*, where she discusses the "culture shock and soul loss" (hooks, 2009: 53) of the southern Black folk when they moved from the southern states of America to the north. In escape of the overt racial hostility in the south and in search of a promise of economic freedom, in the north they found racism to be as present there, and a much harsher urban economic reality than the rural south, meaning it was both increasingly difficult for Black people to own land, and an industrialised cityscape that promoted a way of life separated from nature.

> Without the space to grow food, to commune with nature, or to mediate the starkness of poverty with the splendor of nature, black people experienced

profound depression. Working in conditions where the body was regarded solely as a tool (as in slavery), a profound estrangement occurred between mind and body.

ibid.

hooks goes onto argue that, too often, the struggles for anti-racism, Black self-recovery, and ecological environmental concerns are viewed as separate (or even competing) movements, which is the unfortunate result of the separation from the land which is a prevailing reality for contemporary city living Black folk, fuelled with a disconnect of knowledge of the importance of the harmonious land-body relationship, as was the way of our rural dwelling ancestors.

Recalling the legacy of our ancestors who knew that the way we regard land and nature will determine the level of our self-regard, black people must reclaim a spiritual legacy where we connect our well-being to the well-being of the earth. This is a necessary dimension of healing.

ibid: 54

The physical movements from the pre-slavery holistic rural lands of West Africa to the rural semi-industrialised systems of slavery in new world of the southern American states and the Caribbean, and from those southern states post-emancipation to the industrialised urban north, are echoed in the transition from the semi-industrialised rural landscape of 1950s Caribbean to hyper-industrial cities in UK. The intergenerational experiences of living in contemporary cities in the UK is not fixed in a linear timeline from pre-/post-slavery to post-war migration, as physical movement is a flux of continual leaving and arrival in all directions, and the distinctions between what is considered rural and industrialised is no longer as pronounced. To be clear, today you could take a photograph in some parts of west Africa, southern and northern US states, the Caribbean, and the UK, and it would be hard to tell the difference. However, the violent or hostile rupture of these physical movements, either in leaving, arrival, or both (as enslaved people, fleeing hostile environments, as economic migrants, or as other forms of refugees) is the connected lack of quality of these physical transitions which requires the healing.

hooks makes the reflection that when we speak about healing, we need to also equate that activity with a restoration and reconnection of our relationship with the natural world. She asserts that wherever it is that Black people find themselves living, that we must find the time to

commune with nature, to appreciate the other creatures who share this planet with humans. Even in my small New York City apartment I can pause to listen to birds sing, find a tree and watch it. We can grow plants – herbs, flowers, vegetables.

ibid.: 53

In the following self-penned fictional account based in London, one of the characters, Uncle Baruti, enacts the embodiment of this flux reality, and Levi represents the ambivalent city dweller, learning more about himself in his older years.

Standing on Africa (fiction)

Do ya remember wen you and ya mates use to shout out ta me?

Levi was daydreaming.

Uh, what was that uncle?

Most morning, when you were maybe 11 or 12, you and ya mates wud walk past my allotment on ya way to school an shout out to me. About 4 or 5 of you. Ya use to call me Bushman!

Levi remembered. Walking up Brook Road on the way to school, on the left-hand side were a row of allotments, and Levi and his mates would see his uncle planting stuff, however, Levi was sure it was his uncle who would always shout out to him, not the other way around. He admitted to himself that, back then, he was a bit embarrassed about his uncle, as all the local kids used to make fun of him, calling him crazy and a Rasta tramp. When they found out Bushman was his uncle, Levi is ashamed to admit it now, but he sometimes joined in the chorus and taunted his uncle to deflect the focus from himself. Whenever he saw his uncle since, that guilt has always been in the back of his mind. Now though, all these years later, his uncle seemed to remember it slightly differently.

> I use to spend all mi time in that allotment. Planting potatoes, carrots and a whole range of veg. I bet dat ya didn't know dat most of the veg you ate was from my allotment.
> No, I didn't.
> All de other allotment people were jealous of me, none of dem could grow tings as fast or big as I could. They all thought I had some secret ingredient I was feeding de earth with. Some mornings I would throw you and ya mates an apple on ya way ta school. Ya 'member?

Levi remembered that bit well. He and his friends never ate the apples thinking that they might be poisoned and threw them in the river next to the school. Uncle Baruti continued to reminisce.

> Ya probably won't 'member this bit either, but one morning I told you de secret, and you is de only person I ever told. I know ya wouldn't understand as you probably not listening, showing off in front ya mates.

Uncle Baruti chuckled to himself. Levi did not have the faintest idea what his uncle was talking about, and he was beginning to think that maybe he was mad after all.

> I had just laid down a new layer of soil and was digging it, getting it ready to plant. I heard ya voice shouting frum de road, "Bushman! Yo, Bushman! What you standing there doing? Yo, Bushman! What you doing?". Well I turned around an told ya exactly what I was doin', even though ya thought I was mad at the time. I told ya the secret. I told you, "I'm just here standing on Africa."

Levi was still puzzled. He still didn't remember the incident and it was probably far too abstract for him to comprehend at the time. Uncle Baruti went onto explain that he managed to get some soil for his allotment from Gambia from a friend who worked at the docks, and that was the secret of him successfully growing so many vegetables.

"When you asked me what I was doing, I simply told you the truth. I was standing on Africa."

Levi couldn't argue with that really or his uncle's reality. He still felt his uncle was slightly mad, but maybe not as much as he first thought.

Soil – Postscript

The notion of soil can be a highly emotive subject for many. Not particularly in relation to the physical aspects of soil itself as a piece of material culture (though horticulturalists, archaeologists, and other scholars have plenty to say about the implications of the physical dynamics of soil, e.g. see Salisbury, 2012), but when it is equated with more ideological and socio-cultural-political considerations such as home, memory, identity, health, land rights, nationhood, ownership, wealth creation, and industrialisation. The very ground beneath our feet is perhaps the most commodified resource on the planet, and the most taken for granted. We play on it when we are children, we fight over it in war, and we are buried in it when we die.

To make a very crude (but observed accurate) cultural generalisation – when white English people pass away, close family members can take a pinch of dirt in their fingers and sprinkle it high over the coffin as it lies in the grave. At African heritage funerals, the hired gravediggers take a break while the congregation at the graveside take the shovels themselves, and dig the huge pile of soil until the lowered casket is covered and the grave hole is completely filled in. This activity is done mostly by the men (though not exclusively, women have been increasingly joining in this practice), all while dressed in our best suits, dresses, shoes, and other church attire. I cannot remember how young I was when I first witnessed this graveside practice (not yet a teenager), or the first time I did it (probably at some point in my

20s). It felt like a rite of passage. I do not remember whose funeral it would have been, but the sweat worked up digging the soil and getting my clothes dirty was a small sacrifice to show that person how much they meant to me.

Soil is personal, and whether it is digging to plant a pot or to bury a loved one, it is our own hands that we are choosing to put to work, and it is our feet choosing to stand in that place. In that precise moment of time and space, we know where we are, and we know why we are there.

17
CONCLUSION

In Chapter 16 we saw Uncle Baruti stand on Gambian soil in London, and feel a connection spanning 2,761.86 miles. Our imaginations and stories can take us anywhere, and objects can aid the time travel process when those stories are non-fiction and coming from "real" people.

Every home of an older person is a domestic museum of memory and ideas. The oldest person we personally know and can speak to is our individual connection to the furthest reach into the past as far as they can remember. When that person sadly passes away, our reach into the past shortens and transfers to the second oldest person we now know, who will then become the oldest, and so on. With each passing of an elder, our possible knowledges of the living past becomes limited, and we are consigned to learning from books and other secondary source materials, rather than hearing stories from the mouths of people who were there. I always say to my students (and anyone who will listen) to interview your parents, grandparents, carers, the older people in your life about their lives. Not only will we find out some interesting things about them we did not know before, but we will also get to hear their voices again. Recording it on a phone will suffice. Suggest to them an object or photograph they can respond to, it can ease self-consciousness and smooth the process.

At the all too frequent funerals of our elders who came to Britain in the post-war period, my generation, who are their children (born predominantly in the 1960s and 1970s), we often look at each other and resign ourselves in the acknowledgment that we are the next generation of elders in waiting. It is a morbid thought, but one day we may have to oversee the house clearances of those who are closest to us. It is impractical to keep everything, but we can keep the stories safe, to learn from ourselves and to pass onto next generations. This book is my contribution to that intergenerational transitional process.

The last word will rightly go to mum. While working on the revisions for this book after the peer review feedback, I was talking to her about my writing, making

DOI: 10.4324/9780367809621-18

FIGURE 17.1 A happy home recipe, 2022

sure she was comfortable with what I wrote in it about her, and about me being at the house more due to her not being in great health. She gave me her blessing. The next day when she came downstairs, she said,

> You know what you were saying about your book … see that sign there, that Grace brought me from Barbados? Go and read it. How about having that at the end of your book? (see Figure 17.1) That could work well, couldn't it? You know I might not be in good health, but when I'm upstairs in bed, I'm not just lying there. I always thinking about something!

She chuckles, and I laugh with her nodding. So true, always thinking about something.

BIBLIOGRAPHY

Abera, T. (2017) Ethiopianism principles. *Online International Interdisciplinary Research Journal*, vol. 7, July Special Issue, pp. 309–315.

Achebe, C. (1971) *Things fall apart*. Heinemann, Oxford.

Adams, M. (2021) Far-right group condemns black Jesus painting at St Albans Cathedral. *The Herts Advertiser*, 13 May.

Adichie, C.N. (2009) The danger of a single story. *TED Talk*, 7 October. Available at: www.youtube.com/watch?v=D9Ihs241zeg. Accessed 2 October 2022.

Adinkra (2007) *West African wisdom: Adinkra symbols and meaning*. Available at: www.adinkra.org/htmls/adinkra/denk.htm. Accessed 27 August 2021.

Adinkra Symbols (2020) *Denkyem*. Available at: www.adinkrasymbols.org/symbols/denkyem/. Accessed 27 August 2021.

Adom, D., Appau Asante, E., & Kquofi, S. (2016) Adinkra: An epitome of Asante philosophy and history. *Research on Humanities and Social Sciences*, vol. 6, no. 14, pp. 42–53, ISSN 2224–5766.

Anderson, B. (2006) *Imagined communities: Reflections on the origin and spread of nationalism*. Verso Books, London.

Anderson, L. & Dent, D. (1958) 'Time for new ideas', *Times*, 8 January. London.

Arestedt, L., Persson, C., & Benzein, E. (2014) Living as a family in the midst of chronic illness. *Scandinavian Journal of Caring Sciences*, vol. 28, pp. 29–37.

Ashton, S.A. (2014) *Radical objects: The Black fist Afro comb*. History Workshop. Available at: www.historyworkshop.org.uk/radical-objects-the-black-fist-afro-comb/. Accessed 14 March 2022.

Attfield, J. (2000) *Wild things: The material culture of everyday life*. Berg, Oxford.

Ayres, R. (1973) *Red, black & green*. Polydor Records.

Barthes, R. (1977) *Image, music, text*, Fontana Press, London.

Barthes, R. (1980) *Camera Lucida*. Vintage, London.

Barthes, R. (2009) *Mythologies*. Vintage, London.

Baucheron, E. & Routex, D. (2013) *The museums of scandals*. Prestel, New York.

BBC Anniversaries (2019) *The wedding of Prince Charles and Lady Diana Spencer*. Available at: www.bbc.com/historyofthebbc/anniversaries/july/wedding-of-prince-charles-and-lady-diana-spencer. Accessed 19 December 2019.

BBC News (2019) *Nailsworth church black Jesus painting "shot" with air rifle*. 7 November. Available at: www.bbc.co.uk/news/uk-england-gloucestershire-50331743. Accessed 11 August 2021.

BBC News 24 (9 March 2021) *BBC News with Katty and Christian*. Available via BBC iPlayer at: www.bbc.co.uk/iplayer/episode/m000t3hn/bbc-news-with-katty-and-christian-09032021. Accessed 10 March 2021.

BBC One (2019) *Call the midwife*. Series 8, Episode 2, first aired 20 January. Neal Street Productions.

BBC Online (2021) *Meghan racism row: Society of Editors boss Ian Murray resigns*. Available at: www.bbc.co.uk/news/uk-56355274. Accessed 11 March 2021.

Beaudoin, S. (2007) *Poverty in world history*. Routledge, Oxon.

Behar, R. (1997) *The vulnerable observer: Anthropology that breaks your heart* (1st Edition). Beacon Press, Boston.

Belafonte, H. & Burgie, I. (1957) *Island in the Sun* (song). Maybellene Records.

BEMSCA (2022) *Bath Ethnic Minority Senior Citizens Association roundtable discussion with author*. Fairfield House. Bath. 23 February.

Benefice (2021) *The Nailsworth Benefice website*. Available at: www.thenailsworthbenefice. co.uk/art-and-architecture. Accessed on 11 August 2021.

Berger, J. (1982) 'The ambiguity of the photograph', in K. Askew & R. Wilk (eds), *The anthropology of media: A reader*. Blackwell Publishers, Oxford, pp. 47–55.

Blake-Hannah, B. (2022) *Growing out: Black hair & Black pride in the swinging Sixties*. Hansib Publications, London.

Boakye, J. (2021) *Musical truth: A musical history of modern Black Britain in 28 songs*. Faber & Faber, London.

Bourdieu, P. (2005) 'Habitus', in J. Hillier & E. Rooksby (eds), *Habitus: A sense of place*. Routledge, London, pp. 43–49.

Bowers, K. (2016) *Imperial exile: Emperor Haile Selassie in Britain 1936–40*. Brown Dog Books, London.

Brake, M. (1974) The skinheads: An English working class subculture. *Youth & Society*, vol. 6, no. 2, pp. 179–200.

Brock, A. (2012) From the Blackhand side: Twitter as a cultural conversation. *Journal of Broadcasting & Electronic Media*, vol. 56, no. 4, pp. 529–549.

Bush, B. (2010) African Caribbean slave mothers and children: Traumas of dislocation and enslavement across the Atlantic World. *Caribbean Quarterly*, vol. 56, no. 1–2, pp. 69–94. DOI: 10.1080/00086495.2010.11672362

Carney, J. (1998) The role of African rice and slaves in the history of rice cultivation in the Americas. *Human Ecology*, vol. 26, no. 4, pp. 525–545.

Carney, J. (2002) *Black rice: The African origins of rice cultivation in the Americas*. University of Illinois Press, Cambridge, Massachusetts.

Carney, J. (2004) 'With grains in her hair': Rice in colonial Brazil. *Slavery & Abolition*, vol. 25, no. 1, pp. 1–27. DOI: 10.1080/0144039042000220900

Carney, J. (2006) African origins of rice cultivation in the Black Atlantic. *Africa: Revista do Centro de Estudos Africanos* USP, S. Paulo, pp. 27–28, 91–114.

Carr, J. (2021) *The world is waiting: Viewers in 68 countries will see Meghan and Harry's bombshell interview with Oprah Winfrey*. Mail Online, 4 March. Available at: www.dailymail. co.uk/news/article-9327181/Viewers-64-countries-Meghan-Harrys-bombshell-interview-Oprah-Winfrey.html. Accessed 10 March 2021.

Carter, B., Harris, C., & Joshi, S. (1993) 'The 1951–1955 Conservative Government and racialization of Black immigration', in W. James & C. Harris (eds), *Inside Babylon: The Caribbean diaspora in Britain*. Verso, London, pp. 55–71.

Catsoulis, J. (2006) 'Color of the cross review', *The New York Times*, November 9.

Chakravorty, S. & Williams, T.N. (2014) Sickle cell disease: A neglected chronic disease of increasing global health importance. *Archives of Disease in Childhood*, vol. 100, no. 1, pp. 48–53. DOI:10.1136/archdischild-2013-303773

Chambers, M. (2007) I wanna be treated normal. (poem) Bristol.

Chancy, M. (1997) *Searching for safe spaces: Afro-Caribbean women in exile*. Temple Press, Philadelphia.

Charles, A. (2020) *Outraged: Why everyone is shouting and no one is talking*. Bloomsbury Publishing Plc, London.

Chatters, L. Taylor, R., & Jayakody, R. (1994) Fictive kinship relations in Black extended families. *Journal of Comparative Family Studies*, vol. 25, no. 3, pp. 297–312. https://doi.org/10.3138/jcfs.25.3.297

Cieraad, I. (eds) (2006) *At home: An anthropology of domestic space*. Syracuse University Press, New York.

Clarke, A. (1998) *Growing up stupid under the Union Jack: A memoir*. Vintage, Canada.

Clarke, J.H. (1974) Marcus Garvey: The Harlem Years. *Transition*, vol. 46, pp. 14–19.

Cliffe, R. (1999) Mayor Ray Cliffe interview. *Footsteps of the Emperor*. HTV. Shawn Sobers (Dir.).

Clifton, T. (1983) *Music as heard: A Study in applied phenomenology*. Yale University Press, New Haven.

Columbia Politics Collective. (2021) *The pandemic has invigorated protest movements—and repressive governments, too*. Columbia Global Reports, 23 April. Available at: https://global reports.columbia.edu/blog/2021/04/cpc-protests-movements/

Conway, D. (2007) Caribbean transnational migration behaviour: Reconceptualising its 'strategic flexibility'. *Population, Space and Place*, vol. 13, pp. 415–431.

Cook, C. (2010) Entertainment in a box: Domestic design and the radiogram and television. *Music in Art*, Spring–Fall, vol. 35, no. 1/2, *Rethinking Music in Art: New Directions in Music Iconography*, Spring–Fall, pp. 261–270.

Coussonnet, C. (2012) "Exclusive interview: Michael McMillan – in the framework of the exhibition Who More Sci-Fi than Us", Uprising Art, 2 July.

Crenshaw, K.W. (1991) 'Mapping the Margins: Inter-sectionality, Identity Politics, and Violence against Women of Color.' *Stanford Law Review* 43: 1241–1299.

Crow, L. (2022) *Extending activist reach and influence through Dwelling Space Activism: An autoethnographic and practice-led enquiry through activism, performance and life praxis*. Thesis, University of the West of England.

Csikszentmihalyi, M. & Rochberg-Halton, E. (1981) *The meaning of things*: Domestic symbols and the self. Cambridge University Press, Cambridge.

Cumberbatch, A.G. (2020) The history of Black British gardeners is one of resistance: From the transatlantic slave trade to Kew Gardens and the Chelsea Flower Show, the long history of Black horticulturists can't be forgotten. *Gal Dem*. Available at: – https://gal-dem.com/the-history-of-black-british-gardeners-is-one-of-resistance/

Cundall, F. (1909) *Jamaica place-names*. Institute of Jamaica, Kingston.

Davies, K.G. (1999) *The Royal African Company*. Routledge/Thoemmes Press, London.

DeGruy, J. (2005) *Post traumatic slave syndrome: America's legacy of enduring injury and healing*. Uptone Press, Portland.

Deleuze, G. & Guattari, F. (2001) *A thousand plateaus: Capitalism and schizophrenia*. Bloomsbury Publishing, New York, London.

Delle, J.A. & Fellows, K.R. (2021) Repurposed metal objects in the political economy of Jamaican slavery. *International Journal of Historical Archaeology*, vol. 25, pp. 998–1023.

De los Santos, J.A.A., Diaz, B.G., & Rosales, E.L. (2022) Coronaphobia and coping among the Bereaved: The mediating role of gardening during the Covid-19 pandemic. *Nurse Media Journal of Nursing*, vol. 12, no. 1, pp. 13–23.

Devilish Publishing. (2022) *Jessie Seymour Irvine – Composer*. Available at: www.devilishpub lishing.com/artists/jessie-seymour-irvine/. Accessed 12 March 2022.

Dodoo, V. (2011) 'Kwame Nkrumah's mission and vision for Africa and the world', in C.S Quist-Adade & F.C. Kwantlen (eds), *From colonization to globalization*. Polytechnic University, Surrey, pp. 64–73.

Doerksen, B. (2002) *Faithful one*. Hosanna! Music.

Douglass, F. (1845) 'The narrative life of Frederick Douglass', in B.T. Du Bois & W.E.B. Douglass (eds), *Three American classics*. Dover Publications, New York, pp. 351–426.

Douglass, F. (1892) *Life and times of Frederick Douglass*. Musaicum Books, sine loco.

Drazin, A. & Frohlich, D. (2007) Good intentions: Remembering through framing photographs in English Homes. *Ethnos*, vol. 72, no. 1, pp. 51–76. DOI: 10.1080/00141840701219536

Du Bois, W.E.B. (1903) 'The souls of Black folk', in B.T. Du Bois & W.E.B. Douglass (eds), *Three American classics*. Dover Publications, New York, pp. 159–331.

Durkheim, E. (1995) *The elementary forms of religious life*. Translation by Karen E. Fields. Free Press, New York.

Ebert, J. (2018) *How many of these design classics do you have in your home?* Ideal Home. Available at: www.idealhome.co.uk/news/design-classics-livingetc-192129. Accessed 14 March 2022.

Egerer, M., Lin, B., Kingsley, J., Marsh, P., Diekmann, L., & Ossola, A. (2022) Gardening can relieve human stress and boost nature connection during the COVID-19 pandemic. *Urban Forestry & Urban Greening*, vol. 68, p. 127483.

Eltis, D., Morgan, P., & Richardson, D. (2007) Agency and diaspora in Atlantic history: Reassessing the African contribution to rice cultivation in the Americas. *American Historical Review*, vol. 112, no. 5, pp. 1329–1358.

Elwell-Sutton, T, Deeny, S, & Stafford, M. (2020) *Emerging findings on the impact of COVID-19 on black and minority ethnic people: COVID-19 chart series*. The Health Foundation. Available at: www.health.org.uk/news-and-comment/charts-and-infographics/emerging-findings-on-the-impact-of-covid-19-on-black-and-min. Accessed 12 March 2021.

Faire, L. (1998) *Making home: Working-class perceptions of space, time and material culture in family life, 1900–1955*. PhD thesis, Department of Economic and Social History, University of Leicester.

Fanon, F. (1962) *The wretched of the Earth*. Penguin Books, London.

Fischler, C. (1988) Food, self and identity. *Social Science Information*, vol. 27, no. 2, pp. 275–292.

Flack, H. (1947) The pre-history of midwifery. [Abridged]: *Proceedings of the Royal Society of Medicine*, vol. XL, no. 713, pp. 27–36.

Florini, S. (2014) Tweets, tweeps, and signifyin': Communication and cultural performance on "Black Twitter". *Television & New Media*, vol. 15, no. 3, pp. 223–237.

Floyd, S. (1995) *The power of Black music: Interpreting its history from Africa to the United States*. Oxford University Press, New York.

Foucault, M. (2002) *The Archaeology of knowledge*. Routledge, Oxon.

Francis, A. (2022) *No regrets over becoming a republic in Barbados, where the Queen's death is a 'passing news item'*. iNews, 20 September. Available at: https://inews.co.uk/news/barbados-republic-no-regrets-where-queen-death-passing-news-1868624. Accessed 1 October 2022.

Freire, P. (1977) *Pedagogy of the oppressed*. Penguin Books, London.

Fuller Jr., N. (1984) *The united-independent compensatory code/system/concept textbook: A compensatory counter-racist code*. Revised edition. NFJ Productions, New York.

Furnas, J.C. (1952) *Voyage to windward: The life of Robert Louis Stevenson*. Faber and Faber, London.

Garvey, A.J. (1923) *The philosophy and opinions of Marcus Garvey*. UNIA-ACL, Atlanta.

Garvey, M. (1925) *African fundamentalism. The Negro World*. 6 June, Front Page Editorial, New York.

Garvey, M. (1983) *The Marcus Garvey and Universal Negro Improvement Association Papers*. Vol. I: 1826–August 1919. Illustrated edition. California University Press, Berkeley.

Geertz, C. (1962) The rotating credit association: A "middle rung" in development. *Economic Development and Cultural Change*, vol. 10, no. 3, pp. 241–263.

Genosko, G. (2016) *Critical semiotics: Theory, from information to affect*. Bloomsbury Academic, an imprint of Bloomsbury Publishing Plc, London, New York.

Gentleman, A. (2017) 'I can't eat or sleep': The woman threatened with deportation after 50 years in Britain, *The Guardian*, 28 November. Available at: www.theguardian.com/uk-news/2017/nov/28/i-cant-eat-or-sleep-the-grandmother-threatened-with-deportation-after-50-years-in-britain. Accessed 1 March 2022.

Gentleman, A. (2019) *The windrush betrayal: Exposing the hostile environment*. Guardian Faber, London.

George, V. (2008) Verna George. *Journal of Caribbean Literatures*, vol. 5, no. 3, pp. 59–64.

Gerbner, K. (2018) *Christian slavery: Conversion and race in the protestant Atlantic world*. University of Pennsylvania Press, Philadelphia.

Gewin, V. (2017) *Rice reveals enslaved Africans' agricultural heritage*. Sapiens. Available at: www.sapiens.org/culture/african-rice-new-world/. Accessed 22 February 2022.

Gilroy, P. (1987) *There ain't no Black in the union Jack*. Hutchinson, London.

Gilroy, P. (1999) *The Black Atlantic: Modernity and double consciousness*. Verso, London.

Goffman, E. (1956) *The presentation of self in everyday life*. University of Edinburgh Social Sciences Research Centre. Monographs; no. 2, Edinburgh.

Golding, E. (2017) *Making a Dutchie – Smile Jamaica – July 4 2017*. Smile Jamaica. TVJ. Available at: www. youtube.com/watch?v=yfwBruXQb2o. Accessed 11 April 2022.

Goodrich, L.M. (1947) From the league to the United Nations. *International Organization*, vol. 1, no. 1, pp. 3–21.

Graham, R. & Smith, S. (2016) The content of our #Characters: Black Twitter as counterpublic. *Sociology of Race and Ethnicity*, vol. 2, no. 4, pp. 433–449.

Grey, B. (2018) *Neil Kenlock Expectations Exhibition interview: Barbara Grey*. Black History Month Interview. Available at: www.blackhistorymonth.org.uk/article/video/neil-kenlock-expectations-exhibition-interview-barbara-grey/

Grip, L. & Hart, J. (2009) The use of chemical weapons in the 1935–36 Italo-Ethiopian War. SIPRI Arms Control and Non-proliferation Programme, October.

Gruzd, A., Wellman, B., & Takhteyev, Y. (2011) Imagining Twitter as an imagined community. *American Behavioral Scientist*, vol. 55, no. 10, pp. 1294–1318. DOI: 10.1177/0002764211409378

Guardian Letters page. (2015a) No Irish, no blacks, no dogs, no proof, October 21. Available at: www.theguardian.com/money/2015/oct/21/no-irish-no-blacks-no-dogs-no-proof. Accessed 20 February 2020.

Guardian Letters page. (2015b) No reason to doubt, no Irish, no black signs, October 28. Available at: www.theguardian.com/world/2015/oct/28/no-reason-to-doubt-no-irish-no-blacks-signs. Accessed 20 February 2020.

Hack, A. (2005) *Golden jubilee anniversary of HIM Haile Selassie's visit to Bath. The Anglo-Ethiopian Society*. News File, Spring. Available at: https://tinyurl.com/anglo-ethiopian. Accessed 13 March 2022.

Hall, S. (1973) *Encoding and decoding in the television discourse*. Paper for the Council of Europe Colloquy on "Training in the critical heading of televisual language". Organized by the Council & the Centre for Mass Communication Research, University of Leicester, September.

Hall, S. (1980) 'Encoding/decoding', in Centre for Contemporary Cultural Studies (ed), *Culture, media, language: Working papers in cultural studies, 1972–1979*. Hutchinson, London, pp. 128–138.

Hall, S. (1992) 'Identity and the Black photographic image', in D.A. Bailey (ed), *Critical decade: Black British photography in the 80s*. Ten.8, Birmingham, pp. 24–32.

Hall, S. (1996) 'The global, the local, and the return of ethnicity', in S. Hall, D. Held, D. Hubert, & K. Thompson (eds), *Modernity: An introduction to modern societies*. Blackwell Publishers, Oxford, pp. 623–629.

Hall, S. (2003) 'The spectacle of the other', in S. Hall (ed), *Representation: Cultural representation and signifying practices*. Sage Publications, London, pp. 223–279.

Hanson, A. (2012) *Elvis's best gospel recordings*. Available at: www.elvis-history-blog.com/elvis-best-gospel.html. Accessed 12 March 2022.

Harri. (2021) *Show me a better voice... Jim Reeves 'He'll Have To Go – Reaction'*. HarriBest Reactions. Available at: www.youtube.com/watch?v=Ia4aEzSAcNM. Accessed 10 March 2022.

Harris, C. (1993) 'Post-war migration and the industrial reserve army', in W. James & C. Harris (eds), *Inside Babylon: The Caribbean diaspora in Britain*. Verso, London, pp. 9–54.

Harris, J. (2016) Bristol mayor Marvin Rees: 'My dad arrived to signs saying: No Irish, no blacks, no dogs', *The Guardian*, 23 May.

Haskins, R. (1986) Ruth Haskins interview. *The Emperor in Bath: The Tuesday feature*. A. Vivian (Director). *BBC Bristol*, 29 April.

Haskins, R. (1999) Ruth Haskins interview. *Footsteps of the Emperor*. HTV. Shawn Sobers (Director).

Havens, T. (2013) *Black television travels: African American media around the globe*. New York University Press, New York.

Hawthorne, W. (2010) From "black rice" to "brown": Rethinking the history of risiculture in the seventeenth- and eighteenth-century Atlantic. *The American Historical Review*, vol. 115, no. 1, pp. 151–163.

Hernandez-Ruiz, E. & Dvorak, A.L. (2020) Music and mindfulness meditation: Comparing four music stimuli composed under similar principles. *Psychology of Music – Sage Journals*, vol. 49, no. 6, pp. 1620–1636.

Highmore, B. (2011) *Ordinary lives: Studies in the everyday*. Routledge, Oxon.

Highmore, B. (2014) *The great indoors: At home in the modern British house*. Profile Books, London.

Himid, L. (2011) *Tailor Striker Singer Dandy*. Available at: https://lubainahimid.uk/portfolio/tailor-striker-singer-dandy/. Accessed 3 March 2022.

Himid, L. (2018) *I'm a painter and a cultural activist*, Tate. Available at: www.youtube.com/watch?v=Nc1i66JYaJE . Accessed 3 March 2022.

Himid, L. (2022) *Black feminist vision: Artist Lubaina Himid*. The Courtauld. Available at: www.youtube.com/watch?v=CArwEMZucI0. Accessed 3 March 2022.

Himid, L. & Higgins, C. (2021) 'I have always thought in conversations': Inside the art of Lubaina Himid, *The Guardian*, 20 November. Available at: www.theguardian.com/artan ddesign/2021/nov/20/i-have-always-thought-in-conversations-inside-the-art-of-luba ina-himid. Accessed 3 March 2022.

Hoare, C. (2021) *Growing spaces*. RRB Photobooks, Bristol.

Holmes, C. (2020) *Super Black: The Vanley Burke Archive*. Firstsite Gallery. Available at: www.youtube.com/watch?v=shfxKPFVy6k. Accessed 6 March 2022.

hooks, b. (2009) *Belonging: A culture of place*. Routledge, Oxon.

House of Names (2022) *Spalding history, family crest & coats of arm*. Available at: www.house ofnames.com/spalding-family-crest. Accessed 12 March 2022.

Humez, J.M. (1993) In search of Harriet Tubman's spiritual autobiography. *NWSA Journal*, vol. 5, no. 2, pp. 162–182.

Hutton, A. (2021) 'We deserve this peace and joy': Black gardeners bloom on TikTok and Instagram. *The Guardian*, 20 June.

Ivens, M. (2001) Barbados splits from the queen, trading one empire for another. *Bloomburg. com*, 4 December. Available at: www.bloomberg.com/opinion/articles/2021-12-04/barbados-splits-from-the-queen-trading-one-empire-for-another-in-china. Accessed 15 March 2022.

Jackson, J.E. (2005) Stigma, liminality, and chronic pain: Mind-body borderlands. *American Ethnologist*, vol. 32, no. 3, pp. 332–353.

Jacobs-Huey, L. (2002) The natives are gazing and talking back: Reviewing the problematics of positionality, voice, and accountability among "native" anthropologist. *American Anthropologist*, vol. 104, no. 3, pp. 791–804.

James, W. (1993) 'Migration, racism and identity formation: The Caribbean experience in Britain', in W. James & C. Harris (eds), *Inside Babylon: The Caribbean diaspora in Britain*. Verso, London, pp. 9–55.

Johnson, D. (2018) *The legendary Blaupunkt (Bluespot) Arkansas radiogram*. Lardsah. Available at: www.youtube.com/watch?v=WxN0tCx8L6I. Accessed 10 March 2022.

Jordon, L. (2011) *Jim Reeves: His untold story*. Pagetuner Books International, USA, sine loco.

Jørgensen, A.M. (2001) 'Sankofa and modern authenticity in Ghanaian film and television', in M.E. Baaz & M. Palmberg (eds), *Same and other: Negotiating African identity in cultural production*. Nordiska Afrikainstitutet, Uppsala, Sweden, pp. 119–141.

Kamimoto, S. (2015) Influence of Reggae Music on the economic activities of EABIC Rastafarians in Jamaica. *Caribbean Quarterly*, vol. 61, no. 1, pp. 42–59. DOI: 10.1080/00086495.2015.11672547

Kenyatta, J. (1938) *Facing Mount Kenya*. Martin Secker & Warburg, London.

Kincaid, J. (1978) Girl. *The New Yorker*. Available at: www.newyorker.com/magazine/1978/06/26/girl. Accessed 2 March 2022.

King, H. (1999) *Footsteps of the emperor*. HTV. Shawn Sobers (Director).

Kinouani, G. (2021) *Living while Black: The essential guide to overcoming racial trauma*. Penguin Random House, London.

Knudsen, B.T., Munsya, S., Lisalusa, L., & Williams, S.C. (2022) Decolonial countervisuality, in B.T. Knudsen, J.R. Oldfield, E. Buettner, & E. Zabunyan (eds), *Decolonizing colonial heritage: New agendas, actors and practices in and beyond Europe*. Routledge, Abingdon, New York, pp. 255–273.

Koepnick, L. (1999) *Walter Benjamin and the aesthetics of power*. University of Nebraska Press, Lincoln.

Kuper, A. (1996) *Anthropology and anthropologists*. Routledge, London.

Kuwornu-Adjaottor, J., Appiah, G., & Nartey, M. (2015) The philosophy behind some Adinkra symbols and their communicative values in Akan. *Philosophical Papers and Review*, vol. 7, no. 3, pp. 22–33. DOI:10.5897/PPR2015.0117

Kwei-Armah, K. (2007) Going back to my roots. BBC News website. Available at: http://news.bbc.co.uk/1/hi/magazine/6480995.stm. Accessed 11 January 2021.

Laguda, I. (2019) If you discover your heroes are racist, leave them and their art in the past, *The Metro*, 31 August. Available at: https://metro.co.uk/2019/08/31/if-you-discover-your-heroes-are-racist-leave-them-and-their-art-in-the-past-10651094/. Accessed 11 March 2022.

LaSusa, Danielle M. (2007) Eiffel tower key chains and other pieces of reality: The philosophy of souvenirs. *The Philosophical Forum*, vol. 38, no. 3, pp. 271–287. DOI:10.1111/J.1467-9191.2007.00267.X

Lawrence, D. (2006) *And still I rise: Seeking justice for Stephen.* Faber and Faber, London.

Legacies of British Slavery database. (2022) *Dr Hinton Spalding.* Centre for the Study of the Legacies of British Slavery, University of Central London. Available at: www.ucl.ac.uk/lbs/person/view/24790. Accessed 12 March 2022.

Leonard, C. (2019) *Political Song | No Blacks, No Dogs, No Irish – Skinny Pelembe.* New Frame, 12 July. Available at: www.newframe.com/political-song-no-blacks-no-dogs-no-irish-skinny-pelembe/

Levy, A. (1994) *Every light in the house burnin'.* Tinder Press, London.

Levy, A. (2004) *Small island.* Review Headline Books Publishing, St Ives.

Lima, M.H. (2012) A written song: Andrea Levy's neo-slave narrative. *ENTERTEXT,* Special Issue on Andrea Levy, no. 9, pp. 135–153.

Littlefield, D. (1981) *Rice and slaves: Ethnicity and the slave trade in colonial South Carolina.* University of Illinois Press, Champaign, Illinois.

Lloyd, G. (1995) The Man of Reason: Male and female in western philosophy. Routledge, London.

Loesser, F. (1947) *The sewing machine song.* Performed by Betty Hutton in The Perils of Pauline. Video clip and lyrics. Available at: www.youtube.com/watch?v=999ph8iRT4o. Accessed 26 February 2022.

MacFarlane, C. (1986) *Invasion.* Macka B. Ariwa Sounds.

Malik, S. (2002) *Representing Black Britain: Black and Asian images on television.* Sage, London.

Maunganidze, M. & Menter, A. (2021) *Rooted in Bristol.* Documentary Film. Afrika Eye.

Mbiti, J, S. (1969) *African religions and philosophy.* Heinemann, London.

McDonald, K. (2021) *Interview with the Dutch pot man Reagall Wolfe in St Mary Jamaica.* Kennygoodvibestv. Available at: www. youtube.com/watch?v=ewKsD4Ss4I0. Accessed 11 April 2022.

McGinty, D. (1993) Black scholars on Black music: The past, the present, and the future. *Black Music Research Journal*, vol. 13, no. 1, pp. 1–13.

McGrath, A. (2001) *In the beginning: The story of the King James Bible.* Hodder & Stoughton, London.

McLuhan, M. (2008) *Understanding media.* Routledge, Oxon.

McMillan, M. (2007) Van Huis Uit/That's the way we do it...!: The Living Room of Migrants in The Netherlands. *Guided Talk*, April.

McMillan, M. (2009) The West Indian front room: Reflections on a diasporic phenomenon. Project Muse. Small Axe 28. March, pp. 135–156.

McMillan, M. (2019) Dub in the front room: Migrant aesthetics of the sacred and the secular. *Open Cultural Studies*, vol. 3, pp. 184–194.

Mercer, K. (1994) Welcome to the Jungle: New positions in Black cultural studies. Routledge, London.

Miller, D. (ed) (2009) *Anthropology and the individual: A material culture perspective.* Berg, Oxford.

Mintz, S.W. (1989) *Caribbean transformations.* Columbia University Press Morningside Edition, New York.

Mir, A. (2020) *Roots in resilience: A brief history of the British-Bangladeshi community in London's east end. UCL – History.* London, 8 December. Available at: www.ucl.ac.uk/history/news/2020/dec/roots-resilience-brief-history-british-bangladeshi-community-londons-east-end

Mitchell, R. & Sobers, S. (2013) Re:Interpretation: the representation of perspectives on slave trade history using creative media, in M. Dresser & A. Hann (eds), *Slavery and the British country house*. English Heritage, Swindon, pp. 132–139.

Morgan-Lindo, S. (2021) People rather buy food now than a pot, *The Star*, 26 February.

Morrison, T. (1975) *A humanist view* (speech). Portland, Oregon, May 30. Black Studies Center public dialogue, Pt. 2.

Motley, M. (2021) *PM of Barbados Mia Motley puts "disingenuous" BBC reporter "in her place"*. Barbados Video. Available at: www. youtube.com/watch?v=SYD2scU3JJY. Accessed 14 March 2022.

Msimang, S. (2020) To be a black mother is to manage the rage of others while growing joyous black children. This is no easy task, *The Guardian*, 7 August.

Muhammad, P.M. (2004) The Trans-Atlantic slave trade: Forgotten crime against humanity as defined by International Law. *American University International Law Review*, vol. 19, no. 4, pp. 883–948.

Mullings, S., Sobers, S., & Thomas, D. (2021) The future of visual anthropology in the wake of Black Lives Matter. *Visual Anthropology Review*, vol. 37, no. 2, pp. 401–421.

Muthayya, S., Sugimoto, J., Montgomery, S., & Maberly, G. (2014) An overview of global rice production, supply, trade, and consumption. *Annals of the New York Academy of Sciences*, vol. 1324, pp. 7–14. DOI: 10.1111/nyas.12540

Mwai, J. & Ashmore, L. (2022) Barbados' new republic: A win for China? *The Diplomat*, 27 January. Available at: https://thediplomat.com/2022/01/barbados-new-republic-a-win-for-china/. Accessed 15 March 2022.

Ñāṇamoli, B. & Bodhi, B. (2009) *The middle length discourses of the Buddha: A translation of the Majjhima Nikāya*. Wisdom Publications in association with the Barre Center for Buddhist Studies, Boston.

Nelson, C. & George Jr, H. (1995) White Racism and "The Cosby Show": A Critique. *The Black Scholar*, vol. 25, no. 2, pp. 59–61.

Nietert, P.J., Silverstein, M.D., & Abboud, M.R. (2002) Sickle cell anaemia epidemiology and cost of illness. *Pharmacoeconomics*, vol. 20, no. 6, pp. 357–366.

Oakley, J. (1996) *Own or other culture*. Routledge, Oxon.

O'Brien Chang, K. & Chen, W. (1998) *Reggae routes: The story of Jamaican music*. Ian Randle Publishers, Kingston, Jamaica.

Ohito, E.O. (2016) Refusing curriculum as a space of death for Black female subjects: A Black feminist reparative reading of Jamaica Kincaid's "Girl". *Curriculum Inquiry*, vol. 46, no. 5, pp. 436–454. DOI: 10.1080/03626784.2016.1236658

Okrah, K.A.A. (2008) Sankofa: Cultural heritage conservation and sustainable African development. *The African Symposium*, vol. 8., no. 2, pp. 24–31.

Okri, B. (2011) *A time for new dreams*. Rider Books, London.

Ombati-Simon, J.M. (2012) *Kenya the beloved: A message to my people*. Xlibris, Indiana.

ONS (2020) *One in eight British households has no garden*. Office for National Statistics, 14 May. Available at: www.ons.gov.uk/economy/environmentalaccounts/articles/oneineightbritishhouseholdshasnogarden/2020-05-14

O'Reilly, J. (2016) Irish-Jamaican couple put a positive spin on the 'No dogs, No blacks, No Irish' message with their brilliant t-shirts, *The Irish Post*, 2 August.

Palmer, C. (2018) *East St Clements Church, Site Details*. Aberdeenshire Council. Available at: https://online.aberdeenshire.gov.uk/smrpub/master/detail.aspx?refno=NJ90NE0 064. Accessed 12 March 2022.

Parker, L. (2019) Who let the dogs in? Antiblackness, social exclusion, and the question of who is human. *Journal of Black Studies*, vol. 50, no. 4, pp. 367–387.

Parkins, N.C. (2010) Push and pull factors of migration. *American Review of Political Economy*, vol. 8, no. 2, pp. 6–24.

Patten, T.O. (2006) Hey girl, am I more than my hair?: African American women and their struggles with beauty, body image, and hair. *NWSA Journal*, vol. 18, no. 2, pp. 24–51.

Pelembe, S. (2019) *No Blacks, no dogs, no Irish* (song). Brownswood Recordings.

Pentreath, R. (2021) Why do we call classical music 'classical music'? *Classical FM*. Available at: www.classicfm.com/discover-music/music-theory/why-do-we-call-it-classical-music/. Accessed 13 March 2022.

Peru, Y. (2020) Black Jesus is a saint – model, son of reggae singer cast as Jesus in 'A Last Supper', *The Gleaner*, 5 July.

Pines, J. (1992) *Black and white in colour: Black people in British television since 1936.* British Film Institute, London.

Pipe, E. (2020) *The rise of grassroots growing projects in Bristol.* B24/7, 31 July.

Pirsig, R. (2004) *Zen and the art of motorcycle maintenance.* Vintage, London.

Plato (2010) *The allegory of the cave.* P & L Publication, Brea.

Points West & BBC News Channel (2020) *Director General response.* Available at: www.bbc.co.uk/contact/complaint/pointswestbbcnewschannel0720. Accessed 16 March 2021.

Powdermaker, H. (1966) *Stranger and friend: The way of an anthropologist.* Norton, New York.

Prentice, R. (2012) "No One Ever Showed Me Nothing": Skill and self-making among Trinidadian garment workers. *Anthropology & Education Quarterly*, vol. 43, no. 4, pp. 400–414.

Prince, M. (2004) *Mary Prince: The history of Mary Prince.* Penguin, London.

Psoinos, M., Hatzidimitriadou, E., Butler, C., & Barn, R. (2011) *Ethnic monitoring in healthcare services in the UK as a mechanism to address health disparities: A narrative review.* Swan IPI, London.

Ragsdale, J.G. (1991) *Dutch ovens chronicled: Their use in the United States.* University of Arkansas Press, Fayetteville.

Ramachandran, S. (2006) Visiting friends and relatives (VFR) market: A conceptual framework. *TEAM Journal of Hospitality & Tourism*, vol. 3, no. 1, pp. 1–10.

Ramsey, G. (1996) Cosmopolitan or provincial?: Ideology in early Black Music historiography, 1867–1940. *Black Music Research Journal*, vol. 16, no. 1, pp. 11–42.

Reed, A. (2020) Returning to our roots: Black Americans are redefining relationship to the land with gardening, farming, *USA Today Life*, 5 August. Available at: https://eu.usatoday.com/story/life/2020/08/05/black-americans-reconnecting-roots-by-gardening-farming-land/5405740002/

Rehling, D.L. (2002) 'When Hallmark calls upon nature: Images of nature in greeting cards', in M. Meister & P.M. Japp (eds), *Enviropop: Studies in environmental rhetoric and popular culture.* Praeger, Westport, pp. 13–30.

Riley, M. (2014) 'Bass culture: An alternative soundtrack to Britishness', in J. Srattonnand & N. Zuberi (eds), *Black popular music in Britain since 1945.* Ashgate, Farnham, pp. 101–114.

Rodney, W. (1988) *How Europe underdeveloped Africa.* Bogle L'Ouvertiure Publications, London.

Rokosz-Piejko, E. (2018) Adapting, remaking, re-visioning: Alex Haley's roots. *Polish Journal for American Studies*, vol. 12, pp. 143–152.

Roper, G. (2013) "Scamming": Wanton criminality or resistance? Making the case for public theology in the light of the legacy of Sam Sharpe. *International Journal of Public Theology*, vol. 7, no. 4, pp. 426–443.

Rose, G. (2002) *Visual methodologies.* Sage, London.

Sadlier, A. (2019) Majority of Americans think it is OK to snoop through someone's bathroom cabinet. *New York Post*, 27 November.

Salazar, J. (2011) Haile Selassie: Appeal to the league of nations. *African Yearbook of Rhetoric*, vol. 2, no. 3, pp. 9–18.

Salisbury, R.B. (2012) Engaging with soil, past and present. *Journal of Material Culture*, vol. 17, no. 1, pp. 23–41.

Saro-Wiwa, K. (1995) *A month and a day: A detention diary*. Penguin, London.

Savishinsky, N. (1994) Rastafari in the promised land: The spread of a Jamaican socioreligious movement among the youth of West Africa. *African Studies Review*, vol. 37, no. 3, pp. 19–50.

Sawhney, N. (2019) Nitin Sawhney at The Royal Albert Hall 'What is classical music?'. *Classical Album Sundays*. Available at: www. youtube.com/watch?v=efiRpde7VfU. Accessed 13 March 2022.

Scarsi, A. (2021) Barbados warned over ditching Queen as China 'gifts' £400m 'No such thing as free lunch'. *Express.co.uk*, 30 November. Available at: www.express.co.uk/news/royal/1528689/barbados-republic-future-china-investments-barbados-cut-ties-queen. Accessed 15 March 2022.

Scott, P. (2008) Did owner-occupation lead to smaller families for interwar working-class households? *Economic History Review*, vol. 61, no. 1, pp. 99–124.

Schwarz, B. (2021) Windrush: Unsolved legacies. *New West Indian Guide*, vol. 95, pp. 289–295.

Selassie, H. (1999) *My life and Ethiopia's progress: Volume 2. Addis Ababa 1966*. Frontline Books, Chicago.

Selassie, T. (2021) *We are those whose clothes make a statement* (poem). Fairfield House, Bath.

Seltzer, S. & Bender, I.B. (2003) Cognitive dissonance in endodontics. *Journal of Endodontic*, vol. 29, no. 11, pp. 714–719.

Semple, K. (2020) China extends reach in the Caribbean, unsettling the U.S. *The New York Times*, 8 November. Available at: www.nytimes.com/2020/11/08/world/americas/china-caribbean.html. Accessed 14 March 2022.

Sesher, S. (2021) Creative arts as activism: Post-Covid Black futures series. *Critical Race and Culture Research Network*. Available at: https://criticalraceculture.com/creative-arts-as-activism/.

Seymour, T. (2013) Why Black British directors and actors leave the UK for Hollywood, *The Guardian*, 29 August.

Sharman, J. (2019) Man who sprayed racist graffiti on Black family's door because 'Brexit was playing on his mind' is jailed, *The Independent*, 16 May.

Sharpless, R. (2017) Going Dutch: A pot's place in the southern kitchen. *Southern Cultures*, vol. 23, no. 3, pp. 111–117.

Shiva, V. (2005) New emperors, old clothes, *The Ecologist*, July. Available at: https://theecologist.org/2005/jul/01/new-emperors-old-clothes. Accessed 24 February 2022.

Shujaa, M.J. & Shujaa, K.J. (2015) *The SAGE Encyclopaedia of African Cultural Heritage in North America*. Sage Publishing, Thousand Oaks.

Siddiqi, A.E.A., Jordan, L.B., & Parker, C.S. (2013) Sickle cell disease – The American saga. *Ethnicity & Disease*, vol. 23, no. 2, pp. 245–248.

Sinclair, L. (2018) "They wanted to jail us all' – Black Panthers photographer Neil Kenlock looks back. *The Guardian*, 7 August.

Sinclair, P. (2017) Making a Dutchie – Smile Jamaica – July 4. *Smile Jamaica*. TVJ. Available at: www. youtube.com/watch?v=yfwBruXQb2o. Accessed 11 April 2022.

Sky News (2021a) *Duchess of Sussex: Royals, racism and speaking her truth*. Available at: www. youtube.com/watch?v=bRJuAh3GpRM. Accessed 10 March 2021.

Sky News (2021b) *Harry and Meghan interview: Royals 'shown for what they are', says comedian Gina Yashere.* Available at: https://news.sky.com/video/royals-shown-for-what-they-are-12240415. Accessed 11 March 2021.

Smiet, K. (2015) Post/secular truths: Sojourner Truth and the intersections of gender, race and religion. *European Journal of Women's Studies*, vol. 22, no. 1, pp. 7–21.

Smith, D. (2019) *My Jamaican Dutch pot.* Available at: https://kit.co/Dell2019/my-jamaican-dutch-pot-plus-more-enjoy. Accessed 10 April 2022.

Smith, S.P. (2018) Instagram abroad: Performance, consumption and colonial narrative in Tourism. *Postcolonial Studies*, vol. 21, no. 2, pp. 172–191.

Sobers, S. (1998a) Deep freeze new family, in G. Edwards (ed), *Origins: Personal stories of crossing the seas.* Origins, Bristol.

Sobers, S. (1998b) 'Silent witness', in G. Edwards (ed), *Origins: Personal stories of crossing the seas.* Origins, Bristol.

Somé, M.P. (1995) *Of water and the spirit: Ritual, magic, and initiation in the life of an African Shaman.* Penguin, London.

SouFLoTV (2015) Jamaican kitchen something we must have. *SouFLoTV.* Available at: www.youtube.com/watch?v=IuiZJLAbgSM. Accessed 7 April 2022.

Stajcic, N. (2013) Understanding culture: Food as a means of communication. *Hemispheres*, no. 28, pp. 5–14.

Stephenson, M.L. & Hughes, H.L. (1995) Holidays and the UK Afro-Caribbean community. *Tourism Management*, vol. 16, no. 6., pp. 429–435.

Stevenson, R.L. (1924) *A child's garden of verses; underwoods, ballads.* C. Scribner's, New York.

Stewart, R. (1976) *Hit song.* Arab Records, Kingston, Jamaica.

Stewart, R. (1979) *Rice and peas.* Corona Records, Queens.

Streetly, A., Sisodia, R., Dick, M., Latinovic, R., Hounsell, K., & Dormandy, E. (2018) Evaluation of newborn sickle cell screening programme in England: 2010–2016. *Archives of Disease in Childhood*, vol. 103, pp. 648–653.

Sweeny, M. & McCouch, S. (2017) The complex history of the domestication of rice. *Annals of Botany*, vol. 100, pp. 951–957. DOI:10.1093/aob/mcm128

Sweetness, T.J. (2019) *How it's made – Jamaican Dutch pots.* Available at: www. youtube.com/watch?v=-GJ8e26Lj6I. Accessed 10 April 2022.

Symbolikon (2001) *Denkyem.* Available at: https://symbolikon.com/downloads/denkyem-adinkra/. Accessed 27 Aug 2021.

Tate (2022) *Life between islands: Caribbean-British Art 1950s – now.* Available at: www.tate.org.uk/press/press-releases/life-between-islands-caribbean-british-art-1950s-now-0. Accessed 13 March 2022.

Temple, C. (2010) The emergence of *Sankofa* practice in the United States: A modern history. *Journal of Black Studies*, vol. 41, no. 1, pp. 127–150.

The Dutch Pot Jamaican Restaurant (2016) *Our story.* Available at: https://dutchpotrestaurants.com/about-us/#:~:text=The%20Dutch%20Pot%20dates%20back,and%20temperature%20is%20always%20consistent. Accessed 10 April 2022.

Thomas, H. (1997) *The slave trade: The history of the Atlantic slave trade 1440–1870.* Picador, London.

Titlestad, M. (2014) The South African life and afterlife of Jim Reeves. *Safundi: The Journal of South African and American Studies*, vol. 15, no. 4, pp. 497–514. DOI: 10.1080/17533171.2014.941716

Tolliver-Jackson, L.J. (2020) Why Black people are turning to gardening during difficult times. USA Network – Florida. *The Palm Beach Post*, 20 June.

Torrington, A. (2014) *Making freedom*. Presentation, 9 December. Black Cultural Archives, London.

Truth, S. (1851) *Ain't I a Woman?* Speech to Women's Convention. Akron, Ohio 1851. Available at: https://sourcebooks.fordham.edu/mod/sojtruth-woman.asp.

Tuhiwai Smith, L. (2006) *Decolonizing methodologies: Research and indigenous peoples.* Zed Books, London.

Tulloch, C. (2018) 'The glamorous 'diasporic intimacy' of habitus: 'Taste', migration and the practice of settlement', in M. Quinn, D. Beech, M. Lehnert, C. Tulloch, & S. Wilson (eds), *The persistence of taste: Art, museums and everyday life after Bourdieu*, 1st edition. Routledge, Oxon, pp. 257–274.

Turner, S. (1994) *The social theory of practices: Tradition, tacit knowledge and prepositions.* Polity Press, Cambridge.

Twitchin, J. (ed) (1990) *The Black and white media book: Handbook for the study of racism and television.* Trentham Books, Chester.

Tyler, J.D. (1971) Cast iron cooking vessels, *The Magazine Antiques*, August, pp. 7–21.

Ullendorff, E. (1995) *From Emperor Haile Selassie to H.J. Polotsky: An Ethiopian and semitic miscellany.* Harrassowitz Verlag, Wiesbaden.

Upsetter (2022) *Roman Stewart: A biography*. Upsetter. Available at: www.upsetter.net/roman/biography.htm. Accessed 22 February 2022.

Vernon, P. (2018) *Campaign for Windrush day is part of our long history of race equality and social justice.* Centre for Labour and Social Studies. Available at: https://classonline.org.uk/blog/item/windrush-patrick-vernon. Accessed 2 March 2022.

Vernon, U. (2015) *Castle Hangnail.* Dial Books, New York.

Wailer, B. (1989) *Bald Head Jesus* (song). Solomonic Music. Kingston, Jamaica

Wallace, M., Wilson, B. and Darlington-Pollock, F. (2022) Social inequalities experienced by children of immigrants across multiple domains of life: A case study of the Windrush in England and Wales. *Comparative Migration Studies*, vol. 10, no. 1. doi:10.1186/s40878-022-00293-1.

Wan, D. (1999) 'Magic medicine cabinet: A situated portal for consumer healthcare', in H.W. Gellersen (eds), *Handheld and ubiquitous computing. HUC 1999.* Lecture Notes in Computer Science, vol 1707. Springer, Berlin, Heidelberg.

Wardle, H. & Obermuller, L.J. (2019) 'Windrush generation' and 'hostile environment': Symbols and lived experiences in Caribbean migration to the UK. *Migration and Society*, vol. 2, pp. 81–89.

Watson, B. (2021) Basil Watson talks influences, favourite creation and historic Windrush monument – Interview with Janet Silvera, *The Gleaner*, 28 November. Available at: https://jamaica-gleaner.com/article/lifestyle/20211128/basil-watson-talks-influences-favourite-creation-and-historic-windrush. Accessed 15 April 2022.

Weaver, M. (2020) Norwich residents hold anti-racism protest at 'Brexit day' poster, *The Guardian*, 31 January. Available at: www.theguardian.com/uk-news/2020/feb/02/norwich-anti-racism-protest-brexit-day-poster

Webster, W. (1998) *Imagining home: Gender, race and national identity, 1945–1964.* UCL Press, London, p. 165.

Weinberg, M. & Jospeh, D. (2016) If you're happy and you know it: Music engagement and subjective wellbeing. *Psychology of Music. Society for Education, Music, Psychology Research*, vol. 45, no. 2, pp. 57–267. DOI: 10.1177/0305735616659552

White, E.V., Gatersleben, B., Wyles, K.J., Murrell, G., Golding, S.E., Scarles, C., & Xu, S. (2021) *Gardens and wellbeing during the first UK Covid-19 lockdown* (Research Report No. 1). Surrey Environmental Psychology Research Group.

White, J. (2020) *Terraformed: Young Black lives in the inner city*. Repeater Books, London.

Williams, N. (2020) *Granddad*. Available at: www.naomi-williams.co.uk/index.php/projects-2/. Accessed 12 April 2022.

Wiwa, K. (2001) *In the shadow of a saint*. Steerforth Press, Westminster.

Wolper, D. & Troupe, Q. (1978) *The inside story or television's 'roots'*. Star Books, London.

Wood, P.H. (1974) *Black majority: Negroes in colonial South Carolina from 1670 through the Stono rebellion*. Norton, New York.

Woolery, T. (2014) *What are judging clothes?* Woolery Kitchen. Available at: www.woolerykitchen.com/blog-posts/article/what-are-judging-clothes. Accessed 26 February 2022.

Wright, C. & Clibborn, S. (2018) Back door, side door or front door? An emerging de-facto low-skilled immigration policy in Australia. *Comparative Labor Law Journal: A Publication of the U.S. National Branch of the International Society for Labor Law and Social Security and the Wharton School, and the Law School of the University of Pennsylvania*, vol. 39, no. 1, pp. 165–188.

Zephaniah, B. (2018) *The life and rhymes of Benjamin Zephaniah: The autobiography*. Simon & Schuster, London.

Zhang, P. (2013) Food as a social medium and a medium of culture. *ETC: A Review of General Semantics*, vol. 70, no. 2, pp. 174–177.

INDEX